Staff Favorites

FOOD & WINE
STAFF FAVORITES

EXECUTIVE EDITOR **Kate Heddings**

EDITOR **Susan Choung**

DESIGNER **Alisha Petro**

COPY EDITOR **Lisa Leventer**

EDITORIAL ASSISTANT **Taylor Rondestvedt**

PRODUCTION DIRECTOR **Joseph Colucci**

PRODUCTION MANAGER **Stephanie Thompson**

FOOD & WINE

EDITOR **Nilou Motamed**

CREATIVE DIRECTOR **Fredrika Stjärne**

EXECUTIVE EDITOR **Pamela Kaufman**

ART DIRECTOR **James Maikowski**

PHOTO EDITOR **Sara Parks**

FRONT COVER

Cast-Iron Roast Chicken with Lentils and Walnut Vinaigrette (recipe, p. 145)

PHOTOGRAPHER **Con Poulos**

FOOD STYLIST **Simon Andrews**

STYLE EDITOR **Suzie Myers**

BACK COVER

PHOTOGRAPHER **Marcus Nilsson**

STYLIST **Alison Attenborough**

For additional photo contributors,
see p. 271.

Published by Time Inc. Books
225 Liberty Street
New York, NY 10281

FOOD & WINE is a trademark of Time Inc.
Affluent Media Group, registered in the
U.S. and other countries.

ISBN 10: 0-8487-4840-9
ISBN 13: 978-0-8487-4840-1

ISSN 2471-643X

Manufactured in the United States of America

FOOD & WINE

Staff Favorites

FOOD & WINE
BOOKS

Candied Ginger,
Coconut and Quinoa
Granola, p. 207

Contents

Recipes in **red** can be made in 30 minutes or less.

MAINS

BRUNCH

DESSERT

Recipes in **red** can be made in 30 minutes or less.

Foreword

The Food & Wine Test Kitchen has perfected literally thousands of recipes over the past 30-plus years, and at long last we've collected the very best of them in a place other than our dog-eared "fave recipes" folders. *Staff Favorites* is where you'll find the dishes that we return to again and again in our home kitchens, be it Tyler Florence's Extra-Crispy Fried Chicken, Thomas Keller's Over-the-Top Mushroom Quiche or Michael Recchiuti's decadently rich Quadruple Chocolate Brownies.

When we asked our staff for their all-time favorite recipes, we realized just how clearly their choices reflect their particular tastes and predilections. It turns out, for instance, that Ray Isle, our stellar wine editor, is a lamb fanatic. He has gone home and made almost every lamb recipe we've ever published! So we trust him when he says that the Green-Olive-and-Lemon-Crusted Leg of Lamb (p. 201) is truly the best. Art director James Maikowski leans toward recipes that can be prepared in advance so he can eat when he's ready, with no last-minute stress. His favorites include a simple White Bean Dip with Herbs (p. 21) as well as the luscious Apple Pie Bars (p. 241). And even after six years in professional pastry kitchens, the Test Kitchen's Emily Tylman still lusts for desserts–especially chocolaty ones. Among her top picks: Triple-Layer Sour Cream Chocolate Cake (p. 232), Grilled Chocolate Sandwiches with Caramel Sauce (p. 255) and Double-Chocolate Cookie Crumble (p. 259).

Selecting the recipes here has been a real labor of love; we hope you'll enjoy each and every one as much as we do. Please share your creations with us via Twitter and Instagram @foodandwine, using the hashtag #foodandwine. We can't wait to see them.

Nilou Motamed
Editor
FOOD & WINE

Kate Heddings
Executive Editor
FOOD & WINE Cookbooks

The Eaters

JUSTIN CHAPPLE

Test Kitchen Senior Editor

As F&W's resident Mad Genius, Justin spends much of his time developing wonderfully oddball cooking hacks.

Favorite Childhood Memory: Buying four avocados for a dollar in his hometown of Stockton, California.

SUSAN CHOUNG

Books Editor

Growing up in Brooklyn, New York, Susan helped out at her parents' Italian and Jewish delis. She still has strong opinions about sandwiches.

Most Patience-Instilling Job: Children's cooking show host in Korea.

KATE HEDDINGS

Food Director

Kate's love affair with Hostess cupcakes and Suzy Q's as a kid morphed into a passion in adulthood for all things sugary (except fudge).

A Perfect Food Day: Kimchi, blue crab, raw green beans and lots of dessert.

JULIA HEFFELFINGER

Assistant Food Editor

A proud Midwesterner, Julia is a sucker for fried pork dumplings and hopes to own a chicken coop someday.

Worth Fighting For: She has been known to get into physical altercations over guacamole.

RAY ISLE

Executive Wine Editor

Ray spends an inordinate amount of time cooking, to ensure that he has enough interesting food to pair with all the wine he "has to" taste.

Ultimate Escape: Going to Northeast Harbor, Maine, to sit by the ocean.

JAMES MAIKOWSKI

Art Director

James, an only child who grew up in the Connecticut River Valley, has a penchant for soft-serve.

Proudest Cooking Moment: Learning how to crack two eggs at a time while making pasta at a food shop.

SUZIE MYERS

Style Editor

Born and bred in London, Suzie still puts the kettle on around 4 o'clock every day for an afternoon cuppa.

In Between Photo Shoots: If she's not eating a confection from a local bakery, then she's prepping one from F&W.

SARA PARKS

Photo Editor

Sara grew up in western Massachusetts, making pies with her mother. She now bakes in her Brooklyn kitchen, trying to perfect her mom's pie crust.

Instagram Pointers: Overhead angles, natural light and no flash *ever* for food.

CHRISTINE QUINLAN

Deputy Editor

Christine has strong feelings about how to cook eggs. But they're nothing compared to her views on lobster rolls.

First Restaurant Job: A breakfast waitress when she was just 14.

FREDRIKA STJÄRNE

Creative Director

A Swedish transplant, Fredrika favors experimentation over recipes. The exception: her grandmother's twisted cardamom buns.

Off-Duty Obsessions: Gardening, surfing and diving into anything related to psychoanalysis.

EMILY TYLMAN

Test Kitchen Assistant

Emily spent eight years in professional kitchens, including Eleven Madison Park and Dominique Ansel in NYC.

Dream World Carb Tour: Baguettes in Paris, bucatini all'amatriciana in Rome, ramen in Japan and japchae in Korea.

TINA UJLAKI

Executive Food Editor

Tina still gets just as excited about a great new dish as she did when she started at F&W 31 years and 20,000 recipes ago.

Can't-Live-Without Foods: Honeycrisp apples, grainy bread, cheese, chocolate.

MAJORITY VOTE Of all the recipes in this book, these chewy Chocolate Brownie Cookies (p. 250) were the hands-down staff favorite.

starters

At F&W we're instantly drawn to starters,
like birds attracted to sparkly objects. That's
because starters pack a lot of flavor into
just a few bites and go so great with cocktails.

ASIAN SNACK MIX
WITH NORI

MAKES   **6 cups**

TIME   **Active 10 min;**
Total 30 min plus cooling

½ cup pecans, broken into large
    pieces (2 oz.)

6   cups rice-flake cereal,
    such as Special K (6 oz.)

5   sheets seasoned nori,
    crumbled (from one .74-oz. bag;
    see Note)

3   Tbsp. shinshu (yellow) or
    shiro (white) miso

2   Tbsp. agave nectar

1   Tbsp. wasabi powder or
    1½ tsp. wasabi paste

1   tsp. kosher salt

¼   cup canola oil

NOTE

If seasoned nori is unavailable,
use plain nori and add 1 teaspoon
of toasted sesame oil to
the food processor in Step 2.

Grace Parisi, cookbook author and former F&W Test Kitchen senior editor, combines rice-flake cereal, seasoned nori (seaweed flavored with sesame oil and salt), pecans, miso and wasabi in this light, munchable, Asian-inspired riff on Chex Mix.

1 Preheat the oven to 350°. Spread the pecans in a pie plate and toast for about 6 minutes, until fragrant. Transfer to a large bowl and let cool slightly. Add the cereal and nori and toss well.

2 In a mini food processor, combine the miso, agave nectar, wasabi and salt. Add the oil and process until smooth. Dollop the mixture over the flakes, pecans and nori and toss with your hands to coat evenly.

3 Spread the mix evenly on a parchment paper–lined rimmed baking sheet. Toast for about 18 minutes, stirring and tossing 2 or 3 times, until browned; the mix will crisp as it cools. Transfer to a bowl and serve. —*Grace Parisi*

MAKE AHEAD

The cooled snack mix can be stored in an airtight container for up to 5 days.

BEER

Hoppy IPA.

> "I'm a pickle and chile fiend, so of course I love pickled jalapeños in my guacamole. Because they're finely chopped, you don't accidentally set your mouth ablaze, which can happen with sliced jalapeños."
>
> —SUSAN CHOUNG, BOOKS EDITOR

GUACAMOLE WITH PICKLED JALAPEÑOS

SERVES **4 to 6**

TIME **15 min**

- 2 **Hass avocados, halved and pitted**
- ¼ **cup chopped cilantro**
- 3 **Tbsp. minced white onion**
- 2 **pickled jalapeños, stemmed and finely chopped**
- 1 **Tbsp. fresh lime juice**
  Sea salt
  Tortilla chips, for serving

Chef Alex Stupak makes extraordinary guacamoles for his Empellón restaurants in New York City. Here, he cleverly mixes in pickled jalapeños, which add both heat and tang to the mashed avocados.

1 Scoop the avocados into a medium bowl and coarsely mash with a fork. Fold in the cilantro, onion, jalapeños and lime juice and season with salt. Serve with tortilla chips. —*Alex Stupak*

VARIATION

Stupak makes another excellent guacamole, swapping in fresh jalapeños for pickled. To add crunch, he stirs in chopped pistachios toasted in olive oil.

SALSA NEGRA

MAKES **1 cup**

TIME **20 min**

¾ cup plus 2 Tbsp. grapeseed oil

¾ oz. chiles de árbol, stemmed

¾ oz. guajillo chiles
(about 3)—stemmed, seeded
and cut into pieces

10 black garlic cloves, peeled and
minced (see Note)

10 fresh garlic cloves, minced

1 Tbsp. white wine vinegar

1 Tbsp. piloncillo
(raw Mexican sugar) or
packed light brown sugar

¾ tsp. cumin seeds
Kosher salt

NOTE

Black garlic is fermented and has
a sweet, molasses-like flavor.
It's available at markets like Trader
Joe's and Whole Foods, and online
from obisone.com.

F&W Best New Chef 2015 Carlos Salgado of Taco Maria in Costa Mesa, California, makes this smoky, spicy, rich salsa negra with black garlic and two types of dried chile. He uses it to spike rice and beans; you'll want to put it on everything.

1 In a large saucepan, combine the oil and both chiles and cook over moderate heat, stirring frequently, until the chiles are fragrant and browned in spots, about 7 minutes. Remove from the heat and stir in both garlics along with the vinegar, sugar, cumin and 1 teaspoon of salt. Cover and let cool.

2 Transfer the chile mixture to a blender and pulse until a coarse paste forms. Season with salt. —*Carlos Salgado*

SERVE WITH

Grilled chicken legs or steak.

MAKE AHEAD

The salsa negra can be refrigerated for up to 5 days.

"When the editors tasted this in the Test Kitchen, we all decided it was going to be our go-to sauce for everything. It's basically a chile sauce, with black garlic. The spreadable, sweet-and-savory black garlic is deeply caramelized throughout and significantly boosts the flavor." —TINA UJLAKI, EXECUTIVE FOOD EDITOR

ZA'ATAR-SPICED BEET DIP
WITH GOAT CHEESE AND HAZELNUTS

MAKES   3 cups

TIME   Active 20 min;
       Total 1 hr 30 min

- 6 **medium beets (1½ lbs.), trimmed**
- 2 **small garlic cloves, minced**
- 1 **small fresh red chile, seeded and minced**
- 1 **cup plain Greek yogurt**
- 3 **Tbsp. extra-virgin olive oil**
- 1½ **Tbsp. pure maple syrup**
- 1 **Tbsp. za'atar (see Note)**
  Kosher salt
- ¼ **cup roasted skinned hazelnuts, chopped**
- 2 **Tbsp. goat cheese, crumbled**
- 2 **scallions, thinly sliced**
  Warm bread, for serving

NOTE

Za'atar is a Middle Eastern blend of sesame seeds, herbs and sumac. It's available at specialty food stores and Middle Eastern markets.

Beets have a strong presence in the cuisine of almost every ethnic group in Jerusalem, explains Yotam Ottolenghi, the chef at Nopi in London. They color pickling juices on the Arab table and form the basis for a soup of Jewish, Iraqi and Kurdish origin. Ottolenghi and his *Jerusalem* cookbook co-author, Sami Tamimi, puree beets with Greek yogurt for this luscious spread.

1 Preheat the oven to 350°. Put the beets in a small roasting pan and add ¼ cup of water. Cover with foil and bake for about 1 hour, until tender. Let cool slightly.

2 Peel the beets, cut into wedges and transfer to a food processor. Add the garlic, chile and yogurt and pulse until blended. Add the olive oil, maple syrup and za'atar and puree. Season with salt. Scrape into a wide, shallow bowl. Scatter the hazelnuts, goat cheese and scallions on top and serve with bread.
—*Yotam Ottolenghi and Sami Tamimi*

WINE

Earthy, dry rosé.

"I was on-set when this dip was being photographed for the magazine. I ran home with a bootleg copy of the recipe and cooked it for friends that weekend. It's simple and earthy, with great texture, and the color makes it totally Instagram-worthy!"
—JAMES MAIKOWSKI, ART DIRECTOR

"This recipe is so incredibly quick and versatile that although I typically serve it as a dip at our staff parties, I've also broiled it on top of french fries, stuffed it into grilled cheese and mixed it into deviled egg filling."
—EMILY TYLMAN, TEST KITCHEN ASSISTANT

PIMENTO CHEESE

MAKES **3 cups**

TIME **25 min plus 1 hr chilling**

- **1 cup mayonnaise**
- **¼ small Vidalia onion, finely chopped**
- **½ tsp. hot sauce**
- **1 lb. sharp cheddar cheese, coarsely shredded**
- **½ cup diced drained pimientos (from one 7-oz. jar)**

Pimientos are large, sweet, heart-shaped peppers that are typically used for canning. Pimento cheese—the simple combination of grated cheddar cheese with mayonnaise and pimientos—is a Southern staple often served on crackers or vegetables. The key to making the best pimento cheese is top-quality sharp cheddar. But Atlanta-based food writer and stylist Angie Mosier says her personal secret is using sweet onions like Vidalia or Walla Walla.

1 In a food processor, blend the mayonnaise, onion and hot sauce. Add the shredded cheese and pulse until finely chopped. Add the pimientos and pulse until combined. Transfer the pimento cheese to a bowl. Refrigerate until firm, at least 1 hour. —*Angie Mosier*

SERVE WITH

Crackers or vegetables.

MAKE AHEAD

The pimento cheese can be refrigerated for up to 3 days.

WHITE BEAN DIP
WITH HERBS

MAKES **About 3 cups**

TIME **10 min**

¼ cup plus 2 Tbsp. extra-virgin olive oil

3 garlic cloves, very finely chopped

1 tsp. finely chopped sage

½ tsp. finely chopped rosemary

Two 19-oz. cans cannellini beans, drained

Kosher salt and cayenne pepper

Cookbook author Grace Parisi likes to make this dip when guests arrive with short notice. Drizzling it with a high-quality olive oil will add depth and complexity, but stick with a less-expensive supermarket brand for sautéing the garlic and herbs in Step 1. Any canned white beans can be used in place of the cannellini.

1 In a medium skillet, heat ¼ cup of the olive oil until shimmering. Add the garlic, sage and rosemary and cook over moderately high heat, stirring, until fragrant and the garlic is just beginning to brown, about 1 minute. Add the beans and toss to coat.

2 Transfer the cannellini beans to a food processor. Add 2 tablespoons of water, season with salt and cayenne and process to a fairly smooth puree. Transfer the dip to a small serving bowl and drizzle the remaining 2 tablespoons of olive oil on top. —*Grace Parisi*

SERVE WITH

Pita chips.

RICOTTA AND ROASTED TOMATO
BRUSCHETTA WITH PANCETTA

SERVES **8**

TIME **Active 15 min; Total 45 min**

10 **oz. multicolored cherry tomatoes**

2 **garlic cloves, thickly sliced**

5 **Tbsp. extra-virgin olive oil,**
   plus more for drizzling

   Kosher salt and pepper

4 **thin slices of pancetta**

32 **sage leaves**

1 **lb. fresh ricotta cheese**

8 **slices of country bread,**
   cut ¾ inch thick and toasted

   Flaky sea salt, for serving

Peak-season tomatoes make all the difference in these simple bruschetta from cookbook author and food stylist Susan Spungen. They're the perfect accompaniment to a bowl of soup or a large salad.

1 Preheat the oven to 325°. In a bowl, toss the tomatoes with the garlic and 1 tablespoon of the olive oil; season with kosher salt and pepper. Transfer the tomatoes to one side of a parchment-lined baking sheet and lay the pancetta slices out on the other side. Bake for 25 minutes, until the pancetta is crisp. Transfer the pancetta to paper towels to drain, then crumble.

2 Roast the tomatoes for about 10 more minutes, until bursting and lightly caramelized. Transfer the tomatoes and any rendered fat from the pancetta to a bowl.

3 Meanwhile, in a small skillet, heat the remaining ¼ cup of olive oil over moderately high heat. Add the sage and fry until bright green and crisp, 30 to 45 seconds. Drain the sage on paper towels; reserve the oil for another use.

4 Spread the ricotta on the toasts and top with the tomatoes and crumbled pancetta. Drizzle with olive oil, sprinkle with sea salt and pepper and top the toasts with the sage leaves. Serve immediately. —*Susan Spungen*

VARIATION

To turn these into two-bite hors d'oeuvres, just cut the bruschetta crosswise into strips.

WINE

Bright, berry-scented sparkling rosé.

SPICY GRILLED SHRIMP
WITH YUZU KOSHO PESTO

SERVES **4 to 6**

TIME **25 min**

- 1½ Tbsp. yuzu kosho (see Note)
- 1½ tsp. minced peeled fresh ginger
- 1 garlic clove, minced
- 1 large stalk of fresh lemongrass, tender inner white part only, minced
- 1½ Tbsp. chopped cilantro
- ½ cup extra-virgin olive oil
- 12 jumbo shrimp (about ¾ lb.), butterflied in the shell

NOTE

Yuzu kosho is a hot, spicy and aromatic Japanese condiment made from chiles and ultra-citrusy yuzu zest. It's available at Japanese markets and from chefshop.com.

Yuzu kosho is the key to this supersimple and utterly delicious recipe from F&W Best New Chef 2011 Ricardo Zarate, co-author of *The Fire of Peru*.

1 In a small bowl, combine the yuzu kosho with the ginger, garlic, lemongrass, cilantro and olive oil. Spread half of the pesto on the shrimp and let stand for 10 minutes.

2 Light a grill or heat a grill pan. Grill the shrimp over high heat, turning once, until lightly charred and cooked through, about 4 minutes. Transfer the shrimp to plates and serve with the remaining pesto. —*Ricardo Zarate*

MAKE AHEAD

The yuzu kosho pesto can be refrigerated for up to 3 days.

WINE

The fragrant, medium-bodied Argentinean white Torrontés is spectacular with grilled seafood like these spicy shrimp.

"This is one of those magical recipes—seven ingredients, 25 minutes, and you have an outstanding dish that's packed with flavor. The yuzu kosho pesto has so much going for it. It's aromatic, citrusy, fiery and pungent, yet it doesn't overwhelm the shrimp."

—TINA UJLAKI, EXECUTIVE FOOD EDITOR

GRILLED BEEF ROLLS
WITH NUOC CHAM DIPPING SAUCE

MAKES **40 rolls**

TIME **Active 1 hr; Total 5 hr**

BEEF ROLLS

- 2 **lbs. ground sirloin**
- 3 **garlic cloves, minced**
- 3 **Tbsp. tomato paste**
- 2 **Tbsp. cornstarch**
- 2 **Tbsp. soy sauce**
- 2 **Tbsp. rice wine or sherry**
- 1 **Tbsp. Asian fish sauce**
- 1 **Tbsp. sambal oelek**
- 1 **Tbsp. sugar**
- 1 **tsp. freshly ground black pepper**
- 40 **jarred brined grape leaves— drained, rinsed and patted dry**

  Vegetable or peanut oil, for brushing

NUOC CHAM

- ¼ **cup sugar**
- ⅓ **cup hot water**
- ⅓ **cup Asian fish sauce**
- 3 **Tbsp. fresh lime juice**
- 3 **garlic cloves, minced**
- 1 **Tbsp. minced jalapeño**
- 1 **Tbsp. finely grated peeled fresh ginger**
- 3 **Tbsp. unsalted roasted peanuts, finely chopped**

  Chopped cilantro and whole mint leaves, for garnish

  Lettuce leaves, for wrapping

For these Vietnamese-style grilled beef rolls (bo la lot), Andrew Zimmern, host of Travel Channel's *Bizarre Foods,* wraps seasoned ground sirloin in briny grape leaves and serves them with a sweet, spicy, tangy dipping sauce. Traditionally, the rolls are wrapped in wild betel leaves, which have a slightly peppery flavor when grilled. They can be found at some Asian markets.

1 MAKE THE BEEF ROLLS In a large bowl, combine the ground beef with all of the remaining ingredients except the grape leaves. Cover with plastic wrap and refrigerate for at least 4 hours or overnight.

2 Snip off any stems from the grape leaves. Spread 4 leaves on a work surface. Form a 1-tablespoon-size log of the beef filling at the stem end of each leaf. Fold the sides of each leaf over the filling, then tightly roll up the leaves to form 4 cylinders. Repeat with the remaining grape leaves and filling.

3 MAKE THE NUOC CHAM In a medium bowl, whisk the sugar into the hot water until dissolved. Whisk in all of the remaining ingredients except the garnishes. Transfer the nuoc cham to a serving bowl.

4 Light a grill. Lightly brush the grill and beef rolls with oil. Arrange the rolls on the grill and cook over moderate heat, turning often to prevent burning, until firm and just cooked through, about 8 minutes. Sprinkle the rolls with cilantro and mint. Serve warm with lettuce leaves for wrapping and the nuoc cham for dipping. —*Andrew Zimmern*

WINE

Spicy, blackberry-inflected Malbec.

GOLDEN GAZPACHO
WITH AVOCADO

SERVES **4**

TIME **Active 15 min; Total 45 min**

- 2 **lbs. yellow or orange cherry tomatoes, halved**
- 1 **small garlic clove, crushed**
- ¼ **cup extra-virgin olive oil**
- 1 **jalapeño, seeded and minced**
- **Kosher salt and pepper**
- **Diced avocado and tortilla chips, for serving**

Justin Chapple, F&W Test Kitchen senior editor and star of the Mad Genius Tips videos, based this eye-catching gazpacho on a salsa recipe. He uses yellow tomatoes, which are less acidic than red ones. Jalapeño gives the soup subtle heat.

1 In a blender, puree the halved tomatoes and crushed garlic with ¼ cup of water. With the machine on, gradually add the olive oil until incorporated. Transfer to a bowl, stir in the jalapeño and season with salt and pepper. Refrigerate until chilled, about 30 minutes. Ladle the gazpacho into bowls and top with diced avocado. Serve with tortilla chips. —*Justin Chapple*

MAKE AHEAD

The gazpacho can be refrigerated overnight.

WINE

Zesty, slightly fizzy Txakoli from Spain.

"With only three ingredients whizzed in a blender, this silky soup could not be any easier. It's a staple in my house during the summer because it's all the things it needs to be at that time of year: cool, light and supremely refreshing." –KATE HEDDINGS, FOOD DIRECTOR

DEVILED EGGS
WITH PICKLED SHRIMP

MAKES	24 deviled eggs
TIME	1 hr 15 min plus overnight pickling

SHRIMP

- ¾ cup fresh lemon juice
- ½ cup water
- ¼ cup plus 2 Tbsp. white wine vinegar
- ½ small Spanish onion, chopped
- 1 garlic clove, crushed
- ½ Tbsp. pickling spice
- 1 small dried red chile
- 12 shelled and deveined medium shrimp

EGGS

- 1 dozen large eggs
- ½ cup mayonnaise
- 1 Tbsp. whole-grain mustard
- 4 cornichons, finely chopped
- 2 Tbsp. finely chopped dill, plus sprigs for garnish
- 1 Tbsp. finely chopped chives
- Kosher salt and pepper
- Hot sauce, for serving

"I have the food of the South in my blood," says star chef Bobby Flay. To amp up this Southern potluck staple, Flay tops his creamy dill-and-chive deviled eggs with tangy pickled shrimp.

1 BRINE THE SHRIMP In a medium saucepan, combine all of the ingredients except the shrimp and bring to a boil. Simmer over moderately low heat for 5 minutes; let cool completely.

2 In a medium saucepan of salted boiling water, blanch the shrimp until nearly cooked through, about 2 minutes. Drain and cool under running water. Add the shrimp to the cooled brine, cover and refrigerate overnight. Drain and cut in half lengthwise.

3 MAKE THE EGGS In a large saucepan, cover the eggs with water and bring to a boil. Simmer over moderately high heat for 8 minutes. Drain the water and shake the pan gently to crack the eggs. Chill the eggs slightly under cold running water, then peel them under running water. Pat dry.

4 Cut the eggs in half lengthwise and remove the yolks; transfer the yolks to a bowl and mash well with a fork. Fold in the mayonnaise, mustard, cornichons and chopped dill and chives; season with salt and pepper. Mound the filling in the egg-white halves and top with the shrimp. Garnish with dill sprigs and serve lightly chilled with hot sauce. —Bobby Flay

MAKE AHEAD

The drained pickled shrimp can be refrigerated for up to 2 days.

> "This dish totally wowed us when we made it way back when. Curried crab never had a better partner than crisp, juicy watermelon. Plus, they look great together, whether you plate them flat or layer them in a small glass bowl." —TINA UJLAKI, EXECUTIVE FOOD EDITOR

CURRIED CRAB AND WATERMELON
SALAD WITH ARUGULA

SERVES **4**

TIME **35 min**

- 3 Tbsp. extra-virgin olive oil
- 2 Tbsp. finely chopped Granny Smith apple
- 1 Tbsp. finely chopped onion
- 1½ tsp. mild curry powder
  Pinch of saffron threads, crumbled (optional)
- ½ cup mayonnaise
- 1 Tbsp. finely chopped cilantro
- 1 Tbsp. finely chopped mint
  Kosher salt and pepper
- 1 lb. jumbo lump crabmeat, picked over
  Four ½-inch-thick half-round watermelon slices from a large watermelon, rind removed
- 2 Tbsp. plus 1 tsp. fresh lime juice
- 5 oz. arugula

This easy yet sophisticated recipe is from Daniel Boulud of Daniel restaurant in New York City. Boulud, an F&W Best New Chef 1988, pairs a curry-spiced crab salad with sweet watermelon and bright cilantro and mint.

1 In a small saucepan, heat 1 tablespoon of the olive oil until shimmering. Add the apple, onion, curry and saffron and cook over moderate heat until the onion is softened, about 5 minutes. Remove from the heat and stir in 1 teaspoon of water; let cool.

2 Scrape the apple mixture into a mini food processor. Add the mayonnaise and process until smooth. Transfer the curried mayonnaise to a medium bowl, add the cilantro and mint and season with salt and pepper. Gently fold in the crabmeat.

3 Cut each watermelon slice into 2 triangles and transfer to 4 plates. Season the watermelon with salt and pepper and sprinkle each serving with 1 teaspoon of lime juice. Mound the crab salad on the watermelon. In another bowl, toss the arugula with the remaining 1 tablespoon of lime juice and 2 tablespoons of oil and season with salt and pepper. Arrange the arugula on the plates and serve. —*Daniel Boulud*

WINE

Fruit-forward New Zealand Sauvignon Blanc.

THREE-PEA SALAD
WITH RICOTTA-PEA PUREE AND BLACK GARLIC

SERVES **6**

TIME **Active 1 hr 30 min;
Total 2 hr 30 min**

LEMON CONFITURE

¾ cup sugar

½ tsp. kosher salt

2 firm lemons, very thinly sliced crosswise on a mandoline and seeded

PEA PUREE

¼ cup extra-virgin olive oil

½ medium onion, minced

Kosher salt

1 cup fresh or thawed frozen peas

2 Tbsp. finely chopped mint

2 Tbsp. finely chopped parsley

½ cup fresh ricotta cheese

2 Tbsp. freshly grated Parmigiano-Reggiano cheese

SALAD

1½ Tbsp. extra-virgin olive oil, plus more for brushing

12 small black garlic cloves, peeled (see Note on p. 16)

1 cup freshly shelled English peas (¼ lb.)

¼ lb. sugar snap peas, trimmed

¼ lb. snow peas, trimmed

Kosher salt

Pea shoots, thinly sliced radishes, small mint leaves, finely chopped chives, chopped marcona almonds and edible flowers, for garnish

This wonderful, complex-tasting warm salad is from F&W Best New Chef 2014 Matthew Accarrino of SPQR in San Francisco. It combines three types of peas with a creamy ricotta-pea puree, sweet-tart lemon confiture and almonds.

1 MAKE THE LEMON CONFITURE Preheat the oven to 350°. In a small saucepan, combine the sugar and salt with ¾ cup of water and bring to a boil, stirring to dissolve the sugar. Transfer to a small baking dish and add the lemon slices in an even layer. Bake for 20 to 25 minutes, until the rinds are translucent and the lemons are tender. Let cool completely.

2 MEANWHILE, MAKE THE PEA PUREE In a medium skillet, heat the olive oil. Add the onion, season with salt and cook over moderate heat, stirring occasionally, until just starting to brown, about 7 minutes. Add the peas and cook, stirring, until warmed through, 3 minutes. Stir in the mint and parsley until just wilted, 1 minute. Transfer the mixture to a mini food processor and let cool completely, then puree until smooth. Scrape the pea puree into a medium bowl and fold in the ricotta and Parmigiano-Reggiano. Season with salt.

3 PREPARE THE SALAD Lightly brush a large square of wax paper with olive oil. Arrange the black garlic cloves on the wax paper 3 inches apart and put another piece of wax paper on top. Using a rolling pin, gently roll the cloves until very flat. Slide the paper onto a plate and freeze until the cloves are slightly firm, about 15 minutes.

4 Meanwhile, in a large saucepan of salted boiling water, blanch the English peas, sugar snaps and snow peas until crisp-tender, about 3 minutes. Drain, transfer to a large bowl and stir in the 1½ tablespoons of olive oil. Coarsely chop 8 of the lemon slices and fold them in. Season with salt.

5 Scoop ⅓-cup mounds of the pea puree onto 6 plates and spoon the warm peas alongside. Peel the top sheet of wax paper off the smashed black garlic and, using a small offset spatula, lay 2 garlic cloves on each mound of pea puree. Arrange 1 slice of lemon confiture on the garlic and garnish the salads with pea shoots, radishes, mint, chives, marcona almonds and edible flowers. Serve right away. —*Matthew Accarrino*

MAKE AHEAD

The ricotta-pea puree can be refrigerated overnight. The lemon confiture can be refrigerated for up to 1 week.

WINE

Zippy, green apple–scented northern Italian Pinot Grigio.

GRILLED FAVA BEAN PODS
WITH CHILE AND LEMON

SERVES **6**

TIME **15 min**

1 **lb. very fresh fava beans
   in the pods, rinsed**
2 **Tbsp. extra-virgin olive oil**
1 **scallion, thinly sliced crosswise**
½ **tsp. crushed red pepper**
   Kosher salt
   Lemon wedges, for serving

"Trust me," says San Diego chef Nate Appleman about this unorthodox recipe. He quickly grills whole fava beans, tosses them with crushed red pepper and serves them hot. They can be eaten whole—the tender pods develop a lovely charred flavor on the grill—but it's also easy to eat them in the traditional way: by popping the beans out of their pods and outer skins.

1 Light a grill. In a large bowl, toss the fava bean pods with the olive oil. Grill the favas over high heat for about 5 minutes, turning occasionally, until softened and charred in spots. Return the beans to the bowl and toss with the scallion and crushed red pepper; season with salt. Transfer to a platter and serve with lemon wedges. —*Nate Appleman*

VARIATION

Serve these grilled fava bean pods with lemony lebneh or lemon-garlic yogurt for dipping.

"Who knew that you could eat a whole fava bean pod? The only thing this recipe really depends on is superfresh, firm fava beans. The pod gets tender and the beans steam within, like an oversize version of the very best edamame you've ever had."

—TINA UJLAKI, EXECUTIVE FOOD EDITOR

ANTIPASTO SALAD WITH BOCCONCINI AND GREEN OLIVE TAPENADE

SERVES **8**

TIME **25 min**

- **3 Tbsp. green olive tapenade from a jar**
- **¼ cup finely chopped peperoncini**
- **½ cup extra-virgin olive oil**
- **1½ cups bocconcini (about 9 oz.)**
- **1 Tbsp. plus 1 tsp. fresh lemon juice**
- **1 Tbsp. plus 1 tsp. red wine vinegar**
- **1 Tbsp. plus 1 tsp. minced garlic**
- **1 tsp. dried oregano**
  Kosher salt and pepper
- **1 small head of iceberg lettuce— halved, cored and finely shredded (4 cups)**
- **6 oz. thinly sliced Genoa salami, cut into narrow strips (1½ cups)**
- **6 small basil leaves**
- **½ cup green olives, such as Picholine**

At Osteria Mozza and Pizzeria Mozza in Los Angeles, chef Nancy Silverton gets the biggest flavors from the simplest ingredients. She does just that with this salad, which combines crisp iceberg lettuce, milky mozzarella, spicy-tangy peperoncini and salty olives and salami.

1 In a medium bowl, mix the green olive tapenade with the peperoncini and ¼ cup of the oil. Add the bocconcini and toss.

2 In a small bowl, whisk the lemon juice with the vinegar, garlic and oregano. Whisk in the remaining ¼ cup of olive oil and season the dressing with salt and pepper.

3 In a large bowl, combine the shredded lettuce and salami. Add the marinated bocconcini and half of the dressing and toss well. Transfer the antipasto salad to a large platter. Top with the basil and olives. Drizzle the remaining dressing around the salad and serve. —*Nancy Silverton*

MAKE AHEAD

The recipe can be prepared through Step 2 and refrigerated overnight.

WINE

Sparkling, berry-scented Lambrusco.

> "Wings get even better when you add the umami kick of miso. The white (shiro) kind is the lightest and mildest form of miso. Mixing it with sugar, lime and fish sauce turns it into a glaze you'll want to slather on everything from pork chops, shrimp and salmon to grilled zucchini." —TINA UJLAKI, EXECUTIVE FOOD EDITOR

STICKY MISO CHICKEN WINGS

SERVES 6

TIME Active 15 min; Total 1 hr

12 chicken wings, tips discarded, wings split

2 Tbsp. canola oil

Kosher salt and pepper

⅓ cup shiro (white) miso

2 tsp. fresh lime juice

1 tsp. finely grated peeled fresh ginger

1 tsp. Asian fish sauce

1 Thai bird chile, minced

3 tablespoons turbinado or light brown sugar

Cilantro leaves, for garnish

Lime wedges, for serving

F&W Test Kitchen senior editor Kay Chun gives these irresistible sweet-sour wings a savory earthiness with miso and fish sauce, and zing with lime juice and ginger.

1 Preheat the oven to 400°. In a large bowl, toss the wings with the oil and season lightly with salt and pepper. Transfer to a rack set over a baking sheet. Bake for about 40 minutes, turning the wings halfway through, until they are golden, crispy and cooked through.

2 Meanwhile, in a small saucepan, combine all of the remaining ingredients except the cilantro and lime. Add 3 tablespoons of water and cook over moderately low heat, whisking frequently, until the sugar is dissolved and the glaze is smooth and slightly thickened.

3 Brush the glaze all over the wings and bake for about 10 minutes longer, until the wings are golden brown and sticky. Transfer the wings to a platter, garnish with cilantro and serve with lime wedges. —*Kay Chun*

WINE

Juicy, floral-inflected Gamay from Beaujolais.

POTATO TARTE FLAMBÉE

SERVES **4 to 6**

TIME **Active 45 min;**
Total 1 hr 50 min

All-purpose flour, for dusting

Two 6-oz. balls of levain dough (sourdough; see Note)

Extra-virgin olive oil, for brushing and drizzling

¼ **cup crème fraîche**

¼ **lb. Red Norland or other red potatoes, sliced crosswise ¹⁄₁₆ inch thick on a mandoline**

¼ **cup lightly packed rosemary leaves**

2 **tsp. finely grated lemon zest, preferably Meyer lemon**

Maldon sea salt (see Note) and pepper

NOTE

You can buy raw levain dough from select bakeries. Maldon sea salt has a great crunch and a remarkably subtle, briny flavor; it is available at most grocery stores and online.

This spectacular vegetarian take on tarte flambée (Alsatian-style pizza with onions and bacon) is from Julianne Jones, the baker at Vergennes Laundry in Vergennes, Vermont. She layers thin potato slices on French sourdough (levain), adding crème fraîche for extra tanginess. The key to achieving a crisp crust is stretching the dough thin and baking it quickly in a very hot oven.

1 On a lightly floured work surface, roll or stretch each piece of levain dough to a 6-by-12-inch rectangle. Lightly brush the dough with olive oil, cover loosely with plastic wrap and let stand at room temperature until slightly puffed, about 45 minutes.

2 Meanwhile, set a pizza stone in the bottom of the oven and turn the oven to 500°, allowing at least 30 minutes for the stone to preheat.

3 Work with 1 dough rectangle at a time. If the dough has shrunk, gently stretch it to a 6-by-12-inch rectangle and transfer to a floured pizza peel. Spread 2 tablespoons of the crème fraîche on the dough and arrange half of the potato slices on top, overlapping them slightly. Sprinkle half of the rosemary and lemon zest over the potatoes and drizzle with 1 tablespoon of olive oil. Season with Maldon sea salt and pepper.

4 Slide the dough onto the hot pizza stone and bake for 8 to 10 minutes, until golden brown and crisp. Slide the tarte flambée onto a work surface, cut into 2-inch strips and serve. Repeat with the remaining dough and toppings.
—*Julianne Jones*

WINE

Ripe, full-bodied Alsace white, such as Pinot Gris.

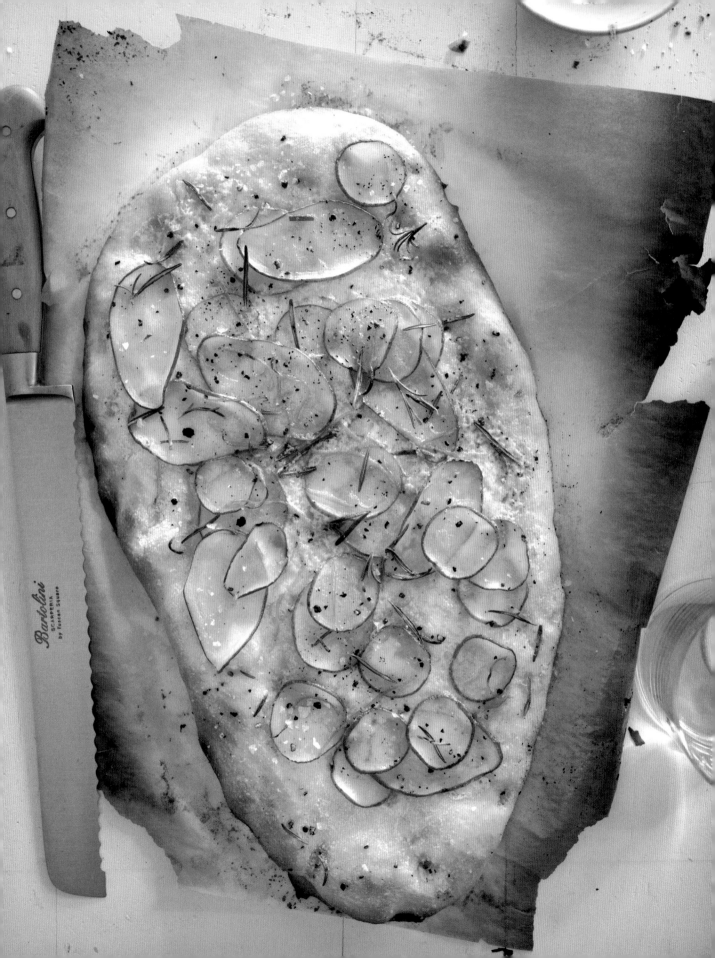

PORK-KIMCHI DUMPLING PANCAKES

SERVES **6 to 8**

TIME **1 hr**

DIPPING SAUCE

- ¼ cup soy sauce
- 1 Tbsp. white vinegar
- 1 Tbsp. sesame seeds
- 1 Tbsp. sugar
- ½ Tbsp. gochugaru (Korean red pepper flakes)

DUMPLINGS

- 10 oz. ground pork
- 2 scallions, minced
- ⅓ cup finely chopped drained kimchi
- 2 garlic cloves, minced
- 1 Tbsp. minced peeled fresh ginger
- 1 large egg, lightly beaten
- 1 Tbsp. soy sauce
- 1 tsp. kosher salt
- ¼ cup firm tofu, finely chopped
- 30 gyoza wrappers
- 1½ Tbsp. cornstarch
- 3 Tbsp. canola oil

Corey Lee of Benu in San Francisco, an F&W Best New Chef 2012, ingeniously reinvents pan-fried dumplings: He adds a batter that turns the dumplings into one round, crisp pancake.

1 MAKE THE DIPPING SAUCE In a small bowl, mix all of the ingredients until the sugar is dissolved.

2 MAKE THE DUMPLINGS In a large bowl, mix all of the ingredients except the wrappers, cornstarch and oil. Arrange 4 wrappers on a work surface; keep the rest covered with a damp paper towel. Brush the edges of the wrappers with water and drop 1 tablespoon of the filling in the centers. Fold over one side of the wrapper to form a half-moon, pressing the edges together. Transfer to a parchment-lined baking sheet and cover with plastic wrap; assemble the remaining dumplings.

3 In a small bowl, stir the cornstarch with 1 cup plus 2 tablespoons of water to make a slurry. Heat 1 tablespoon of the oil in an 8-inch nonstick skillet. Arrange 10 dumplings around the edge of the skillet, overlapping them slightly (there should be almost no empty space). Cook over moderate heat until golden on the bottom. Drizzle one-third of the slurry over and around the dumplings, cover the skillet and cook for 1 minute. Uncover and cook until the dumplings are cooked through and the slurry forms a thin crust, about 4 minutes. Carefully invert the dumpling pancake onto a plate. Repeat to make 2 more pancakes. Serve with the dipping sauce. —*Corey Lee*

MAKE AHEAD

The uncooked dumplings can be refrigerated for 4 hours or frozen for up to 1 month; allow additional cooking time if starting with frozen dumplings.

WINE

Crisp Grüner Veltliner from Austria has the same tangy acidity as kimchi and works well with these savory pancakes.

ZUCCHINI QUESADILLA
WITH SPICY SALSA ROJA

SERVES **2**

TIME **Active 20 min; Total 45 min**

- 1 **lb. tomatoes, cored and quartered**
- 1 **small onion, peeled and quartered**
- 4 **garlic cloves**
- ¼ **cup canola oil**
- 6 **dried chiles de árbol, stemmed**
- 1 **chipotle chile in adobo**
- 2 **Tbsp. apple cider vinegar**
- 1 **tsp. sugar**
- **Kosher salt**
- **Two 10-inch flour tortillas**
- ½ **cup shredded Monterey Jack cheese**
- 2 **small zucchinis, thinly sliced crosswise**
- **Chopped cilantro and thinly sliced Fresno chiles, for garnish**

Walter Manzke makes all kinds of innovative Mexican food at Petty Cash Taqueria in L.A. Here, he adds thin zucchini slices to a cheesy quesadilla, which livens it up a bit; his bold, spicy salsa gives it an excellent punch.

1 Preheat the broiler. On a rimmed baking sheet, toss the tomatoes, onion and garlic with 2 tablespoons of the oil. Broil 6 inches from the heat for 20 minutes, until the tomatoes and onion are softened and nicely charred.

2 In a small skillet, toast the árbol chiles over moderately low heat, stirring, until lightly charred, 3 minutes; transfer to a blender. Add the broiled tomatoes, onion and garlic along with the chipotle chile, vinegar and sugar and puree until smooth. Transfer the salsa roja to a bowl and season with salt.

3 In a large cast-iron skillet, heat 1 tablespoon of the oil. Place 1 tortilla in the skillet and scatter the cheese and zucchini evenly on top. Drizzle with some of the salsa roja and top with the second tortilla. Cook over moderately high heat until crisp on the bottom, 3 minutes. Flip the quesadilla, add the remaining 1 tablespoon of canola oil and cook until the cheese is melted, 2 minutes. Slice the quesadilla into wedges and transfer to a plate. Garnish with the cilantro and Fresno chiles and serve with the remaining salsa roja. —*Walter Manzke*

COCKTAIL

A simple tequila drink, like a limey margarita or a paloma (made with grapefruit juice and soda).

"This quesadilla is my weeknight go-to. The zucchini cuts the richness and makes me feel a little less guilty about piling on the cheese. I like to make extra salsa for breakfast tacos the next morning, for spicing up cocktail sauce for shrimp or even for stirring into a Bloody Mary." —JULIA HEFFELFINGER, ASSISTANT FOOD EDITOR

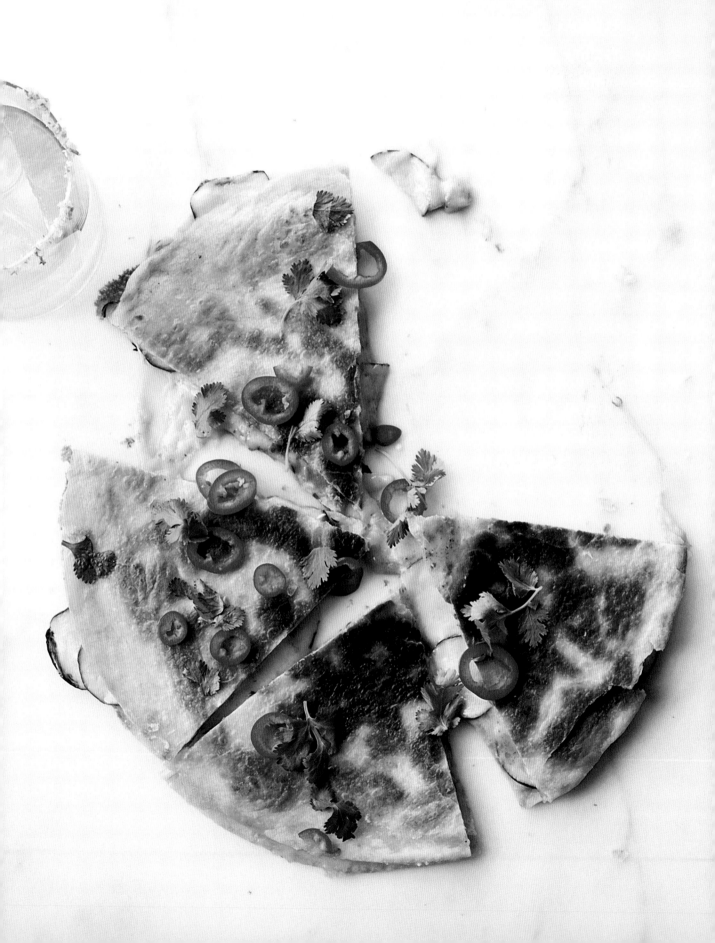

BACONY TORTILLAS WITH MELTED CHEESE AND CRISPY MUSHROOMS

SERVES **4**

TIME **Active 1 hr; Total 2 hr**

BACONY TORTILLAS

- **1 cup all-purpose flour,
  plus more for dusting**
- **¾ tsp. kosher salt**
- **2 Tbsp. cold rendered bacon fat,
  from 4 oz. bacon (see Note)**
- **2 Tbsp. vegetable shortening**
- **½ cup warm water**

MUSHROOMS AND CHEESE

- **2 Tbsp. unsalted butter**
- **6 oz. chanterelle, hen-of-the-
  woods or black trumpet
  mushrooms, cut into large pieces**
- **2 thyme sprigs**
  Kosher salt
- **8 oz. Chihuahua or Fontina cheese,
  shredded**
- **1 serrano chile, thinly sliced**
- **¼ cup cilantro leaves**

NOTE

If bacon fat is unavailable, double
the amount of vegetable shortening.

In this recipe from Ford Fry, chef at The Optimist in Atlanta, bacon fat helps make homemade tortillas tender and gives them a deep flavor. They're fantastic for scooping up melty cheese and crispy mushrooms.

1 MAKE THE TORTILLAS In a stand mixer, combine the 1 cup of flour and the salt. Using your hands, rub the bacon fat and vegetable shortening into the flour until the mixture is crumbly. Using the dough hook, slowly mix in the water at medium speed until a ball forms, adding more flour if necessary; the dough will be moist but should start to pull away from the side of the bowl. Continue kneading until the dough is smooth, shiny and elastic, about 10 minutes. Cover the bowl with plastic wrap; let rest for 45 minutes.

2 Scoop slightly rounded tablespoons of the dough and roll between pieces of parchment paper into 4-inch rounds. Working in batches, heat a cast-iron skillet and cook the tortillas over moderately high heat, turning once, until lightly browned, about 1 minute. Transfer to a kitchen towel and keep warm.

3 PREPARE THE MUSHROOMS AND CHEESE In a medium skillet, melt the butter. Add the mushrooms and thyme and cook over moderately high heat, undisturbed, until lightly browned, about 2 minutes. Season the mushrooms with salt and cook, tossing occasionally, until browned and crisp, about 6 minutes. Transfer to a paper towel–lined plate; discard the thyme sprigs.

4 Preheat the broiler. In a small cast-iron skillet or ovenproof dish, broil the cheese 8 inches from the heat until just melted, about 1 minute. Top the cheese with the mushrooms, chile and cilantro and serve immediately, with the warm tortillas. —*Ford Fry*

MAKE AHEAD

The tortillas can be made up to 6 hours ahead and kept covered at room temperature. Reheat before serving.

BEER

Pair this rich dish with a refreshing pale ale.

salads +sides

We think salads and sides are the unsung heroes of a meal. Sometimes nothing satisfies like the cool crunch of a salad. And what would meat loaf be without mashed potatoes?

SUMMER SALAD WITH HERBS AND PITA CRISPS

SERVES **4 to 6**

TIME **40 min**

- ¼ cup plus 2 Tbsp. extra-virgin olive oil
- 1 tsp. finely grated garlic
- 2 pita breads, each split into 2 rounds
- Kosher salt and pepper
- ½ lb. haricots verts, green beans or wax beans, trimmed
- 1 mint sprig plus 2 cups chopped mint
- 2 Tbsp. fresh lemon juice
- 1 shallot, minced
- 1 Kirby cucumber, chopped
- 6 cups packed chopped baby romaine (6 oz.)
- 2 cups parsley leaves
- 12 multicolored cherry tomatoes, halved
- 1 cup sunflower sprouts or chopped purslane

For this riff on fattoush (a Middle Eastern toasted pita bread salad), F&W Test Kitchen senior editor Kay Chun cleverly rubs the inside of a wooden salad bowl with a mint sprig, then makes the dressing right in the bowl. This lets the dressing absorb the natural mint oils.

1 Preheat the oven to 375°. In a small bowl, mix the olive oil with the garlic. Brush the pita with 2 tablespoons of the garlic oil. Toast in the oven for 5 to 7 minutes, until crisp and golden. Transfer the pita to a plate; season with salt and pepper. Let cool, then break into big crisps.

2 Meanwhile, in a medium saucepan of salted boiling water, blanch the beans until crisp-tender, about 2 minutes. Drain and chill in a bowl of ice water. Drain and pat dry; halve the beans crosswise.

3 Rub the mint sprig all over the inside of a large wooden bowl; discard the sprig. In the bowl, mix the remaining ¼ cup of garlic oil with the lemon juice and shallot; season with salt and pepper. Add the chopped mint, beans, cucumber, romaine, parsley, tomatoes, sprouts and pita crisps. Toss to coat, then serve. —Kay Chun

VARIATION

For a fall or winter version of this salad, replace the summer vegetables with any combination of roasted root vegetables, squash, brussels sprouts and red onion.

WINE

Spritzy, citrusy Portuguese white, such as Vinho Verde.

FALL HARVEST SALAD

SERVES **10 to 12**

TIME **Active 25 min; Total 40 min**

¼ cup plus 3 Tbsp. vegetable oil, preferably peanut

2 cups peeled butternut squash (10 oz.), cut into 1-inch cubes

Kosher salt and pepper

2 Tbsp. sherry vinegar

1 Tbsp. coarsely chopped tarragon

1 Tbsp. chopped flat-leaf parsley

10 oz. mixed salad greens or mesclun

1 cup coarsely chopped pecans

½ cup roasted pumpkin seeds

This salad from Shawn McClain, the chef at Green Zebra in Chicago, epitomizes fall flavors, with its chunks of butternut squash, pumpkin seeds, pecans and greens. The easiest way to peel the butternut squash is with a sturdy Y-peeler.

1 In a large nonstick skillet, heat 2 tablespoons of the oil. Add the squash in an even layer, season with salt and pepper and cook over moderately high heat until browned on the bottom, about 5 minutes. Turn the squash cubes and cook over moderately low heat until browned on the other side and just tender, about 7 minutes.

2 In a small bowl, combine the vinegar with the tarragon, parsley and the remaining 5 tablespoons of oil; season the dressing with salt and pepper. In a large bowl, toss the salad greens with the pecans, pumpkin seeds and roasted squash. Pour the dressing over the salad and toss well. Serve right away. —*Shawn McClain*

MAKE AHEAD

The dressing can be kept at room temperature for up to 2 hours. The cooked squash can be refrigerated overnight. Bring to room temperature before using in the salad.

WINE

Pinot Noir's balance of crisp fruit, light spiciness and moderate tannins makes it very versatile—ideal with all the big flavors in this salad.

> "Every summer, when the snow peas are superfresh and the unruly pot of mint on the deck needs to be tamed, I eat this salad and am quickly reminded why I waited all year to make it."
>
> —JAMES MAIKOWSKI, ART DIRECTOR

FRESH SNOW PEA SALAD
WITH PANCETTA AND PECORINO

SERVES 6 to 8

TIME 35 min

- 1 lb. snow peas, strings removed, pods sliced on the diagonal ¼ inch wide
- ¼ cup plus 1 Tbsp. extra-virgin olive oil
- 4 oz. thickly sliced pancetta, cut into ¼-inch dice
- ½ small white onion, finely chopped
- 2 Tbsp. fresh lemon juice
- ½ tsp. lemon oil (see Note) Kosher salt and pepper
- ½ cup mint leaves, torn
- 2 oz. shaved Pecorino Sardo cheese

NOTE

Olive oil pressed or infused with lemon is available at specialty food stores and most supermarkets.

Daniel Humm, the chef at Eleven Madison Park in New York City, creates a terrific summer salad that's crisp and lemony, with bits of meaty pancetta and lots of fresh mint.

1 Soak the snow peas in a bowl of ice water for 10 minutes. Meanwhile, in a medium skillet, heat 1 tablespoon of the olive oil. Add the pancetta and cook over moderate heat until lightly browned and the fat has rendered, about 5 minutes. Spoon off all but 1 tablespoon of the fat in the skillet. Add the onion and cook, stirring occasionally, until softened, about 5 minutes.

2 Drain the snow peas and pat dry. In a medium bowl, whisk the remaining ¼ cup of olive oil with the lemon juice and lemon oil and season with salt and pepper. Add the snow peas, pancetta, onion and half of the mint and season with salt and pepper; toss well. Garnish with the remaining mint, shave the pecorino on top and serve. —*Daniel Humm*

TIP

Since the snow peas aren't cooked, it's best to buy them when they're very fresh, preferably from a farmers' market—they will be more tender.

WINE

Crisp and fragrant Italian white, such as Arneis from Piedmont.

FRENCHIE SALAD

SERVES **4 to 6**

TIME **Active 30 min; Total 1 hr**

PICKLED MUSTARD SEEDS

- 2 Tbsp. yellow mustard seeds
- ¼ cup distilled white vinegar

DRESSING

- 4 oz. cherry tomatoes
- ¾ cup plus 1 Tbsp. extra-virgin olive oil
- 1 Tbsp. red wine vinegar
- 1 Tbsp. Dijon mustard
- 1 Tbsp. fresh orange juice
- Kosher salt and pepper

SALAD

- 4 slices of thick-cut bacon (4 oz.), cut into 1-inch dice or strips
- 2 oz. blue cheese, crumbled (⅓ cup)
- ¼ cup crème fraîche
- 4 heads of Little Gem or baby romaine lettuce (1 lb.), leaves separated
- Kosher salt and pepper
- Chopped chives, for garnish

At French Louie in Brooklyn, chef Ryan Angulo creates dishes that are both French and American, as in this hearty salad. It's an homage to the frisée salad as well as a take on the American steakhouse wedge salad.

1 PICKLE THE MUSTARD SEEDS In a small saucepan, combine the mustard seeds and vinegar and bring to a boil. Remove the saucepan from the heat and let stand for 1 hour.

2 MAKE THE DRESSING Preheat the oven to 450°. In a small ovenproof skillet or baking dish, toss the tomatoes with 1 tablespoon of the oil. Roast for 30 minutes, until the tomatoes have popped and are browned in spots. Transfer to a blender. Add the remaining ingredients; puree until smooth.

3 MAKE THE SALAD In a small skillet, cook the bacon over moderate heat until browned and crisp, 5 to 7 minutes. Transfer to paper towels to drain. In a small bowl, blend the blue cheese with the crème fraîche until smooth. Dollop the mixture onto plates and spread slightly. In a large bowl, toss the lettuce with half of the dressing; season with salt and pepper. Arrange the lettuce on top of the blue cheese mixture. Garnish with the pickled mustard seeds, the bacon and chives. Serve the remaining dressing on the side. —*Ryan Angulo*

MAKE AHEAD

The dressing can be refrigerated for up to 3 days.

WINE

Medium-bodied southern French white, like Picpoul de Pinet.

GARLICKY CAESAR SALAD

SERVES **6**

TIME **15 min**

- ¼ cup mayonnaise
- 3 Tbsp. freshly grated pecorino, plus thin shavings for serving (optional)
- 1 anchovy fillet, drained, plus more fillets for serving (optional)
- 1 tsp. red wine vinegar
- 1 small garlic clove, smashed
- ⅛ tsp. Worcestershire sauce
- ⅛ tsp. Tabasco
  Freshly ground white pepper
- 3 chilled large hearts of romaine (about 1 lb.), leaves left whole
  Freshly ground black pepper

Frank Falcinelli created his take on this classic some 25 years ago: romaine hearts with a pungent dressing made from anchovy, Worcestershire, Tabasco and, irreverently, jarred mayonnaise. The recipe is now a cornerstone of the menu at his Frankies restaurants in New York City.

1 In a blender, combine the mayonnaise with the 3 tablespoons of grated pecorino, 1 anchovy, 2 tablespoons of water and the vinegar, garlic, Worcestershire and Tabasco. Process until smooth. Season the dressing with white pepper.

2 In a large salad bowl, toss the romaine with the dressing and season with black pepper. Garnish with pecorino shavings and anchovy fillets and serve right away. —*Frank Falcinelli and Frank Castronovo*

VARIATION

The dressing would also be delicious on a kale Caesar salad.

"This salad re-creates the restaurant experience in your kitchen: It doesn't hold back, it gives you what you want. The creamy, tangy dressing also brings together jarred mayonnaise, anchovies and white pepper, all fortuitous nods to my Scandinavian heritage." —FREDRIKA STJÄRNE, CREATIVE DIRECTOR

> "This dish simply has everything going for it. Green apples add a touch of sweetness, hazelnuts are toasty and quinoa provides a bit of protein. It also has escarole, one of my favorite salad greens. The crisp, sweet leaves have a slightly bitter edge and don't wilt when dressed." —TINA UJLAKI, EXECUTIVE FOOD EDITOR

ESCAROLE SALAD
WITH RED QUINOA AND HAZELNUTS

SERVES 4 to 6

TIME Active 20 min; Total 40 min

- ¼ cup red quinoa, rinsed and drained
- ¼ cup plus 2 Tbsp. extra-virgin olive oil
- 3 Tbsp. apple cider vinegar
- 1 Tbsp. plus 1 tsp. honey
- Fine sea salt and pepper
- 1 head of escarole, chopped into bite-size pieces
- 1 Granny Smith apple— halved, cored and thinly sliced on a mandoline
- ½ cup toasted hazelnuts, chopped

Marco Canora, the health-minded chef at Hearth in New York City, likes quinoa, a high-protein seed, because it mimics the satisfying texture and starchiness of a grain. He uses it in this crunchy and fresh winter salad.

1 In a medium saucepan of boiling water, cook the quinoa just until tender, about 10 minutes. Drain well and spread out on a baking sheet to cool.

2 In a large bowl, whisk the olive oil with the vinegar and honey. Season with salt and pepper. Add the escarole, apple, hazelnuts and quinoa and toss to coat. Season with salt and pepper and serve. —*Marco Canora*

VARIATION

For this super-versatile salad, you can swap in pear for the apple and black quinoa for the red. Or, to convert it to a main-course salad, toss in julienned ham or shredded chicken.

WINE

The toasty character of Chardonnay harmonizes with the hazelnuts in this salad and accentuates the bright crunch of the apple.

FARRO AND GREEN OLIVE SALAD
WITH WALNUTS AND RAISINS

SERVES **6 to 8**

TIME **40 min**

1¼ cups farro (½ lb.)

Fine sea salt

1 cup walnuts (3½ oz.)

2½ cups pitted green olives, preferably Castelvetrano, chopped (11 oz.)

4 scallions, white and light green parts only, finely chopped

⅓ cup snipped chives

2 Tbsp. golden raisins

½ tsp. crushed red pepper

¼ cup extra-virgin olive oil

3 Tbsp. fresh lemon juice

1 Tbsp. honey

Freshly shaved pecorino cheese, for serving

Heidi Swanson, creator of the culinary blog 101 Cookbooks, loads this salad with so many olives that there's a piece in every single bite. It's worth seeking out bright green Castelvetrano olives (available at most olive bars), which have a meaty texture and mild, buttery flavor.

1 Preheat the oven to 375°. In a medium saucepan, combine the farro with 4 cups of water and ½ teaspoon of salt. Bring to a boil and simmer, partially covered, until the farro is tender, about 20 minutes. Drain well and spread on a baking sheet to cool.

2 Meanwhile, place the walnuts in a pie plate and toast in the oven for 5 to 7 minutes, until lightly golden and fragrant. Let cool, then coarsely chop.

3 In a large bowl, combine the farro, walnuts, olives, scallions, chives, raisins, crushed red pepper, olive oil, lemon juice and honey and season with salt. Toss well. Transfer the salad to a platter, garnish with cheese and serve. —*Heidi Swanson*

MAKE AHEAD

The salad can be refrigerated overnight. Bring it to room temperature before serving.

WINE

Ripe, citrusy Sauvignon Blanc.

WARM SPELT AND RED CABBAGE
WITH RICOTTA SALATA

SERVES **6**

TIME **Active 30 min;
Total 1 hr 30 min plus
overnight soaking**

SPELT

1 **Tbsp. extra-virgin olive oil**

1⅓ **cups spelt (not pearled), soaked
overnight and drained**

½ **small yellow onion, finely
chopped**

1 **thyme sprig**

Kosher salt

CABBAGE

2 **Tbsp. unsalted butter**

2 **Tbsp. extra-virgin olive oil**

1 **medium red onion, finely diced**

1 **lb. red cabbage, cut into 1-inch
pieces (4 cups)**

2 **Tbsp. red wine vinegar**

Kosher salt and pepper

1½ **tsp. chopped thyme**

1 **cup walnuts (4 oz.)**

4 **oz. ricotta salata cheese,
crumbled (1 cup)**

Spelt is a highly nutritious, ancient strain of wheat. Cooked as grains, it's nutty and chewy, almost like barley. Cookbook author Grace Parisi combines thyme-scented spelt with toasted walnuts, wilted red cabbage and salty crumbles of ricotta salata cheese. You can swap in other whole grains, such as farro, wheat berries or barley.

1 COOK THE SPELT In a large saucepan, heat the olive oil. Add the spelt and cook over moderate heat, stirring, until lightly toasted; it will turn slightly opaque just before browning. Add the yellow onion and thyme and cook over low heat, stirring, until the onion is softened, about 5 minutes. Add 2 cups of water and ½ teaspoon of salt and bring to a boil. Cover and cook over very low heat until the water is absorbed and the spelt is tender but still chewy, about 50 minutes. Drain well. Discard the thyme sprig, fluff the spelt and season with salt.

2 MEANWHILE, MAKE THE CABBAGE Preheat the oven to 350°. In a large skillet, melt the butter in the oil. Add the red onion and cook over high heat, stirring, until softened, about 4 minutes. Add the cabbage and vinegar, season with salt and pepper and cook, stirring occasionally, until the cabbage is barely wilted, about 6 minutes. Add the thyme and ½ cup of water, cover and cook over low heat, stirring occasionally, until the cabbage is tender and the water has evaporated, about 20 minutes.

3 Meanwhile, spread the walnuts in a pie plate and toast in the oven for about 12 minutes, until golden. Let cool, then coarsely chop. Fold the spelt, toasted walnuts and ricotta salata into the cabbage and season with salt and pepper. Transfer to a bowl and serve. —*Grace Parisi*

MAKE AHEAD

The cooked spelt can be refrigerated for up to 5 days or frozen for up to 1 month.

KALE SALAD WITH GARLICKY PANKO

SERVES **6**

TIME **30 min**

½ cup plus 2 Tbsp. extra-virgin olive oil

1 garlic clove, thinly sliced

½ cup panko

  Kosher salt and pepper

1 bunch of curly kale

¼ cup rice vinegar

3 oz. feta cheese, crumbled

6 fried eggs (optional)

At Mei Mei in Boston, siblings Margaret, Irene and Andy Li like to cook with all kinds of Asian ingredients, including the panko and rice vinegar they add to this kale salad.

1 In a large nonstick skillet, heat 2 tablespoons of the olive oil. Add the garlic and cook over moderate heat, stirring, until fragrant, 30 seconds. Stir in the panko and cook, stirring, until golden and crisp, 3 minutes. Season with salt and pepper and transfer to a plate to cool.

2 Cut the stems from the kale and tear the leaves into pieces. In a large bowl, whisk the vinegar with the remaining ½ cup of oil and season with salt and pepper. Add the kale and massage the leaves with the dressing using your fingers. Season with salt and pepper and toss. Transfer to a platter, top with the feta, garlicky panko and fried eggs, if using, and serve.
—Margaret, Irene and Andy Li

TIP

Rubbing curly kale leaves with a rice vinegar dressing and salt makes them amazingly tender. The technique also works with shaved brussels sprouts and cabbage.

"This simple salad is surprisingly satisfying–the garlicky panko topping will make even the biggest kale-hater want seconds. I top the salad with a fried egg for weeknight meals or serve it alongside a big steak and roasted potatoes for a steakhouse dinner at home." —JULIA HEFFELFINGER, ASSISTANT FOOD EDITOR

> "After a day of sampling heavy and exotic foods at work (I'm not complaining), this supereasy, crunchy vegetable salad is exactly what I want for dinner. It's also one of my favorite sides for a richer cut of grilled pork or beef, like Korean short ribs."
>
> —JULIA HEFFELFINGER, ASSISTANT FOOD EDITOR

BROCCOLINI, MUSHROOM AND SESAME SALAD

SERVES **4**

TIME **15 min**

- 1 **bunch of Broccolini (12 oz.), trimmed**
- 2 **cups sliced button mushrooms**
- 2 **Tbsp. toasted sesame seeds**
- 1½ **Tbsp. apple cider vinegar**
- 1½ **Tbsp. toasted sesame oil**
- 1½ **Tbsp. soy sauce**
- ¼ **tsp. crushed red pepper**
- 1 **garlic clove, grated or minced**
- 1 **scallion, thinly sliced**
  Kosher salt and pepper

Judy Joo, host of the Cooking Channel's *Korean Food Made Simple,* makes a tangy Asian vinaigrette that's a superb (and quick) way to dress up Broccolini and mushrooms.

1 In a saucepan of salted boiling water, blanch the Broccolini until bright green and crisp-tender, about 2 minutes. Drain and transfer to a large bowl; let cool slightly. Add all of the remaining ingredients and toss to coat. Season with salt and pepper and serve. *—Judy Joo*

VARIATION

If Broccolini is unavailable, substitute thin spears of broccoli.

WINE

Bold southern Italian white, such as Falanghina.

"We think Jamie Oliver pioneered the fantastic, meant-to-be, much-copied matchup of sweet roasted carrots and creamy avocado. It has the perfect combo of textures and flavors. If you want to add something, grilled scallions would be delicious, as would a squeeze of lime." —TINA UJLAKI, EXECUTIVE FOOD EDITOR

ROASTED CARROT AND AVOCADO SALAD
WITH GRAPEFRUIT GREMOLATA

SERVES **4 to 6**

TIME **45 min**

- ¼ cup plus 2 Tbsp. extra-virgin olive oil
- 3 Tbsp. fresh grapefruit juice plus 2 tsp. finely grated grapefruit zest
- 1½ tsp. ground coriander
- 1½ lbs. medium carrots, cut into ¼-inch-thick rounds
- Kosher salt and pepper
- ¼ cup roasted almonds, chopped
- ⅓ cup chopped parsley
- 2 medium Hass avocados, peeled and cut into wedges

Roasted carrots and raw avocados are an unexpected combination. In this recipe from F&W Test Kitchen senior editor Kay Chun, a grapefruit dressing adds tang and sweetness, while roasted almonds add a healthy crunch.

1 Preheat the oven to 450°. In a small bowl, whisk the olive oil, grapefruit juice and coriander. On a baking sheet, toss the carrots with 3 tablespoons of the dressing. Spread the carrots in a single layer and roast for about 20 minutes, turning once, until golden and tender. Season with salt and pepper.

2 Meanwhile, in a small bowl, mix the almonds, grapefruit zest and parsley. Transfer the carrots to a platter along with the avocados. Drizzle with the remaining dressing, top with the grapefruit gremolata and serve. —*Kay Chun*

VARIATION

You can swap in carrots of varying colors, and if they're young enough, they can be roasted whole.

WINE

Bright, citrusy sparkling wine, like Prosecco.

BEET SALAD WITH CANDIED MARCONA ALMONDS

SERVES 8

TIME Active 45 min; Total 2 hr

2½ lbs. medium red or golden beets, scrubbed and trimmed

½ cup plus 2 Tbsp. extra-virgin olive oil

1 Tbsp. unsalted butter, plus more for greasing

2 Tbsp. sugar

1 Tbsp. light corn syrup

Kosher salt and cayenne pepper

1 cup marcona almonds

½ cup fresh tangerine juice

2 Tbsp. sherry vinegar

1 Tbsp. Dijon mustard

1 Tbsp. minced shallots

1 small head of frisée (4 oz.), torn into bite-size pieces

Young pecorino cheese

Steve Corry, the chef at Five Fifty-Five in Portland, Maine, loves to toss roasted beets with a complex sherry vinegar. To help mellow the vinegar's tang, Corry reduces tangerine juice to a syrup and adds it to the dressing. Inspired by peanut brittle, he candies marcona almonds to top the salad. The nuts are also fantastic on their own.

1 Preheat the oven to 350°. In a large baking dish, toss the beets with 2 tablespoons of the olive oil. Cover with foil and bake for 1½ hours, until tender. When cool enough to handle, peel the beets and cut them into ½-inch wedges.

2 Meanwhile, line a large rimmed baking sheet with parchment paper and lightly butter the paper. In a medium saucepan, combine the 1 tablespoon of butter with the sugar, corn syrup and a pinch each of salt and cayenne and boil, stirring, until the sugar is dissolved. Off the heat, add the almonds and stir until evenly coated with the syrup. Scrape the almonds onto the parchment-lined baking sheet in an even layer. Bake with the beets for about 12 minutes, until golden and bubbling. Let the nuts cool for about 25 minutes, then break into small clusters.

3 In a small saucepan, simmer the tangerine juice over moderate heat until reduced to 2 tablespoons, about 15 minutes. Let cool, then transfer to a large bowl. Whisk in the vinegar, mustard and shallots. Gradually whisk in the remaining ½ cup of olive oil and season the dressing with salt. Add the beets and frisée and toss.

4 Transfer the salad to a platter or bowl. Garnish with the candied almonds, shave the pecorino on top and serve. —*Steve Corry*

MAKE AHEAD

The peeled roasted beets can be refrigerated overnight. Bring to room temperature before serving. The candied almonds can be stored in an airtight container at room temperature for up to 2 days.

SAIGON BEEF SALAD

SERVES 12

TIME 1 hr 30 min

- ¼ cup soy sauce
- 1 cup plus 2 Tbsp. vegetable oil
- 7 garlic cloves, coarsely chopped
  Two 2½-lb. sirloin steaks
- 8 shallots, thinly sliced
  One 2-inch piece of fresh ginger, peeled and coarsely chopped
- 2 Tbsp. sugar
- 1 large jalapeño, coarsely chopped
- ½ cup fresh lime juice
- ⅓ cup Asian fish sauce
  Kosher salt and pepper
- 3 lbs. cabbage, cored and shredded
- 1 cup coarsely chopped mint
- 1 cup coarsely chopped cilantro
- 4 cups mung bean sprouts
- 1½ cups chopped unsalted peanuts

This Vietnamese-style salad was created by Marcia Kiesel, co-author of *Simple Art of Vietnamese Cooking*. It's a fantastic dish for parties since it doesn't have to be served right away. Instead of the steak, you can toss the salad with shrimp or chicken or even pork.

1 In a shallow dish, combine the soy sauce with 2 tablespoons of the oil and 4 of the garlic cloves. Coat the steaks with the marinade and refrigerate for at least 1 hour or overnight.

2 In a medium saucepan, heat the remaining 1 cup of oil until shimmering. Working in 3 batches, fry the shallots over moderately high heat, stirring, until browned, about 4 minutes per batch; lower the heat if necessary. Drain on paper towels.

3 In a mini food processor, combine the remaining 3 garlic cloves with the ginger, sugar and jalapeño and process to a paste. Blend in the lime juice and fish sauce.

4 Light a grill or preheat the broiler. Season the steaks with salt and pepper and grill over moderately high heat or broil until nicely browned and medium-rare, about 5 minutes per side. Let the steaks rest for 10 minutes, then slice them ¼ inch thick. Stack the slices and cut them lengthwise into ¼-inch-wide strips. In a very large bowl, combine the steak, cabbage, mint and cilantro. Toss with the dressing and sprinkle with the bean sprouts, peanuts and fried shallots. —*Marcia Kiesel*

SERVE WITH

This salad is a complete dish on its own, but you can also serve it with white, brown or fried rice and green beans, sugar snaps or snow peas.

WINE

Fragrant and fruity white, such as Altesse from Savoie in France.

> "This recipe can serve six, but if you're like me and you find it totally addictive, it will only serve two! It's really a perfect meal–one that makes you feel virtuous but completely sated. I especially love the nuttiness of the pumpkin seeds combined with the sweet crunch of the snap peas."
> —KATE HEDDINGS, FOOD DIRECTOR

QUINOA SALAD WITH
SUGAR SNAP PEAS

SERVES 6

TIME Active 15 min; Total 40 min

½ lb. sugar snap peas

1½ cups quinoa, rinsed and drained

¼ cup plus 1 Tbsp.
extra-virgin olive oil

3 Tbsp. white wine vinegar

Kosher salt and pepper

½ cup salted roasted
pumpkin seeds

½ cup minced chives

This easy five-ingredient quinoa salad from cookbook author and former F&W Test Kitchen supervisor Marcia Kiesel features crunchy sugar snap peas and salty roasted pumpkin seeds. It can be made in advance and enjoyed at room temperature for picnics, cookouts or a healthy brown bag lunch.

1 In a small saucepan of salted boiling water, simmer the peas until bright green and crisp-tender, about 1 minute. Drain and spread out on a large plate to cool, then pat dry. Cut the peas on the diagonal into 1-inch pieces.

2 In a small saucepan, combine the quinoa with 2 cups of water and bring to a boil. Cover and cook over low heat until all of the water has evaporated and the quinoa is tender, about 15 minutes. Uncover and fluff the quinoa, then transfer to a large bowl and let cool to room temperature.

3 In a small bowl, combine the oil and vinegar and season with salt and pepper. Add the peas to the quinoa along with the pumpkin seeds, chives and dressing; stir to combine. Season with salt and pepper and serve at room temperature or lightly chilled. —Marcia Kiesel

MAKE AHEAD

The salad can be refrigerated for up to 6 hours.

WINE

Vegetable-focused dishes like this quinoa-and-snap-pea salad are terrific with Sauvignon Blanc's lightly herbal, citrusy flavors. Pour something from New Zealand's Marlborough region.

> "This is the perfect summer salad to go with fried chicken and anything off the grill, from ribs and fish to pork or veal chops. If you have extra basil hanging around, or a few avocados looking for a home, you could chop them up and toss them in with the butter beans." —TINA UJLAKI, EXECUTIVE FOOD EDITOR

BUTTER BEAN SALAD
WITH LIME AND MINT

SERVES 8

TIME   35 min plus 2 hr chilling

- 6 cups fresh butter beans or three 10-oz. boxes frozen baby lima beans
- ½ cup extra-virgin olive oil
- ¼ cup plus 2 Tbsp. fresh lime juice
- ¼ cup plus 2 Tbsp. buttermilk
   Kosher salt and pepper
- 1 cup chopped mint

The secret to this delicate and refreshing butter bean salad is the dressing, made with cold, tangy buttermilk, olive oil and lime juice. Cookbook authors Matt Lee and Ted Lee call it "the flavors of a Southern summer."

1 Bring a large saucepan of salted water to a boil. Add the butter beans and cook until tender, 8 to 10 minutes. Drain and rinse the beans under cold running water. Drain well and pat dry.

2 In a large bowl, whisk the olive oil with the lime juice and buttermilk; season with salt and pepper. Stir in the beans, cover and refrigerate for at least 2 hours, until well chilled. Fold in the mint just before serving.
—*Matt Lee and Ted Lee*

MAKE AHEAD

The butter bean salad can be refrigerated for up to 2 days. Add the chopped mint just before serving.

WINE

A white or rosé Sancerre is the perfect complement to this summery salad.

CHARRED BROCCOLI
WITH BLUE CHEESE DRESSING
AND SPICED CRISPIES

SERVES **6**

TIME **50 min**

DRESSING

- ⅓ **cup heavy cream**
- **Pinch of crushed red pepper**
- **Pinch of dark brown sugar**
- 3 **oz. smoked or Maytag blue cheese, crumbled (see Note)**
- ⅓ **cup sour cream**
- **Kosher salt**

BROCCOLI

- 2 **lbs. broccoli, cut into 1½-inch florets with stems**
- ¼ **cup unseasoned rice vinegar**
- 1½ **Tbsp. harissa**
- ½ **tsp. finely grated lemon zest plus 1½ Tbsp. fresh lemon juice**
- 1½ **Tbsp. soy sauce**
- 1 **Tbsp. Dijon mustard**
- 1½ **tsp. Sriracha**
- ½ **cup extra-virgin olive oil**
- ⅓ **cup minced shallots**
- **Kosher salt and pepper**
- 2 **Tbsp. unsalted butter**
- 1 **cup crisped rice cereal, such as Rice Krispies**

NOTE

Izard likes using Rogue Creamery Smokey Blue Cheese (roguecreamery.com).

F&W Best New Chef 2011 Stephanie Izard of The Girl & the Goat in Chicago amps up broccoli with a punchy vinaigrette, creamy blue cheese dressing and a terrifically crunchy, butter-toasted Rice Krispies topping.

1 MAKE THE DRESSING In a small saucepan, warm the heavy cream until hot. Whisk in the crushed red pepper, sugar and one-third of the blue cheese until melted. Let cool completely, then whisk in the sour cream and the remaining cheese. Season the dressing with salt.

2 PREPARE THE BROCCOLI In a large saucepan of salted boiling water, blanch the broccoli until crisp-tender, about 2 minutes. Drain well and spread out on a large baking sheet to cool.

3 In a blender, combine the vinegar, harissa, lemon zest and juice, soy sauce, mustard and Sriracha and puree. With the blender on, gradually add the olive oil until incorporated. Transfer the vinaigrette to a medium bowl and stir in the shallots. Season with salt and pepper.

4 In a medium skillet, melt the butter. Add the cereal and 1½ teaspoons of the harissa vinaigrette and cook over moderately high heat, stirring, until lightly browned, about 3 minutes. Season with salt and transfer to a paper towel–lined plate to drain.

5 Light a grill or heat a grill pan. In a large bowl, toss the broccoli with half of the remaining vinaigrette and season with salt. Grill the broccoli over moderately high heat, turning occasionally, until lightly charred all over, about 5 minutes.

6 Spread the blue cheese dressing on a platter and scatter the broccoli on top. Garnish with the spiced crispies and serve, passing the remaining harissa vinaigrette at the table. —*Stephanie Izard*

MAKE AHEAD

The blue cheese dressing can be refrigerated overnight.

BEER

To go with the funkiness of the blue cheese in this salad, pour a saison or farmhouse ale.

FLASH-ROASTED BROCCOLI
WITH SPICY CRUMBS

SERVES **6**

TIME **30 min**

2 oz. sliced pepperoni

1 garlic clove, sliced

1 cup panko

¼ cup plus 2 Tbsp. extra-virgin olive oil

2 lbs. broccoli, trimmed and cut into long spears

Kosher salt

2 Tbsp. Dijon mustard

This genius recipe is from cookbook author and former F&W Test Kitchen senior editor Grace Parisi. She pulses pepperoni with breadcrumbs in a food processor to add a ton of extra flavor and a great crunch to broccoli spears.

1 Preheat the oven to 425°. In a mini food processor, pulse the pepperoni with the garlic until finely chopped. Add the panko and pulse just to combine.

2 In a medium skillet, heat 2 tablespoons of the olive oil. Add the crumb mixture and cook over moderate heat, stirring, until crisp and golden, about 5 minutes. Scrape onto a plate and let cool.

3 Meanwhile, in a bowl, toss the broccoli with the remaining ¼ cup of olive oil and season with salt. Spread the broccoli on a baking sheet and roast for about 15 minutes, turning once, until tender and browned in spots. Spread the mustard on one side of the broccoli, then press the broccoli into the spicy crumbs. Transfer the broccoli to a platter, sprinkle with any remaining crumbs and serve. —*Grace Parisi*

VARIATION

You can swap in salami for the pepperoni and cauliflower spears for the broccoli.

"I make this dish every year for Thanksgiving and it gets raves. I think with the glut of rich, carby food on the table, my family's happy to have something bright and punchy. My niece and nephew can never get enough of the togarashi-spiced Rice Krispies, so I make extra for them." —SUSAN CHOUNG, BOOKS EDITOR

SPICY BRUSSELS SPROUTS
WITH MINT

SERVES **4 to 6**

TIME **25 min**

- 2 **Tbsp. vegetable oil**
- ½ **cup crisped rice cereal, such as Rice Krispies**
- ¼ **tsp. togarashi (see Note) or cayenne pepper**
- **Kosher salt**
- ¼ **cup Asian fish sauce**
- 2 **Tbsp. sugar**
- 1 **Tbsp. rice vinegar**
- 1 **Tbsp. fresh lime juice**
- 1 **small garlic clove, minced**
- 1 **small fresh red chile, minced**
- ¼ **cup chopped cilantro**
- 2 **Tbsp. chopped mint**
- 4 **cups roasted or boiled brussels sprouts (about 2 lbs.), halved lengthwise**

NOTE

Togarashi, a Japanese blend of chiles and sesame, is available at Asian markets.

The key to this dish from Momofuku founder David Chang, an F&W Best New Chef 2006, is to almost burn the brussels sprouts; the charred flavor is irresistible. Chang bolsters the sweet-and-salty vinaigrette with fresh herbs and chiles.

1 In a large skillet, heat 1 tablespoon of the oil until shimmering. Add the cereal and togarashi and cook over high heat, stirring, until browned, about 30 seconds. Season with salt. Transfer to a plate and wipe out the skillet.

2 In a small bowl, combine the fish sauce, sugar, rice vinegar, lime juice, garlic, chile and 2 tablespoons of water and stir until the sugar is dissolved. Add the cilantro and mint.

3 Add the remaining 1 tablespoon of oil to the skillet and heat until nearly smoking. Add the brussels sprouts and cook over high heat, stirring, until charred in spots and heated through, about 5 minutes. Transfer to a large bowl and toss with the vinaigrette. Just before serving, sprinkle the spiced cereal on top and serve right away. —*David Chang*

RED CABBAGE SLAW

SERVES **6**

TIME **20 min plus 4 hr macerating**

¼ cup fresh lime juice

¼ cup white wine vinegar

2 Tbsp. Asian fish sauce

2 Tbsp. sugar

1¾ lbs. red cabbage, cored and very thinly sliced

1 cup finely chopped parsley

Kosher salt

At Namu Gaji in San Francisco, chef Dennis Lee makes inventive Korean food. But he prepares simple dishes like this Burmese-Thai slaw for his family's holiday barbecue. Crunchy, fresh and slightly sweet, it's the perfect accompaniment to rich meats.

1 In a large bowl, whisk the lime juice with the vinegar, fish sauce and sugar. Add the cabbage, parsley and a generous pinch of salt and toss well. Cover and refrigerate for at least 4 hours. Season with salt and serve. —*Dennis Lee*

MAKE AHEAD

The cabbage slaw can be refrigerated overnight.

"This slaw is great with grilled anything, but I always reach for it as a side when I'm grilling or roasting salmon. I love how the colors look together on the plate." —JAMES MAIKOWSKI, ART DIRECTOR

PARKER HOUSE ROLLS TOPPED WITH CHEDDAR AND OLD BAY

MAKES **15 large rolls**

TIME **Active 30 min; Total 1 hr plus 2 hr rising**

- 1 **cup milk**
- 1 **envelope active dry yeast (2½ tsp.)**
- 3 **Tbsp. sugar**
- 1 **large egg, beaten**
- 1 **stick unsalted butter, melted, plus more for greasing**
- 3½ **cups all-purpose flour, plus more for kneading**
- 1½ **tsp. table salt**
- ¾ **cup shredded sharp cheddar cheese (about 2 oz.)**
- 1 **tsp. Old Bay seasoning**

When asked about the seasoning on these fluffy, buttery rolls, F&W Best New Chef 2010 Jonathon Sawyer of Greenhouse Tavern in Cleveland said, "Old Bay isn't really a Cleveland thing, but sometimes it's the right ingredient. I remember my mother's Parker Houses being laced with salty, savory Old Bay and a mean aged cheddar."

1 In a microwave-safe cup, heat the milk until warm but not hot, about 20 seconds. Add the yeast and sugar and let stand until foamy, about 5 minutes. Scrape the mixture into a stand mixer fitted with the dough hook. Add the egg and 6 tablespoons of the melted butter and beat at low speed just until combined. Add the 3½ cups of flour and the salt and beat at low speed until the dough is evenly moistened, about 2 minutes. Increase the speed to medium and knead until a soft, smooth dough forms, about 10 minutes.

2 Transfer the dough to a floured work surface and pat it into a 10-inch square. Fold one-third of the dough into the center and the other third on top, like folding a letter. Turn the dough and fold again; you should have a small square. Butter the bowl and return the dough to it. Cover with plastic wrap and let stand in a warm place until doubled in bulk, about 1 hour.

3 Butter a 9-by-13-inch baking pan. On a well-floured work surface, roll out the dough to a 15-inch square. Working from the bottom, tightly roll the dough into a log. Using a floured knife, cut the log into thirds. Cut each third into 5 slices. Arrange the rolls spiral side up in the baking pan in 3 rows of 5. Cover loosely with buttered plastic wrap and let rise for about 1 hour, until billowy.

4 Preheat the oven to 375°. Remove the plastic wrap and bake the rolls for 15 minutes. Sprinkle the cheddar cheese on top and bake for 15 minutes longer, until golden and cooked through; cover the rolls with foil for the last 5 minutes to prevent overbrowning. Brush the rolls with the remaining 2 tablespoons of melted butter and sprinkle them with the Old Bay seasoning. Transfer the baking pan to a rack to let the rolls cool before serving. —*Jonathon Sawyer*

MAKE AHEAD

The baked rolls can be kept at room temperature overnight. Rewarm before serving.

BACON, ONION AND WALNUT KUGELHOPF

SERVES **10**

TIME **Active 1 hr; Total 5 hr**

4 slices of bacon, cut crosswise into ¼-inch strips

1 small onion, finely chopped

¾ cup lukewarm milk

¼ cup sugar

1 tsp. active dry yeast

1 large egg

1 tsp. table salt

2⅔ cups all-purpose flour

1½ sticks unsalted butter, at room temperature— 11 Tbsp. cut into small pieces, 1 Tbsp. melted

⅔ cup coarsely chopped walnuts (about 3 oz.)

17 whole almonds

The rich, buttery, fluted bread known as kugelhopf was a staple of superstar pastry chef Pierre Hermé's childhood in Alsace. His version is studded with walnuts, onions and bacon and topped with almonds. It's traditionally baked in hand-painted earthenware molds, but steel, nonstick aluminum or glass molds are fine too.

1 In a medium skillet, cook the bacon over moderate heat, stirring, until lightly browned, about 7 minutes. Using a slotted spoon, transfer the bacon to paper towels. Add the onion to the skillet and cook, stirring, until softened but not browned, about 5 minutes; using a slotted spoon, transfer to paper towels.

2 In a stand mixer fitted with the paddle, combine the milk, sugar and yeast and let stand for 5 minutes. Add the egg and salt and beat at medium speed until blended. Gradually add the flour and continue beating until the dough is elastic, about 4 minutes. Gradually add the 11 tablespoons of softened butter, beating until the dough comes cleanly off the side of the bowl, about 8 minutes. At low speed, beat in the bacon, onion and walnuts until evenly distributed throughout the dough. Cover the bowl with plastic wrap and let the dough rise at warm room temperature until doubled in bulk, 2 to 3 hours.

3 Generously butter a 9-inch kugelhopf mold or fluted tube pan and set the almonds in the indentations in the bottom. Punch down the dough, shape it into a ball and make a hole in the middle. Set the ring of dough in the mold, cover and let rise until the dough almost reaches the top of the mold, about 1 hour.

4 Preheat the oven to 375°. Bake the kugelhopf for about 40 minutes, until golden brown. Transfer to a rack and let stand for 10 minutes, then unmold. Brush with the melted butter while still warm and serve at room temperature. —*Frédérick and Pierre Hermé*

MAKE AHEAD

The unbuttered kugelhopf can be wrapped in foil and stored at room temperature for up to 1 day; do not use the melted butter.

CHIPOTLE-ROASTED BABY CARROTS

SERVES **6**

TIME **Active 20 min; Total 1 hr**

30 **thin baby carrots
(2 to 3 bunches), tops discarded,
carrots scrubbed**

2 **chipotle chiles in adobo, minced,
plus 1 tsp. adobo sauce from
the can**

1 **Tbsp. unsulfured molasses**

2½ **Tbsp. extra-virgin olive oil
Kosher salt and pepper**

3 **Tbsp. sesame seeds**

4 **oz. watercress,
stems discarded
Plain Greek yogurt, for serving**

When he makes this stunning salad at Empellón Cocina, F&W Best New Chef 2013 Alex Stupak roasts baby carrots with mole poblano, a complex sauce that includes dried chiles, raisins and chocolate. Here, the carrots are roasted simply with smoky chipotles in adobo.

1 Preheat the oven to 350°. On a rimmed baking sheet, toss the carrots with the chipotles, molasses and 2 tablespoons of the olive oil; season with salt and pepper. Roast for 30 to 35 minutes, until the carrots are crisp-tender and browned. Transfer to a plate and let cool completely.

2 Meanwhile, in a small skillet, toast the sesame seeds over moderate heat, tossing, until golden, 3 to 5 minutes. Stir in the remaining ½ tablespoon of oil and season with salt; let cool.

3 On the plate, toss the carrots with the 1 teaspoon of adobo sauce. Arrange the carrots on 6 plates and scatter the watercress on top. Garnish with the sesame seeds and serve with yogurt. —*Alex Stupak*

MAKE AHEAD

The roasted carrots can be kept at room temperature for up to 4 hours.

"I love to toss these carrots with avocado and wrap them in warm corn tortillas to eat like tacos. Or, if I'm feeling fancy, I serve them on a smear of Mexican crema, the way Alex Stupak does at his restaurant."

—JUSTIN CHAPPLE, TEST KITCHEN SENIOR EDITOR

SUNCHOKE-KALE HASH
WITH FARRO

SERVES **10**

TIME **Active 40 min;**
Total 1 hr 15 min

¾ **cup farro**

2½ **lbs. large sunchokes,**
     peeled and cut into 2-inch pieces

Kosher salt and pepper

1 **lb. Tuscan kale,**
    tough stems discarded

3 **Tbsp. extra-virgin olive oil**
    blended with 3 Tbsp.
    vegetable oil

1 **small red onion, sliced**
    ¼ inch thick

1 **Tbsp. unsalted butter**

½ **lb. oyster mushrooms,**
    halved if large

Comfort food is rarely healthy, or vegetarian. This soul-satisfying winter hash is both. The recipe, from F&W Best New Chefs 2009 Jon Shook and Vinny Dotolo of Animal and Son of a Gun in Los Angeles, combines crispy sunchokes, silky oyster mushrooms, tender kale and chewy farro. It's wonderful served with grilled steak or on its own as a meatless main course.

1 In a medium saucepan, cover the farro with 2 inches of water. Bring to a boil, cover and cook over low heat until the farro is tender, about 25 minutes. Drain the farro.

2 Meanwhile, in a large saucepan, cover the sunchokes with water and add a large pinch of salt. Boil over high heat until the sunchokes are tender, about 10 minutes. Drain and let cool slightly, then slice the sunchokes ¼ inch thick.

3 Fill the large saucepan with water and bring to a boil. Add the kale and cook until just tender, about 3 minutes. Drain and let cool slightly, then squeeze the kale dry and coarsely chop it.

4 In a small skillet, heat 2 tablespoons of the blended oil. Add the onion and a pinch of salt and cook over moderately low heat, stirring occasionally, until browned, about 12 minutes.

5 In a large nonstick skillet, melt the butter in 2 tablespoons of the blended oil. Add the sunchokes in an even layer and cook over high heat until browned on the bottom, about 3 minutes. Turn the sunchokes, reduce the heat to moderately high and continue cooking until starting to brown, about 2 minutes. Push the sunchokes to the side of the skillet.

6 Add 1 more tablespoon of the blended oil and the oyster mushrooms to the large skillet. Season with salt and pepper and cook over moderately high heat until browned, about 3 minutes. Add the remaining 1 tablespoon of blended oil along with the farro, kale and onion and cook, stirring, until heated through. Season with salt and pepper and serve. —*Jon Shook and Vinny Dotolo*

MAKE AHEAD

The recipe can be prepared through Step 4 one day ahead; refrigerate the components separately.

WINE

Melon-scented, full-bodied Chenin Blanc.

ROASTED DELICATA SQUASH
WITH QUINOA SALAD

SERVES **4**

TIME **Active 30 min; Total 1 hr**

- 2 **Delicata squash (about 1 lb. each), halved lengthwise and seeded**
- 2 **Tbsp. extra-virgin olive oil**
  Kosher salt and pepper
- 1 **cup quinoa**
- 2 **Tbsp. golden raisins**
- 1 **Tbsp. sherry vinegar**
- 1 **tsp. honey**
- 1 **Granny Smith apple, finely diced**
- 1 **large shallot, minced**
- 1 **garlic clove, minced**
- 2 **Tbsp. chopped mint**
- 2 **Tbsp. chopped parsley**
- 2 **oz. arugula (2 cups)**

Quinoa is definitely a superfood: A grain-like seed, it's a "complete" protein containing all eight essential amino acids. Another plus: It cooks much more quickly than most grains. To create a terrific, healthy side that can double as a vegetarian main course, F&W Best New Chef 1998 Michael Symon of Cleveland's Lola tosses quinoa with arugula, apple, raisins and fresh herbs, then spoons the salad into a halved baked squash (a great source of iron and vitamins A and C).

1 Preheat the oven to 350°. Brush the cut sides of the squash with 1 teaspoon of the olive oil and season the cavities with salt and pepper. Place the squash cut side down on a baking sheet and roast for about 45 minutes, until tender.

2 Meanwhile, in a medium saucepan, bring 2 cups of lightly salted water to a boil. Add the quinoa, cover and simmer for 10 minutes. Stir in the raisins and simmer, covered, until the water is absorbed, about 5 minutes. Transfer the quinoa to a large bowl and let cool.

3 In a small bowl, whisk the vinegar and honey with the remaining 1 tablespoon plus 2 teaspoons of olive oil and season with salt and pepper. Add the dressing to the quinoa along with the apple, shallot, garlic, mint and parsley and toss well. Add the arugula and toss gently. Set the squash halves on plates, fill with the salad and serve. —*Michael Symon*

MAKE AHEAD

The quinoa can be refrigerated overnight. Bring to room temperature and add the arugula just before serving.

WINE

Fruity, light-bodied Beaujolais.

MISO-ROASTED EGGPLANTS
WITH TOMATOES, DILL, SHISO AND BLACK VINEGAR

SERVES **4**

TIME **1 hr**

DRESSING
- **1 Tbsp. sugar**
- **¼ cup plus 2 Tbsp. black vinegar**
- **¼ cup plus 2 Tbsp. canola oil**
- **1 Tbsp. soy sauce**

EGGPLANTS
- **3 Tbsp. shiro (white) miso**
- **1½ Tbsp. mirin**
- **¼ cup plus 2 Tbsp. canola oil**
- **1 lb. Asian eggplants, halved lengthwise**

SALAD
- **1 heirloom tomato, cut into ½-inch dice**
- **½ pint cherry tomatoes, halved**
- **⅓ cup chopped dill, plus more for garnish**
- **¼ cup chopped shiso, plus more for garnish**
- **1 Tbsp. minced scallions**
- **Kosher salt**

For this lovely vegetarian dish, F&W Best New Chef 2014 Cara Stadler of Tao Yuan in Brunswick, Maine, tops long, skinny Asian eggplants with a bright salad drizzled with Chinese black vinegar. Typically made from fermented rice, wheat, barley and sorghum, black vinegar is slightly sweet, with a rich, malty flavor. It's available at Asian markets and online from amazon.com.

1 MAKE THE DRESSING Preheat the oven to 350°. In a small saucepan, combine the sugar with 1 teaspoon of water. Cook over low heat, swirling the pan, until the sugar melts and an amber caramel forms, about 4 minutes. Whisk in the black vinegar. Remove from the heat and let cool to room temperature. Whisk in the oil and soy sauce.

2 PREPARE THE EGGPLANTS In a small bowl, mix the miso with the mirin. In a large nonstick skillet, heat 3 tablespoons of the oil. Add 1 eggplant half, cut side down, and cook over moderate heat until deep golden, 3 to 4 minutes. Transfer the eggplant cut side up to a baking sheet. Repeat with the remaining 3 tablespoons of oil and eggplants. Spread the miso mixture on the cut sides of the eggplants and roast for 15 minutes, until the eggplants are very tender. Transfer to a platter.

3 MEANWHILE, MAKE THE SALAD In a large bowl, toss the tomatoes with the ⅓ cup of dill, ¼ cup of shiso, the scallions and two-thirds of the dressing; season with salt.

4 Spoon the salad over the warm eggplants and drizzle with the remaining dressing. Garnish with dill and shiso and serve. —*Cara Stadler*

MAKE AHEAD

The dressing can be refrigerated overnight.

WINE

Lively cru Beaujolais, such as Morgon or Fleurie.

"These spicy potato wedges fulfill every Buffalo wing craving. I preheat the baking sheet before adding the potatoes–it prevents sticking and helps the potatoes get even crispier. For the hot sauce, I use Frank's RedHot or Sriracha, or habanero sauce to make it superspicy." —JUSTIN CHAPPLE, TEST KITCHEN SENIOR EDITOR

CRISPY BUFFALO-STYLE POTATOES

SERVES **4 to 6**

TIME **Active 15 min; Total 50 min**

- **3** baking potatoes, scrubbed and cut into ½-inch wedges
- **2** Tbsp. extra-virgin olive oil
  Kosher salt and pepper
- **3** Tbsp. unsalted butter, melted
- **2** Tbsp. hot sauce
  Blue cheese dressing, for serving

For her fun take on Buffalo chicken wings, F&W's Kay Chun tosses oven fries with a delicious two-ingredient sauce.

1 Preheat the oven to 450°. On a rimmed baking sheet, toss the potatoes with the olive oil and season with salt and pepper. Roast for 20 minutes. Flip the potatoes and roast for 15 to 20 minutes longer, until golden and crisp.

2 In a large bowl, combine the butter and hot sauce and season with salt and pepper. Add the potatoes and toss to coat. Serve with blue cheese dressing. —*Kay Chun*

VARIATION

Toss the sauce with large roasted cauliflower florets for Buffalo-style cauliflower.

> "I was hooked on this gratin after I tasted it in the Test Kitchen. It's visually stunning, which will seduce me every time! I also love how the small amount of cream combined with chicken broth brings out the flavor of the vegetables, and makes it healthy as well."
> —FREDRIKA STJÄRNE, CREATIVE DIRECTOR

ROOT VEGETABLE GRATIN

SERVES **8**

TIME **Active 25 min;
Total 2 hr 15 min**

2 **large sweet potatoes, peeled**
1 **butternut squash neck
(2¼ lbs.) from a large butternut
squash, peeled**
1 **medium rutabaga (2 lbs.), peeled
and halved lengthwise**
   Nonstick cooking spray
   Kosher salt and pepper
½ **cup low-sodium chicken broth**
¼ **cup heavy cream**
¾ **cup panko**
1½ **Tbsp. extra-virgin olive oil**

Former F&W Test Kitchen associate Melissa Rubel Jacobson uses a mandoline to cut the vegetables into thin slices for this colorful alternative to potato gratin; they turn tender when baked with chicken broth and a little cream.

1 Preheat the oven to 375°. Using a mandoline, slice the potatoes and squash lengthwise ⅛ inch thick. Slice the rutabaga crosswise ⅛ inch thick.

2 Spray an 8-by-12-inch glass baking dish with cooking spray. Arrange half of the potatoes in the dish, overlapping them slightly; season with salt and pepper. Top with half of the rutabaga and squash, seasoning each layer. Repeat the layering. Pour the broth over and around the vegetables.

3 Cover tightly with foil and bake for 1 hour, until the vegetables are almost tender when pierced. Remove the foil and pour the cream over the gratin. Bake for about 30 minutes longer, until the liquid has thickened.

4 Preheat the broiler. Mix the panko with the oil and season with salt and pepper; sprinkle over the gratin. Broil 3 inches from the heat for 2 minutes, until golden, rotating for even browning. Let the gratin stand for 10 minutes, then serve. —*Melissa Rubel Jacobson*

WINE

Lightly sweet root vegetables go great with fruity whites. Try a California Chenin Blanc or a Pinot Gris from Alsace.

FRIED RICE WITH SHALLOTS

SERVES **4**

TIME **25 min**

3 **Tbsp. peanut oil,
   plus more for frying**

3 **shallots, thinly sliced (¾ cup)**

¼ **tsp. ground turmeric**

4½ **cups cold cooked jasmine rice
   (see Note)**

   Kosher salt

1 **cup frozen petite peas, thawed**

   Lime wedges, for serving

NOTE

If you don't have leftover rice on hand, you'll need to cook 1½ cups of rice.

The Burmese make a simple breakfast dish by stir-frying leftover rice with crispy fried shallots, sweet peas and earthy turmeric. To make the dish more substantial, Naomi Duguid, author of the cookbook *Burma,* likes to top the rice with fried eggs. The flavor of the rice is mild, which makes it a versatile partner to fish, poultry and vegetarian dishes.

1 In a small skillet, heat ¼ inch of peanut oil until shimmering. Add ¼ cup of the sliced shallots and fry over moderately high heat, stirring occasionally, until golden brown and crisp, about 2 minutes. Using a slotted spoon, transfer the fried shallots to paper towels to drain.

2 In a wok or large skillet, heat the 3 tablespoons of oil until shimmering. Add the turmeric and the remaining ½ cup of shallots and stir-fry over moderately high heat until the shallots are softened, about 5 minutes. Add the rice and 1 teaspoon of salt and stir-fry over high heat for 1 minute. Add the peas and stir-fry until the rice and peas are hot, 2 to 3 minutes. Stir in the fried shallots and season with salt. Transfer the rice to a bowl and serve with lime wedges.
—*Naomi Duguid*

VARIATION

Turmeric makes this lovely rice dish very fragrant. Now that fresh turmeric is more readily available, you can experiment with it here.

mains

After a day in the Test Kitchen eating
a bite of this and a bite of that,
sitting down to a real main course can
be such a satisfying experience.

HOT NIÇOISE SALAD

SERVES 4

TIME 45 min

- ½ lb. green beans
- 1 cup grape tomatoes, halved
- ½ cup pitted Niçoise olives (3 oz.)
- 1 cup roasted red or yellow bell peppers, cut into strips
-   Two 2-oz. cans flat anchovies packed in olive oil, drained and chopped
- ½ cup torn basil leaves
- ½ cup plus 2 Tbsp. extra-virgin olive oil
-   Kosher salt and pepper
-   Four 6-oz. tuna steaks (1 inch thick)
- 4 large eggs
- 2 Tbsp. fresh lemon juice

"One cold day in London, I was dreaming about Niçoise salad," says actress and lifestyle guru Gwyneth Paltrow. "But it didn't seem right to be eating something so crisp and chilly in the dead of winter." So she transformed the classic salad into a hearty one-dish dinner by roasting tuna steaks on a tangle of beans, tomatoes, anchovies and olives.

1 Preheat the oven to 400°. Put the green beans in a steamer basket and steam over 1 inch of boiling water until crisp-tender, about 4 minutes; transfer to a large roasting pan.

2 Lightly squeeze the tomatoes and add them to the roasting pan. Add the olives, bell peppers, anchovies and basil, toss with ¼ cup of the olive oil and season with salt and pepper. Brush the tuna steaks with 1 tablespoon of the olive oil and season with salt and pepper. Set the tuna on the vegetables. Nestle 4 ramekins among the vegetables and crack an egg into each one. Drizzle the eggs with 1 tablespoon of the olive oil and season with salt and pepper.

3 Roast the tuna, vegetables and eggs in the center of the oven for about 15 minutes, until the fish is slightly rare in the center and the egg whites are set but the yolks are still runny.

4 Meanwhile, in a small bowl, whisk the remaining ¼ cup of olive oil with the lemon juice and season with salt and pepper. Drizzle the dressing over the vegetables and tuna. Transfer to plates and serve immediately. *—Gwyneth Paltrow*

WINE

Fragrant, strawberry-inflected Provençal rosé.

INDIAN-SPICED CHICKPEA SALAD
WITH YOGURT AND HERBS

SERVES **6**

TIME **20 min**

Two 15-oz. cans chickpeas— rinsed, drained and patted dry

2 **Tbsp. peanut oil**

1 **tsp. mustard seeds**

¾ **tsp. cumin seeds**

¾ **tsp. fennel seeds**

¼ **tsp. crushed red pepper**

¾ **cup plain whole-milk yogurt**

1½ **Tbsp. fresh lemon juice**

2 **scallions, thinly sliced**

¼ **cup chopped cilantro**

¼ **cup chopped mint**

1 **tsp. kosher salt**

Jerry Traunfeld, the chef at Poppy in Seattle, was inspired by a trip through India to create this creamy chickpea salad. He flavors it with plenty of aromatic herbs and Indian spices, among them mustard, cumin and fennel seeds.

1 Pour the chickpeas into a large bowl. In a small skillet, heat the peanut oil until shimmering. Add the mustard seeds, partially cover the skillet and cook over moderately high heat until the mustard seeds stop popping, about 1 minute. Add the cumin and fennel seeds and the crushed red pepper and cook until the mixture is fragrant, about 30 seconds. Pour the hot oil and spices over the chickpeas. Stir in the yogurt, lemon juice, scallions, cilantro, mint and salt. Serve at room temperature. —*Jerry Traunfeld*

WINE

Bright, citrusy Sauvignon Blanc.

GERMAN LENTIL SOUP

MAKES   **4 quarts**

TIME   **Active 40 min;
Total 1 hr 30 min**

- 2 **Tbsp. pure olive oil (see Note)**
- 1½ **lbs. shoulder lamb chops**
- 1 **lb. russet potatoes, peeled and cut into ¼-inch dice**
- 4 **garlic cloves, coarsely chopped**
- 2 **red bell peppers, cut into ¼-inch dice**
- 2 **carrots, cut into ¼-inch dice**
- 1 **large onion, coarsely chopped**
- 1 **celery rib, cut into ¼-inch dice**
  One 28-oz. can crushed tomatoes
- 1 **lb. brown lentils, rinsed**
- 10 **cups chicken stock or low-sodium broth**
- 1 **bunch of flat-leaf parsley, stems discarded, leaves chopped**
  Kosher salt and pepper

NOTE

You can substitute lard for the olive oil. Prairie Pride Farm sells leaf lard, the best kind, which comes from around the pig's kidneys. Store it in the refrigerator or the freezer.

Cookbook author Lydie Marshall got this recipe from a friend who'd emigrated from Germany. Her version substitutes olive oil for the traditional lard and red bell peppers for some of the potatoes. For a memorably rich soup, use lard, as in the original German recipe.

1 In a large enameled cast-iron casserole, heat the olive oil. Add the lamb chops and cook over moderately high heat until browned, about 4 minutes per side. Transfer the chops to a plate.

2 Add the potatoes, garlic, peppers, carrots, onion and celery to the casserole and cook over moderate heat, stirring, for 5 minutes. Add the lamb chops, tomatoes, lentils, chicken stock and parsley and bring to a boil. Add 1 tablespoon of salt and a few grindings of pepper. Cover and simmer over low heat until the lentils are tender, 50 minutes to 1 hour. Remove the lamb chops and discard the bones. Cut the meat into large pieces and return it to the soup. Season with salt and pepper and serve hot. —*Lydie Marshall*

MAKE AHEAD

The soup can be refrigerated for up to 3 days.

WINE

Rustic, earthy red, such as Côtes du Rhône.

> "This creamy, vegetable-packed stew is one of my essential winter recipes: It can be made in under an hour, requires almost no prep and leaves me feeling satisfied and healthy."
>
> —JULIA HEFFELFINGER, ASSISTANT FOOD EDITOR

CHICKPEA-VEGETABLE STEW

SERVES **4**

TIME **35 min**

- 2 **Tbsp. extra-virgin olive oil**
- 1 **cup frozen pearl onions, thawed and halved**
- 1 **red bell pepper, diced**
- ½ **lb. fingerling potatoes, halved lengthwise**
- 2 **garlic cloves, minced**
- 1 **Tbsp. finely chopped peeled fresh ginger**
- 1 **Tbsp. harissa**
- 3 **cups chicken stock or low-sodium broth**
  - **One 15-oz. can chickpeas, drained and rinsed**
- ¾ **cup unsweetened coconut milk**
- 2 **Tbsp. fresh lemon juice**
  - **Kosher salt and pepper**
- 1 **Tbsp. minced cilantro**
  - **Toasted bread, for serving**

"Talk about Meatless Monday!" says F&W Best New Chef 2006 Cathal Armstrong of Restaurant Eve in Alexandria, Virginia. "This is a great vegetable dish that I cooked for the CEO of Whole Foods." He gives the stew heft with fingerling potatoes and chickpeas, creaminess with coconut milk and subtle heat with harissa, a Tunisian chile paste.

1 In a large saucepan, heat the olive oil. Add the onions and bell pepper and cook over moderately high heat, stirring, until browned, about 5 minutes. Add the potatoes, garlic, ginger and harissa and cook, stirring, until the harissa darkens, about 2 minutes. Add the stock and chickpeas and bring to a boil. Cover and simmer over moderately low heat until the potatoes are tender, 12 to 14 minutes.

2 Add the coconut milk to the saucepan and bring to a simmer. Stir in the lemon juice and season with salt and pepper. Sprinkle the stew with the cilantro and serve with toasted bread. —*Cathal Armstrong*

WINE

Try a fresh, fruit-forward sparkling wine like Crémant d'Alsace.

WHITE BEAN AND HAM STEW

SERVES **8**

TIME **Active 40 min; Total 3 hr**

4 meaty smoked ham hocks
(about 3½ lbs.)

½ lb. dried cannellini or borlotti
beans (1¼ cups), picked over
and rinsed

2 medium red-skinned potatoes,
peeled and cut into 1-inch pieces

1 large leek, white and pale green
parts only, cut into 1-inch pieces

1 large celery rib, cut into
½-inch pieces

1 large carrot, cut into
½-inch pieces

1 large parsnip, cut into
½-inch pieces

½ lb. Savoy cabbage, cut into
2-inch pieces

Kosher salt and pepper

Eight ¼-inch-thick slices of
peasant bread, lightly toasted

2 cups shredded Gruyère or
Comté cheese

The hearty stew called garbure, from southwestern France, is loaded with vegetables, beans and meat, the exact ingredients depending on availability. In this recipe from his cookbook *Essential Pépin*, master chef Jacques Pépin includes ham hocks and cabbage and tops the dish with toasted bread smothered in melted Gruyère cheese. It's traditional to add some red wine to the last few spoonfuls of broth and sip it straight from the bowl.

1 In a large pot, combine the smoked ham hocks and cannellini beans with 3 quarts of water and bring to a boil. Cover and simmer over low heat for 1 hour. Add the potatoes, leek, celery, carrot, parsnip, cabbage and ½ teaspoon of salt. Cover the stew and simmer over low heat for 1 hour longer.

2 Transfer the ham hocks to a plate. Simmer the stew uncovered over moderate heat until thickened and the beans and vegetables are very tender, about 45 minutes.

3 Meanwhile, discard the skin and bones from the hocks and cut the meat into bite-size pieces. Add the meat to the stew as it simmers. Season the stew with pepper.

4 Preheat the broiler. Ladle the hot stew into 8 heatproof soup bowls and place the bowls on a large cookie sheet. Cover each bowl with a toast and spread the cheese on top. Broil 4 inches from the heat, rotating the bowls as necessary, until the cheese is lightly browned, about 3 minutes. Serve right away.
—Jacques Pépin

MAKE AHEAD

The stew can be refrigerated for up to 3 days. Reheat thoroughly, adding a little stock or water if necessary, before topping and broiling.

WINE

Bright, juicy Beaujolais goes well with rustic dishes like this stew because its acidity can stand up to the heartiness of the dish. Look for an exuberant, red-fruited cru Beaujolais, such as a Juliénas or Chiroubles.

GRILLED EGGPLANT PARMESAN

SERVES **4**

TIME **45 min**

- 1 **large eggplant (1½ lbs.), peeled and sliced crosswise ¼ inch thick**
- 4 **large plum tomatoes, sliced crosswise ¼ inch thick**

  Extra-virgin olive oil, for brushing

  Kosher salt
- ⅓ **cup chopped green olives**

  1 to 2 **Tbsp. chopped oil-packed Calabrian chiles or other hot chiles**
- ¼ **cup finely shredded basil, plus whole leaves for garnish**
- 6 **oz. Fontina cheese, thinly sliced**

  Crusty bread, for serving

For this modern take on eggplant parm, cookbook author and former F&W Test Kitchen senior editor Grace Parisi first grills the vegetables, then bakes them with gooey Fontina cheese. The result is a quicker and much lighter version of the fried kind that Parisi's Calabrian grandmother used to make.

1 Preheat the oven to 450° and heat a grill pan. Brush the eggplant and tomato slices with olive oil and season lightly with salt. Grill the eggplant in batches over moderately high heat, turning once, until softened and lightly charred, about 4 minutes. Grill the tomatoes, turning once, until lightly charred but still intact, about 2 minutes.

2 In a small bowl, combine the olives, chiles and shredded basil. Line a large rimmed baking sheet with parchment paper. In the center, arrange half of the eggplant in a 9-inch square, overlapping the slices slightly. Top with half of the grilled tomatoes, olive mixture and Fontina. Repeat with the remaining ingredients, ending with the cheese.

3 Bake in the center of the oven for about 15 minutes, until bubbling and golden. Let stand for 10 minutes. Garnish with basil leaves and serve with crusty bread.
—Grace Parisi

WINE

Medium-bodied, berry-rich Italian red, such as Dolcetto d'Alba.

"I love the free-form nature of this dish as well as the piquant olives and spicy Calabrian chiles that are layered between the grilled eggplant and plum tomatoes." —TINA UJLAKI, EXECUTIVE FOOD EDITOR

CAULIFLOWER STEAKS
WITH HERB SALSA VERDE

SERVES **2**

TIME **35 min**

¼ cup chopped flat-leaf parsley

2 Tbsp. chopped cilantro

2 Tbsp. chopped tarragon

1½ Tbsp. drained capers, coarsely chopped

6 cornichons, chopped

1 small garlic clove, minced

1 Tbsp. Dijon mustard

1 Tbsp. grainy mustard

⅓ cup extra-virgin olive oil

1 large head of cauliflower

Kosher salt and pepper

2 Tbsp. canola oil

½ cup dry white wine

½ tsp. finely grated lemon zest plus 4½ Tbsp. fresh lemon juice

1 tsp. red wine vinegar

"I can fool my family into thinking we're eating a meaty meal with this dish," says chef Alex Guarnaschelli of Butter in New York City. "And they're a tough crowd." She treats thick slices of cauliflower like beef steaks, searing and topping them with a tangy salsa verde whisked with Dijon mustard.

1 In a large bowl, whisk the parsley with the cilantro, tarragon, capers, cornichons, garlic, mustards and olive oil.

2 Cut the cauliflower from top to bottom into four ½-inch-thick steaks. Generously season them with salt and pepper. In a very large skillet, heat the canola oil until very hot. Add the cauliflower in a single layer and cook over high heat until browned, 2 to 3 minutes. Carefully flip the steaks, add the wine and cook until it has evaporated and the cauliflower is easily pierced with a knife, 3 to 5 minutes.

3 Transfer the cauliflower to a platter and sprinkle with the lemon zest. Stir the lemon juice and vinegar into the salsa verde and season with salt and pepper. Spoon the sauce on the cauliflower and serve. —*Alex Guarnaschelli*

WINE

Concentrated, minerally white, such as Chablis.

"The idea of cooking thick slices of vegetables as you would a steak is one of those great restaurant trends that translates so well to a home kitchen. Start with the tightest heads of cauliflower you can find, which might be on the smaller side. They're much easier to slice thickly, and they make a prettier steak." —TINA UJLAKI, EXECUTIVE FOOD EDITOR

QUINOA AND BROWN RICE BOWL
WITH VEGETABLES AND TAHINI

SERVES **6**

TIME **1 hr**

- 1 cup long-grain brown rice
- 1 cup red quinoa
- ¼ cup extra-virgin olive oil
- 1 small onion, finely diced
- 1 carrot, sliced crosswise ¼ inch thick
- ¼ lb. shiitake mushrooms, stems discarded, caps thinly sliced
- 1 small zucchini, halved lengthwise and sliced crosswise ¼ inch thick
   Kosher salt
- 1 head of broccoli, stems peeled and sliced into coins, heads cut into small florets
   One 12-oz. bunch of kale, large stems discarded
- ¼ cup tahini, at room temperature
- ½ cup fresh lemon juice
- 2 garlic cloves, minced
- ¼ tsp. crushed red pepper
- 1 ripe avocado, cut into ½-inch dice
- 1 cup mung bean sprouts

"While in Los Angeles filming the second season of *Top Chef Just Desserts,* I discovered Café Gratitude, a vegan café with a cult following," says *Top Chef* judge and F&W special projects director Gail Simmons. "For me, its fresh, simple food was the perfect antidote to all that sugar. I became addicted to aptly named dishes like I Am Fortified—a bowl of whole grains with lots of cooked vegetables. When I got back to New York, I developed my own version."

1 In a medium saucepan, cover the brown rice with 2 inches of water and bring to a boil. Cover and cook over low heat until the rice is just tender, about 40 minutes. Drain and return the rice to the saucepan; keep covered.

2 Meanwhile, in a small saucepan, combine the quinoa with 2 cups of water and bring to a boil. Cover and cook over low heat until the quinoa is tender and the water is absorbed, about 20 minutes.

3 In a large skillet, heat 2 tablespoons of the oil. Add the onion and cook over moderate heat until translucent, about 4 minutes. Add the carrot and cook until starting to soften, about 3 minutes. Add the shiitake, cover and cook until tender, about 4 minutes. Add the zucchini, season with salt and cook, stirring a few times, until tender, about 3 minutes. Transfer to a bowl.

4 Heat the remaining 2 tablespoons of oil in the skillet. Add the broccoli, cover and cook over moderate heat, stirring a few times, until deep green, about 5 minutes. Add the kale, cover and cook, stirring a few times, until the broccoli and kale are just tender, about 4 minutes. Season with salt, then stir in the other vegetables.

5 In a small bowl, whisk the tahini with the lemon juice, garlic, crushed red pepper and 2 tablespoons of warm water. Season with salt.

6 Transfer the brown rice and quinoa to bowls. Top with the cooked vegetables, diced avocado and bean sprouts. Serve, passing the tahini sauce at the table. —*Gail Simmons*

WINE

Fresh, zesty Sauvignon Blanc.

QUINOA RISOTTO WITH LEMON AND ROASTED TOMATOES

SERVES **4**

TIME **1 hr**

1½ cups white quinoa, rinsed

Kosher salt and pepper

½ cup panko

¼ cup plus 2 Tbsp. extra-virgin olive oil

1½ tsp. minced rosemary

2 garlic cloves, minced

4 canned whole peeled tomatoes, drained and halved lengthwise

1 lemon

1 large shallot, finely chopped

2 cups chicken stock or low-sodium broth

¼ cup crème fraîche, plus more for garnish

1 tsp. finely grated lemon zest

⅓ cup freshly grated Parmigiano-Reggiano cheese, plus more for garnish

Chopped flat-leaf parsley, for garnish

L.A. chef and Lima native Ricardo Zarate, an F&W Best New Chef 2011, puts a clever Peruvian spin on risotto, using quinoa in place of rice and adding lots of bright flavor with fresh lemon and lemon zest.

1 Preheat the oven to 375°. In a small saucepan, combine the quinoa with 2½ cups of water and a large pinch of salt and bring to a boil. Cover and cook over low heat until the water is absorbed and the quinoa is tender, about 20 minutes. Let stand, covered, for 15 minutes, then fluff with a fork.

2 Meanwhile, in a small bowl, mix the panko with 2 tablespoons of the olive oil, ½ teaspoon of the rosemary, half of the garlic and a generous pinch each of salt and pepper. Arrange the tomatoes cut side up on a rimmed baking sheet and top with the panko mixture. Bake for 25 minutes, until the crumbs are lightly browned; keep warm.

3 Peel the lemon with a sharp knife, being sure to remove all of the bitter white pith. Working over a bowl, cut in between the membranes to release the sections. Cut the lemon sections into ¼-inch pieces.

4 In a medium saucepan, heat the remaining ¼ cup of olive oil until shimmering. Add the shallot and remaining garlic and cook over moderate heat, stirring, until softened, about 4 minutes. Add the remaining 1 teaspoon of rosemary and cook for 1 minute.

5 Stir the quinoa and stock into the shallot mixture and bring just to a boil. Simmer over moderate heat, stirring, until the quinoa is suspended in a thickened sauce, about 5 minutes. Stir in the ¼ cup of crème fraîche, the lemon zest, lemon sections and ⅓ cup of grated cheese. Season with salt and pepper. Spoon the quinoa risotto into bowls and top with the tomatoes. Garnish with crème fraîche, grated cheese and chopped parsley and serve.
—*Ricardo Zarate*

WINE

Bright, fragrant Pinot Blanc from Oregon or Alsace.

BUCATINI ALL'AMATRICIANA

SERVES **4**

TIME **30 min**

½ lb. thinly sliced pancetta,
   coarsely chopped

1 red onion, thinly sliced

3 garlic cloves, thinly sliced

1½ tsp. crushed red pepper

12 oz. prepared tomato sauce
   Kosher salt

1 lb. bucatini

½ cup flat-leaf parsley leaves
   Freshly grated Pecorino Romano
   cheese, for serving

At New York City's Babbo, star chef Mario Batali serves a simple, brilliant version of this classic dish, tossing the long, hollow pasta strands with house-cured guanciale (pork jowl) and a spicy house-made tomato sauce. The even simpler version of the recipe here calls for pancetta and a good jarred tomato sauce.

1 In a large, deep skillet, cook the pancetta over moderate heat, stirring frequently, until lightly browned, about 6 minutes. Using a slotted spoon, transfer the pancetta to a plate. Pour off all but 2 tablespoons of the fat in the skillet. Add the onion, garlic and crushed red pepper and cook over moderately high heat, stirring occasionally, until the onion is lightly browned, about 6 minutes. Return the pancetta to the skillet. Add the tomato sauce, season with salt and simmer until very thick, about 10 minutes.

2 Meanwhile, in a pot of salted boiling water, cook the pasta until al dente. Drain the pasta, reserving ½ cup of the cooking water.

3 Add the pasta to the sauce along with the parsley and the reserved cooking water. Stir over moderately high heat until the pasta is evenly coated, about 2 minutes. Serve the pasta in bowls, passing the cheese at the table.
   —*Mario Batali*

WINE

Medium-bodied Italian red, such as Barbera d'Alba.

"This pasta recipe could not be easier. It calls for jarred tomato sauce, but of course you can swap in homemade. Look for meaty pancetta, and be sure not to cook it until crisp or it will be tough."
—TINA UJLAKI, EXECUTIVE FOOD EDITOR

PAPPARDELLE WITH SUMMER SQUASH AND ARUGULA-WALNUT PESTO

SERVES **4 to 6**

TIME **45 min**

¾ cup walnut halves

4 cups packed arugula leaves (4 oz.)

¾ cup extra-virgin olive oil, plus more for drizzling

½ tsp. finely grated garlic

½ cup freshly grated Parmigiano-Reggiano cheese, plus shavings for garnish

Kosher salt and pepper

12 oz. pappardelle

3 firm, fresh medium zucchini and/or yellow squash (1¼ lbs.), very thinly sliced lengthwise on a mandoline

3 Tbsp. fresh lemon juice

This recipe is a fantastic showcase for flavorful, peak-of-summer squash. F&W Test Kitchen senior editor Kay Chun cuts zucchini and yellow squash lengthwise into long, thin ribbons on a mandoline, then tosses them with hot pasta so they just barely cook.

1 In a small skillet, toast the walnuts over moderately low heat until golden, about 5 minutes. Finely chop ½ cup of the walnuts; coarsely chop the rest for garnish.

2 In a food processor, pulse 2 cups of the arugula until finely chopped; scrape into a large bowl and stir in the ¾ cup of olive oil, the garlic, grated cheese and finely chopped walnuts. Season the pesto with salt and pepper.

3 In a large pot of salted boiling water, cook the pappardelle until al dente. Drain the pasta and add to the pesto in the bowl. Add the zucchini and toss to coat. Stir in the lemon juice and the remaining 2 cups of arugula and season with salt and pepper. Transfer the pasta to a platter, drizzle with olive oil and garnish with the coarsely chopped walnuts and cheese shavings. —*Kay Chun*

WINE

Ripe California Chardonnay.

"This is my go-to pasta recipe in the summer. It's perfect for warmer weather because it's packed with fresh flavors, and the thin ribbons of zucchini keep it light." —JUSTIN CHAPPLE, TEST KITCHEN SENIOR EDITOR

ORECCHIETTE WITH SAUTÉED GREENS AND SCALLION SAUCE

SERVES **4**

TIME **30 min**

- ¾ **lb. orecchiette**
- 4 **Tbsp. unsalted butter**
- 1 **bunch of scallions, thinly sliced**
- 3 **garlic cloves, thinly sliced**
- ¾ **cup dry white wine**
  Kosher salt and pepper
- 2 **Tbsp. extra-virgin olive oil**
  One 5-oz. bag baby arugula
- 6 **large Swiss chard leaves, stems and central ribs discarded, leaves coarsely chopped**
- ¼ **cup mascarpone cheese**

At Redd in Napa Valley, chef Richard Reddington fills homemade ravioli with ricotta, mascarpone, arugula, spinach and Swiss chard, then serves them in a green garlic and white wine sauce. This simplified version calls for store-bought orecchiette tossed with arugula and chard (both are tastier than spinach) and uses scallions in the sauce instead of green garlic, which can be hard to find.

1 In a large pot of salted boiling water, cook the orecchiette until al dente. Drain, reserving ¼ cup of the cooking water.

2 Meanwhile, in a medium saucepan, melt the butter. Add the scallions and garlic and cook over low heat until softened, about 5 minutes. Add the wine and cook over moderate heat until reduced by half, about 5 minutes. Add ½ cup of water, transfer to a blender and puree the mixture until smooth. Season the scallion sauce with salt and pepper.

3 Wipe out the pasta pot and heat the olive oil in it. Add the arugula and Swiss chard and cook over high heat until wilted, about 5 minutes. Add the pasta, scallion sauce and the reserved pasta cooking water and simmer, tossing and stirring, until the sauce is thick, about 3 minutes. Stir in the mascarpone, season with salt and pepper and serve. —*Richard Reddington*

WINE

Lightly grassy Sauvignon Blanc from the Loire Valley.

"My friend refers to this dish as 'sometimes food.' As in it's so rich and luxurious that you want to save it for a splurge. I love the extra chew you get from the thicker bucatini pasta." —JAMES MAIKOWSKI, ART DIRECTOR

BUCATINI CARBONARA

SERVES **2**

TIME **30 min**

- 6 oz. bucatini or perciatelli
- 1 Tbsp. extra-virgin olive oil
- 4 oz. pancetta, sliced ¼ inch thick and cut into ¼-inch dice
- 1 shallot, very finely chopped
- 1 garlic clove, very finely chopped
- 1 cup heavy cream
- 2 Tbsp. freshly grated Parmigiano-Reggiano cheese, plus more for serving
- 4 large egg yolks
  Kosher salt and pepper
- 2 Tbsp. coarsely chopped parsley

Classic Italian carbonara is a minimalist dish, combining just pancetta or guanciale (cured pork jowl), egg yolks and cheese. F&W Best New Chef 2009 Linton Hopkins of Holeman and Finch in Atlanta unapologetically makes his version extra-indulgent with cream, shallot and garlic.

1 In a large pot of salted boiling water, cook the pasta until al dente. Drain, reserving 3 tablespoons of the cooking water.

2 Meanwhile, in a large skillet, heat the oil. Add the pancetta and cook over moderate heat until most of the fat has been rendered, about 7 minutes. Add the shallot and garlic and cook over moderate heat for 1 minute. Add the cream and simmer over moderate heat until slightly thickened, about 2 minutes. Add the hot pasta and stir to coat, 1 minute. Remove from the heat. Stir in the reserved pasta cooking water, the 2 tablespoons of grated cheese and the egg yolks. Season with salt. Transfer the pasta to bowls and sprinkle with the parsley and pepper. Serve, passing more cheese at the table.
—Linton Hopkins

WINE

Carbonara pairs best with a tannic red to refresh the palate after each luxurious bite. Pour a robust Vino Nobile di Montepulciano from Tuscany.

RIGATONI WITH LEMONY KALE-AND-PECORINO PESTO

SERVES **4 to 6**

TIME **30 min**

1½ lbs. Tuscan kale, stemmed

1 lb. rigatoni

3 large garlic cloves

¼ cup pine nuts, toasted

⅔ cup extra-virgin olive oil

1½ oz. Pecorino Toscano cheese, coarsely grated (½ cup), plus more for serving

1 Tbsp. finely grated lemon zest (from 1 lemon)

Pinch of Aleppo pepper, plus more for seasoning

Kosher salt and black pepper

This pesto is particularly great in the fall and winter, when basil isn't flourishing in gardens. Chef Chris Cosentino of Cockscomb in San Francisco adds Pecorino Toscano, a hard sheep-milk cheese that's nuttier and milder than Pecorino Romano.

1 Bring 2 large pots of generously salted water to a boil. Fill a large bowl with ice water. Add the kale to one of the pots and cook for 1 minute, until bright green and just tender. Drain and immediately transfer to the ice water. When cool, drain again. Transfer the kale to a work surface with some water clinging to the leaves and chop it.

2 Meanwhile, cook the rigatoni in the other pot of boiling water until almost al dente. Reserve ½ cup of the cooking water, then drain the pasta.

3 Transfer the kale to a blender. Add the garlic and pine nuts and pulse until coarsely chopped. Add the oil and process until smooth. Transfer the pesto to a large bowl and stir in the ½ cup of pecorino and the lemon zest. Season to taste with the Aleppo pepper, salt and black pepper.

4 Return the pasta to the pot. Add the pesto and cook over moderate heat, stirring constantly, for 2 minutes, adding some of the pasta cooking water if it seems dry. Spoon the pasta into bowls, top with additional cheese and Aleppo pepper and serve. —*Chris Cosentino*

WINE

Lively, aromatic French white like Roussette de Savoie.

> "My friend Paul's recipe is the Mack Daddy of mac 'n' cheeses. I like to use smaller ramekins and serve this with fried chicken as an insanely impressive side dish." —JUSTIN CHAPPLE, TEST KITCHEN SENIOR EDITOR

ANDOUILLE MAC AND CHEESE

SERVES 4

TIME Active 1 hr; Total 1 hr 30 min

- 1½ cups whole milk
- 1½ cups heavy cream
- 4 Tbsp. unsalted butter
- ⅓ cup all-purpose flour
- 1 garlic clove, minced
- ½ tsp. finely chopped thyme
- Pinch of cayenne
- Pinch of freshly grated nutmeg
- Pinch of white pepper
- 1½ cups shredded mild white cheddar cheese (6 oz.)
- 1½ cups shredded sharp cheddar cheese (6 oz.)
- Kosher salt and black pepper
- 3 Tbsp. canola oil
- 1 cup panko
- 6 oz. andouille sausage, diced
- ¾ cup finely diced red bell pepper
- ½ cup finely diced onion
- ¼ cup thinly sliced scallions, plus more for garnish
- ¼ cup finely chopped cilantro, plus leaves for garnish
- ¼ cup finely chopped parsley
- 1 lb. medium pasta shells
- Hot sauce
- Thinly sliced hot red chiles or jalapeños, for garnish

At The Heron in New York's Catskill Mountains, chef Paul Nanni mixes andouille sausage into his spicy, Cajun-inspired macaroni and cheese.

1 Preheat the oven to 450°. In a small saucepan, bring the milk and heavy cream to a simmer. Keep warm over very low heat.

2 In a medium saucepan, melt the butter. Whisk in the flour and cook over moderate heat until bubbling, 1 to 2 minutes. Add the garlic, thyme, cayenne, nutmeg and white pepper and whisk until the roux is lightly browned, 3 to 5 minutes. Gradually whisk in the milk and cream until the sauce is smooth and bring to a boil. Simmer over moderate heat, whisking, until no floury taste remains, 5 to 7 minutes. Remove from the heat and whisk in the mild cheddar and ½ cup of the sharp cheddar. Season the sauce with salt and black pepper.

3 In a large skillet, heat 1 tablespoon of the oil. Add the panko and toast over moderately high heat, stirring, until lightly browned, about 3 minutes. Transfer to a plate. Wipe out the skillet.

4 Heat the remaining 2 tablespoons of oil in the skillet. Add the andouille, bell pepper and onion and cook over moderate heat until the vegetables are lightly browned, about 5 minutes. Stir in the ¼ cup of sliced scallions and the chopped cilantro and parsley.

5 In a large pot of salted boiling water, cook the pasta until al dente. Drain well, then return the pasta to the pot. Stir in the cheese sauce and the andouille mixture. Season with hot sauce, salt and black pepper.

6 Spoon the pasta into four 12-ounce gratin dishes set on a baking sheet. Top with the remaining 1 cup of sharp cheddar and the toasted panko. Bake until piping hot, 15 to 20 minutes. Let stand for 5 minutes. Garnish with scallions, cilantro and red chiles and serve with hot sauce. —*Paul Nanni*

WINE

Bold Italian red, such as Primitivo Salentino.

CREAMY WHITE LASAGNA

SERVES 10

TIME **Active 1 hr 30 min;**
Total 3 hr 30 min

PASTA

3½ cups all-purpose flour,
  plus more for dusting

1½ tsp. kosher salt

3 large eggs, lightly beaten

BÉCHAMEL

2 sticks unsalted butter

1 medium onion, finely chopped

2 rosemary sprigs

2 thyme sprigs

3 garlic cloves, crushed

  Kosher salt

1 cup all-purpose flour

2 quarts whole milk

ASSEMBLY

  Extra-virgin olive oil

½ lb. imported Fontina cheese,
  shredded (2½ cups)

5 oz. Grana Padano cheese, freshly
  grated (1¼ cups)

In this tomato-free lasagna from chef Gerard Craft of Pastaria in St. Louis, delicate pasta turns silken when baked in a creamy, cheesy white sauce. Craft likes to dress up the lasagna with seasonal toppings like wild mushrooms.

1 MAKE THE PASTA In a food processor, pulse the 3½ cups of flour with the salt. Add the eggs and ½ cup of water and pulse until the dough starts to come together. Turn the dough out onto a work surface and knead until smooth and elastic, 10 minutes. If it's too sticky to work with, lightly dust it with flour. Wrap the dough in plastic and let rest at room temperature for 1 hour.

2 MEANWHILE, MAKE THE BÉCHAMEL In a large saucepan, melt the butter. Add the onion, rosemary, thyme, garlic and a pinch of salt and cook over moderate heat, stirring occasionally, until the onion is softened but not browned, about 8 minutes. Add the flour and cook, stirring constantly, until the roux is light golden, 3 to 5 minutes. Gradually whisk in the milk and bring to a boil, then simmer over moderately low heat, stirring frequently, until no floury taste remains, about 20 minutes. Press the béchamel through a fine sieve into a bowl; discard the solids. Season with salt and let cool.

3 ASSEMBLE THE LASAGNA Cut the dough into 8 equal pieces; work with 1 piece at a time, keeping the rest covered with a towel. Flatten the dough slightly. Run it through a pasta machine a total of 6 times: Start at the widest setting, then run through successively narrower settings. Dust the sheet with flour and lay it on a parchment paper–lined baking sheet. Repeat with the remaining dough, separating the sheets with parchment.

4 In a large pot of salted boiling water, cook the pasta sheets until just al dente, 1 to 2 minutes. Drain in a colander and cool under running water, then drain again. Return the pasta to the baking sheet and toss with olive oil to prevent the sheets from sticking together.

5 Preheat the oven to 350°. Brush a deep 9-by-13-inch baking dish with oil; spread with ½ cup of the béchamel. Arrange a layer of pasta over the béchamel, trimming to fit. Spread one-fifth of the remaining béchamel over the pasta; sprinkle with ½ cup of the Fontina and ¼ cup of the Grana Padano. Repeat the layering 4 more times, ending with the cheeses.

6 Tightly cover the baking dish with foil and bake the lasagna for 45 minutes, until bubbling. Remove from the oven and uncover. Preheat the broiler. Broil the lasagna 6 inches from the heat until lightly browned on top, 2 to 4 minutes. Let rest for 15 minutes, then cut into squares and serve. —*Gerard Craft*

WINE

Vibrant, spicy Italian red, like Langhe Nebbiolo.

SPAGHETTI WITH SUNDAY SAUCE

SERVES **8 to 10**

TIME **Active 50 min; Total 5 hr**

- 2 **Tbsp. extra-virgin olive oil**
- 3 **lbs. bone-in, English-cut beef short ribs, cut into 2-inch pieces (see Note)**
  Kosher salt and pepper
- 2 **medium onions, finely chopped**
- 2 **Tbsp. tomato paste**
- 3 **garlic cloves, minced**
- 1 **tsp. dried oregano**
  Two 28-oz. cans whole peeled tomatoes, crushed by hand, juices reserved
- 1 **medium carrot, peeled**
- 2 **lbs. spaghetti**

NOTE

Ask your butcher to cut the short ribs as specified.

When butcher Pat LaFrieda was growing up, the meat in the family's weekly spaghetti sauce varied based on what his dad brought home from the butcher shop—one weekend, it might be spicy Italian sausage; the next, it might be spareribs. The slow-cooked beef short ribs that Pat uses in this recipe from his cookbook, *Meat,* give the dish a lovely richness.

1 In a large enameled cast-iron casserole, heat the olive oil until shimmering. Season the short ribs with salt and pepper and add them to the casserole in a single layer. Cook over moderately high heat, turning occasionally, until browned, about 10 minutes. With tongs, transfer the short ribs to a plate.

2 Pour off all but 1 tablespoon of fat from the casserole. Add the onions and a generous pinch of salt and cook over moderate heat, stirring occasionally, until browned, 12 to 15 minutes. Add the tomato paste, garlic and oregano and cook, stirring, until fragrant, about 2 minutes. Add the crushed tomatoes with their juices and the carrot and bring to a boil.

3 Return the short ribs and their juices to the casserole, cover partially and simmer over low heat, turning the short ribs occasionally, until the meat is very tender and the sauce is thick, about 4 hours.

4 Transfer the short ribs to a plate; discard the carrot. Discard the bones and cut the meat into 1½-inch chunks. Return the meat to the sauce and season with salt and pepper; keep warm over low heat.

5 In a large saucepan of salted boiling water, cook the spaghetti until al dente. Drain the pasta, reserving ½ cup of the cooking water. Transfer the spaghetti to the pot with the sauce, toss well and cook for 1 to 2 minutes. Add a splash of the reserved cooking water if the sauce is too thick. Serve immediately.
—*Pat LaFrieda*

WINE

Bright, medium-bodied Sangiovese, such as Chianti Colli Senesi.

THAI SEAFOOD NOODLE SALAD

SERVES **6**

TIME **1 hr**

- 6 oz. rice vermicelli
- 2 red Thai chiles, thinly sliced
- 2 garlic cloves, thinly sliced
- ¼ cup sugar
- ½ cup fresh lime juice
- ⅓ cup Asian fish sauce
- 2 Tbsp. boiling water
- ½ lb. medium shrimp, shelled and deveined
- ½ lb. bay scallops
- ½ lb. small squid, bodies cut into ½-inch rings, tentacles halved
- 3 plum tomatoes, seeded and diced
- 1 cup bean sprouts
- 1 cup mint leaves
- ½ small red onion, thinly sliced
- ½ cup salted roasted peanuts
- 6 lettuce leaves, for serving
  Cilantro leaves, for garnish

Cookbook author and journalist Anya von Bremzen packs the classic flavors of Thai cuisine—sweet, salty, spicy, sour—in the dressing for this salad. She tosses it with a delicious combo of rice noodles, shrimp, scallops, squid and peanuts.

1 In a medium bowl, cover the vermicelli in cold water and soak for 30 minutes. Meanwhile, in a mortar, pound the chiles and garlic to a paste with 1 tablespoon of the sugar. Add the lime juice, fish sauce, boiling water and the remaining 3 tablespoons of sugar and pound until the sugar is dissolved. Let the dressing stand for 30 minutes.

2 Bring a large saucepan of water to a boil. Fill a bowl with ice water. Add the shrimp to the boiling water and cook until white throughout and curled, 2 to 3 minutes. Using a slotted spoon, transfer the shrimp to the ice water. Add the scallops to the boiling water and cook until white and firm, 2 to 3 minutes. Transfer the scallops to the ice water. Add the squid to the boiling water and cook just until firm, about 45 seconds. Transfer the squid to the ice water. Drain all of the seafood and pat dry.

3 Bring a fresh saucepan of water to a boil and refill the bowl with ice water. Drain the vermicelli, add to the boiling water and cook just until al dente, 1 minute. Drain and transfer to the ice water. Drain again and pat dry. Cut the vermicelli into 3-inch lengths.

4 In a large bowl, toss the seafood with the vermicelli, tomatoes, bean sprouts, mint, red onion, peanuts and chile dressing. Arrange the lettuce leaves on a platter and fill with the seafood salad. Garnish with cilantro leaves and serve.
—*Anya von Bremzen*

MAKE AHEAD

All of the components can be prepared up to 1 day ahead and refrigerated separately. Toss the salad just before serving.

WINE

Because Thai recipes combine so many flavors, they tend to pair best with adaptable white wines like Spanish Albariño, known for its perky acidity, medium body and depth of citrusy flavor.

SPICY PEANUT NOODLES

SERVES **6**

TIME **20 min**

- 1 **lb. spaghetti**
- ¾ **cup creamy peanut butter**
- ½ **cup unseasoned rice vinegar**
- 3 **Tbsp. plus 1 tsp. sugar**
- ¼ **cup plus 2 Tbsp. soy sauce**
- 1 **Tbsp. toasted sesame oil**
- 2 **tsp. crushed red pepper**
  One 2-inch piece of fresh ginger, peeled and coarsely chopped
- 1 **large garlic clove**
- 3 **celery ribs, thinly sliced**
- ½ **cup coarsely chopped cilantro leaves and tender stems**
  Lime wedges, for serving

"My mother used to make this," says Joanne Chang of Flour Bakery + Cafe in Boston. "I learned to re-create it in college, far away from any Chinese markets." Pantry staples like spaghetti and peanut butter are perfect stand-ins for the traditional ingredients. To give spaghetti the soft texture of Chinese noodles, cook it a few minutes longer than the box advises.

1 In a pot of salted boiling water, cook the spaghetti until tender. Drain and cool under cold running water. Drain well.

2 In a blender, puree the peanut butter with 6 tablespoons of the vinegar, 3 tablespoons of the sugar, ¼ cup of water and the soy sauce, sesame oil, crushed red pepper, ginger and garlic. Transfer ½ cup of the peanut dressing to a large bowl and toss with the noodles.

3 In a medium bowl, toss the celery with the cilantro and the remaining 2 tablespoons of vinegar and 1 teaspoon of sugar.

4 Transfer the noodles to bowls and drizzle with the remaining peanut dressing. Top with the celery and serve with lime wedges. —*Joanne Chang*

MAKE AHEAD

The peanut dressing can be refrigerated for up to 2 days.

WINE

Tart, citrusy Riesling from Australia.

"I've served this dish to people aged 5 to 75, and everyone loves it. You can add chicken, vegetables, sesame seeds or nuts and use almost any kind of noodle. It's perfect for picnics since it can be served at room temp or slightly chilled."

—CHRISTINE QUINLAN, DEPUTY EDITOR

SOBA NOODLES WITH MISO-ROASTED TOMATOES

SERVES **4**

TIME **30 min**

- ⅓ cup canola oil
- 3 Tbsp. unseasoned rice vinegar
- 2 Tbsp. white (shiro) miso
- 1 Tbsp. minced peeled fresh ginger
- 1 Tbsp. toasted sesame oil
- 1 Tbsp. honey
- 2 tsp. finely grated lime zest plus 2 Tbsp. fresh lime juice
- Kosher salt
- 2 pints cherry tomatoes
- 8 oz. soba noodles
- 4 scallions, thinly sliced
- 1 Tbsp. toasted sesame seeds

Ashley Rodriguez, a pastry chef and author of the blog Not Without Salt, creates a tangy, bright sauce for soba noodles by roasting cherry tomatoes in a mix of miso, ginger, sesame, lime juice and honey. Try adding shrimp for an even more substantial dish.

1 Preheat the oven to 425°. In a small bowl, whisk the canola oil, vinegar, miso, ginger, sesame oil, honey, lime zest and lime juice until smooth. Season the miso dressing with salt.

2 On a rimmed baking sheet, toss the tomatoes with 3 tablespoons of the miso dressing and season with salt. Roast for 20 minutes, stirring, until the tomatoes are charred in spots. Scrape into a large bowl.

3 Cook the soba in a pot of boiling water just until al dente, about 4 minutes. Drain and cool under cold running water. Add the soba, scallions and half of the remaining dressing to the tomatoes and toss well. Season with salt, transfer to a platter and garnish with the sesame seeds. Serve with the remaining dressing. —*Ashley Rodriguez*

MAKE AHEAD

The tomatoes can be roasted and refrigerated overnight. Rewarm before using.

WINE

Minerally, peppery Austrian white, such as Grüner Veltliner.

CALIFORNIA BLTS

SERVES 4

TIME 45 min

12 slices of bacon, halved crosswise

½ cup mayonnaise

1 Tbsp. finely chopped tarragon

1 Tbsp. fresh lemon juice

Kosher salt and pepper

8 slices of multigrain sandwich bread, toasted

1 Hass avocado—peeled, pitted and sliced

2 Persian cucumbers, thinly sliced on the diagonal

1 medium tomato, thinly sliced

4 small Bibb lettuce leaves

½ cup mixed sprouts, such as radish, sunflower and alfalfa

Justin Chapple, the star of F&W's Mad Genius Tips videos, makes his BLTs chock-full of bacon by weaving the strips into a lattice before baking them. He gives the sandwiches a Californian spin with avocado and lemon-herb mayo.

1 Preheat the oven to 400°. Line a large rimmed baking sheet with parchment paper or foil. For each lattice, weave 6 strips of bacon, 3 in each direction, on the prepared baking sheet.

2 Set an ovenproof rack upside down on the bacon to keep it flat. Bake for 15 to 20 minutes, until browned and crisp. Remove the rack, then transfer the bacon lattices to paper towels to drain.

3 Meanwhile, in a small bowl, whisk the mayonnaise with the tarragon and lemon juice. Season with salt and pepper.

4 Spread the tarragon mayonnaise on each slice of toast. Arrange the sliced avocado, cucumbers and tomato on 4 slices of the toast and sprinkle with salt and pepper. Top with the bacon lattices, Bibb leaves and sprouts. Close the sandwiches and serve. —*Justin Chapple*

WINE OR BEER

Either a ripe, cherry-fruited California Pinot Noir or a hop-forward ale would be a perfect match for these bold BLTs.

"This recipe is a deluxe upgrade of the BLTs I grew up eating. The bacon-weave technique is a smart way to get bacon in every bite and works in all kinds of sandwiches, from fried egg on a roll to a turkey club."
—KATE HEDDINGS, FOOD DIRECTOR

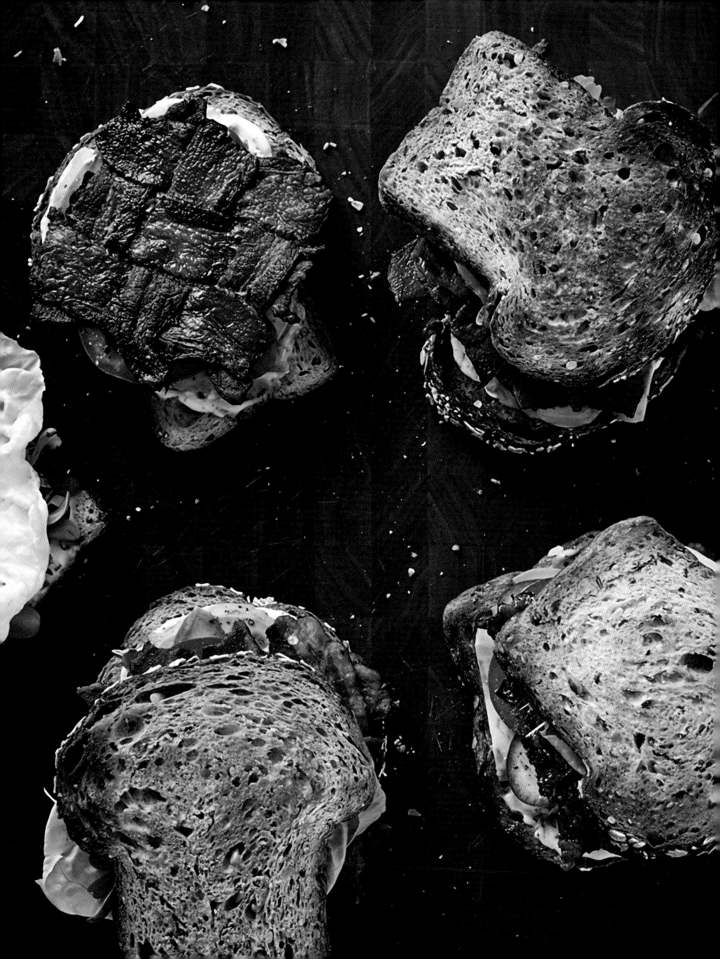

GARLICKY KALE-AND-PROVOLONE GRINDERS

SERVES 4

TIME   Active 20 min; Total 40 min

- 2 **Tbsp. extra-virgin olive oil**
- 7 **oil-packed anchovy fillets**
- 5 **garlic cloves, minced**
- 1 **lb. green kale (2 bunches), stemmed and leaves torn into large pieces (about 18 cups)**
- ½ **lb. thinly sliced provolone cheese**

  One 12-inch ciabatta loaf, halved horizontally

  Sliced radishes, chopped green olives and mayonnaise, for serving

Curly green kale, often eschewed for its bitter taste and fibrous texture, finds redemption in this flavor-packed sandwich. F&W's Kay Chun cooks the salad staple until tender, then layers the wilted greens with melty cheese, briny olives, crunchy radishes and mayo.

1 In a large nonstick skillet, heat the olive oil. Add the anchovies and garlic, then add the kale in batches and cook over moderate heat, stirring, until the kale is wilted, about 3 minutes. Add 1 cup of water, cover and cook until tender, about 15 minutes. Top the kale with the cheese in an even layer. Cover and cook until the cheese melts, about 2 minutes. Using a large slotted spoon, transfer the kale and cheese to the bottom half of the ciabatta. Top with radishes, olives and the top half of the ciabatta spread with mayonnaise. Close the sandwich, cut into 4 pieces and serve. —*Kay Chun*

WINE

The bright, iodine-like flavor of a dry sherry, such as fino or manzanilla, is a classic match for anything involving anchovy.

PIZZA WITH BAKED MEATBALLS

SERVES 4

TIME 45 min

1 Tbsp. extra-virgin olive oil,
  plus more for brushing

1 large egg

2 Tbsp. panko

2 garlic cloves, minced

¼ cup finely chopped flat-leaf
  parsley

1 cup freshly grated Parmigiano-
  Reggiano cheese

  Kosher salt and pepper

1 lb. ground beef chuck

  One 28-oz. can crushed
  tomatoes

  Two 8-oz. balls of pizza dough,
  at room temperature

1 cup basil leaves

"*Avanzi* means 'leftovers' in Italian," says Matt Jennings, chef at Townsman in Boston. When he lived in Florence, Jennings often made this *avanzi* pizza on Fridays with leftovers from the week of cooking. He urges people to get creative: "Char cucumbers and sprinkle feta on top. I've even put toasted ground nuts, dried fruit and canned beans on the *avanzi*—although not necessarily at the same time!"

1 Preheat the oven to 450°. Brush a large ceramic baking dish with olive oil. In a large bowl, whisk the egg. Stir in the panko, garlic, parsley, ¼ cup of the cheese, 1 teaspoon of salt and ½ teaspoon of pepper. Add the ground beef and gently knead to combine. Form the mixture into 1-inch meatballs and transfer to the baking dish. Bake for about 10 minutes, turning once, until browned.

2 Meanwhile, in a large saucepan, heat the 1 tablespoon of olive oil. Add the crushed tomatoes and cook over moderately high heat until bubbling.

3 Add the meatballs to the tomato sauce, cover partially and simmer over moderately low heat until the meatballs are cooked through, about 10 minutes. With a large spoon, mash the meatballs into large chunks. Remove from the heat.

4 Meanwhile, brush 2 large baking sheets with olive oil and preheat in the upper and lower thirds of the oven. On a lightly floured work surface, cut each ball of dough in half. Roll each piece into a 10-inch round or oval. Arrange the rounds on the heated sheets and bake for about 7 minutes, shifting the sheets halfway through, until lightly golden on top.

5 Spread the meatball sauce over the crusts, leaving a ½-inch border. Sprinkle with the remaining ¾ cup of cheese. Bake for about 5 minutes, until the crust is crisp on the bottom and the cheese is melted. Scatter the basil leaves over the pizzas and serve hot. —*Matt Jennings*

WINE

Vibrant, floral-tinged, light red, such as Freisa from Piedmont.

TOMATO, ZUCCHINI AND SALAMI PIZZA

MAKES Two 12-inch pizzas

TIME Active 50 min; Total 2 hr 45 min

DOUGH

- 1½ Tbsp. extra-virgin olive oil, plus more for greasing
- ¾ tsp. active dry yeast
- 2½ cups all-purpose flour, plus more for dusting
  Kosher salt

SAUCE

- 1 Tbsp. extra-virgin olive oil
- 1 small onion, finely chopped
- 3 garlic cloves, finely chopped
  One 15-oz. can diced tomatoes
- 1 cup tomato puree
  Pinch of crushed red pepper
  Pinch of sugar
- 10 large basil leaves, torn
  Kosher salt and black pepper

PIZZA

- 8 slices of provolone cheese (6 oz.)
- 20 thin slices of spicy salami (4 oz.)
- ½ lb. baby zucchini with flowers (flowers optional)—zucchini thinly sliced, flowers halved lengthwise and pistils snipped off
- ½ lb. cherry tomatoes
  Kosher salt and pepper
  Dried oregano and extra-virgin olive oil, for serving

This crisp pizza is from Katie Quinn Davies, the Sydney-based talent behind the blog and book *What Katie Ate*. It's the ideal summer pie, with toppings that include both sliced zucchini and zucchini blossoms.

1 MAKE THE DOUGH Grease a large bowl with olive oil. In a small bowl, whisk ¾ cup of warm water with the yeast and let stand until foamy, about 5 minutes. In another large bowl, whisk the 2½ cups of flour with a large pinch of salt. Make a well in the center of the flour and pour in the yeast mixture and the 1½ tablespoons of olive oil. Stir with a fork until the dough just starts to come together. Turn the dough out onto a generously floured work surface and knead until very smooth, about 5 minutes. Transfer the dough to the greased bowl, cover with plastic wrap and let rise in a warm place until doubled in bulk, about 1 hour.

2 MEANWHILE, MAKE THE SAUCE In a large saucepan, heat the olive oil. Add the onion and garlic and cook over moderate heat, stirring occasionally, until just softened, about 4 minutes. Add the diced tomatoes, tomato puree, crushed red pepper, sugar and basil and bring to a boil. Simmer over moderately low heat, stirring occasionally, until thickened and reduced to 2 cups, about 18 minutes. Season the sauce with salt and black pepper.

3 MAKE THE PIZZAS Preheat the oven to 450° for at least 30 minutes. Grease a large rimmed baking sheet. Cut the pizza dough into 2 pieces. On a lightly floured work surface, roll or stretch out 1 piece of the dough to a 12-inch round; transfer to the prepared baking sheet. Spread half of the sauce over the dough and top with half of the cheese, salami, zucchini and tomatoes. Season with salt and pepper. Bake the pizza for 15 to 18 minutes, until the crust is browned. Garnish with dried oregano and a drizzle of olive oil. Repeat with the remaining dough and toppings. Serve hot. —*Katie Quinn Davies*

WINE

Fresh, fragrant sparkling wine like Prosecco.

BLACK COD WITH MISO

SERVES **6**

TIME **30 min plus overnight marinating**

- **3 Tbsp. mirin**
- **3 Tbsp. sake**
- **½ cup shiro (white) miso**
- **⅓ cup sugar**
- **Six 6- to 7-oz. skinless black cod fillets, about 1½ inches thick**
- **Vegetable oil, for grilling**
- **Pickled ginger, for serving**

This sweet and silky fish dish, which has been cloned at restaurants all over the world, is fairly simple to make, though it's somewhat time-consuming: F&W Best New Chef 1989 Nobu Matsuhisa of the Nobu restaurant empire recommends marinating the black cod in a good deal of the sake-miso marinade for two to three days. But the fish is also spectacular if you marinate it only overnight in just enough sake and miso to coat.

1 In a small saucepan, bring the mirin and sake to a boil. Whisk in the miso until dissolved. Add the sugar and cook over moderate heat, whisking, just until dissolved. Transfer the marinade to a large baking dish and let cool. Add the fish and turn to coat. Cover and refrigerate overnight.

2 Preheat the oven to 400°. Heat a grill pan and oil it. Scrape the marinade off the fish. Grill the fish over high heat until browned, about 2 minutes. Flip the fish onto a heavy rimmed baking sheet and roast for 10 minutes, until flaky. Transfer to plates and serve with pickled ginger. —*Nobu Matsuhisa*

MAKE AHEAD

The marinade can be refrigerated for up to 1 week.

WINE

Spicy, full-bodied Gewürztraminer.

SEARED SOLE WITH LIME SAUCE

  3 Tbsp. Asian fish sauce

1½ Tbsp. palm sugar or packed light
    brown sugar

  ¼ cup finely chopped cilantro

  6 fresh red Thai bird chiles, minced
     (seeded for less heat)

  6 garlic cloves, minced

1½ Tbsp. fresh lime juice

  1 tsp. crushed red pepper

     Four 7-oz. skinless sole fillets,
     preferably grey sole

     Kosher salt and black pepper

  ¼ cup extra-virgin olive oil

This Thai-inspired sauce is a quick miracle for any flaky white fish. L.A. chef Kuniko Yagi prefers making the sauce with spicy Thai bird chiles; for less fire, you can remove the seeds or substitute serranos.

1 In a small saucepan, stir the fish sauce and sugar over high heat until the sugar dissolves, about 1 minute. Remove the pan from the heat and stir in the cilantro, chiles, garlic, lime juice and crushed red pepper.

2 Heat a large skillet until hot. Season the sole with salt and black pepper. Add 2 tablespoons of the olive oil to the skillet and swirl to coat the bottom. Add 2 of the fillets and cook over high heat until lightly browned outside and just white throughout, 1 to 2 minutes per side; transfer to plates. Wipe out the skillet and repeat with the remaining olive oil and sole. Pour the lime sauce on the sole and serve. —*Kuniko Yagi*

SERVE WITH

Steamed white rice and sautéed bok choy or Chinese mustard greens.

MAKE AHEAD

The lime sauce can be refrigerated for up to 3 days.

WINE

Fruit-rich Loire white, such as Anjou Blanc.

"I'm crazy about the sauce for this fish! It takes you through a pinball machine of flavors, pinging sweet, then salty, tangy and hot. The sauce is meant to be poured over the fish, but I'm not mad when some of it touches the rice and vegetables on my plate."

—SUSAN CHOUNG, BOOKS EDITOR

PIMENTÓN-ROASTED RED SNAPPER
WITH HERB SALAD

SERVES **4**

TIME **Active 40 min; Total 1 hr 15 min**

¼ cup plus 1 Tbsp. extra-virgin olive oil

2 tsp. pimentón de la Vera (sweet smoked Spanish paprika)

1 tsp. finely grated lemon zest

6 cups kosher salt (30 oz.), plus more for seasoning

3 large egg whites, beaten

One 2-lb. whole red snapper, cleaned

Ground black pepper

½ lemon, sliced

3 large bay leaves

5 medium celery ribs, thinly sliced on the diagonal

1 cup celery leaves

1 cup parsley leaves

½ cup tarragon leaves

2 Tbsp. fresh lemon juice

F&W's Justin Chapple brushes a whole red snapper with pimentón oil to give it a terrific smoky flavor, then packs it in salt before roasting to seal in moisture. Mixed with egg whites and patted on whole fish, kosher salt hardens in the oven to become a crust that protects food from dry heat without making it taste too salty.

1 Preheat the oven to 425°. In a small bowl, whisk 3 tablespoons of the olive oil with the pimentón and lemon zest. In a large bowl, mix the 6 cups of kosher salt with the egg whites and ½ cup of water until it resembles moist sand.

2 Spread a ¼-inch-thick layer of the salt mixture in the center of a large rimmed baking sheet. Season the fish inside and out with black pepper and brush all over with the pimentón oil. Stuff the cavity with the lemon slices and bay leaves and lay the snapper on the salt. Mound the remaining salt mixture on top, lightly packing it to completely cover the fish.

3 Bake the fish for about 30 minutes, until an instant-read thermometer inserted into the fish through the salt registers 135°. Remove from the oven and let stand for 10 minutes. Crack the salt crust and discard it. Brush off any excess salt and transfer the fish to a platter.

4 In a large bowl, toss the celery with the celery leaves, parsley, tarragon, lemon juice and the remaining 2 tablespoons of olive oil. Season the salad with salt and pepper and serve alongside the fish. —*Justin Chapple*

WINE

Vibrant, herb-scented Chilean Sauvignon Blanc.

GLAZED MACKEREL WITH FRIED EGGPLANT AND MOJO

SERVES **4 to 6**

TIME **1 hr 30 min**

MOJO

6 **garlic cloves, minced**

1 **habanero chile, seeded and minced**

1 **Tbsp. cumin seeds**

Kosher salt and pepper

2 **Tbsp. extra-virgin olive oil**

½ **cup each of fresh orange and lime juices**

1 **Tbsp. each of minced cilantro and mint**

EGGPLANT AND FISH

1½ **lbs. eggplant, cut into ½-inch dice**

Kosher salt and pepper

1 **cup fresh orange juice**

2 **Tbsp. fresh lime juice**

1 **Tbsp. finely chopped peeled fresh ginger**

1 **Fresno chile or jalapeño, seeded and thinly sliced**

1 **tsp. soy sauce**

2 **Tbsp. extra-virgin olive oil, plus more for brushing**

Canola oil, for frying

1 **cup cornstarch**

½ **cup chopped cilantro**

Four 6-oz. Spanish mackerel fillets

This terrific mackerel recipe is from F&W Best New Chef 2013 Jose Enrique of Jose Enrique in San Juan, Puerto Rico. The dish has a great array of textures and flavors: flaky fish fillets, airy fried eggplant and a superspicy garlic-and-citrus mojo sauce.

1 MAKE THE MOJO In a mortar, smash the garlic to a paste with the habanero, cumin seeds and ½ teaspoon of salt. In a small saucepan, heat the olive oil until shimmering. Add the garlic-chile paste and whisk over moderately high heat for 30 seconds. Let stand off the heat for 10 minutes. Whisk in the citrus juices and let cool, then stir in the cilantro and mint; season with salt and pepper.

2 PREPARE THE EGGPLANT AND FISH In a large bowl, cover the eggplant with water and add a small handful of salt. Let soak for 45 minutes.

3 Meanwhile, in a small saucepan, bring the citrus juices, ginger, chile, soy sauce and the 2 tablespoons of olive oil to a boil. Simmer over moderate heat, stirring, until reduced to ⅔ cup, about 12 minutes. Season the orange glaze with salt and let cool.

4 In a large saucepan, heat 1 inch of canola oil to 375°. Drain the eggplant and pat dry. In a colander set over a large bowl, toss the eggplant with the cornstarch, shaking off the excess. Working in 2 batches, fry the eggplant over moderately high heat, turning, until lightly browned and crisp, 5 minutes per batch. Using a slotted spoon, transfer the eggplant to a paper towel–lined baking sheet to drain.

5 Light a grill or heat a grill pan. In a large skillet, heat half of the orange glaze. Add the fried eggplant and toss over high heat until hot, 3 minutes. Fold in the cilantro and season with salt; keep warm.

6 Brush the mackerel with olive oil and season with salt and pepper. Oil the grill grate or grill pan. Grill the fish skin side down until lightly charred on the bottom, about 4 minutes. Brush the fish with some of the remaining orange glaze, flip and grill, brushing with more of the orange glaze, until just cooked through, about 3 minutes longer. Transfer to a platter and serve right away, with the fried eggplant and mojo. —*Jose Enrique*

MAKE AHEAD

The mojo can be refrigerated for up to 1 week.

WINE

Zesty Albariño from Spain's Galicia is a great match for oily fish like mackerel.

GRAPE LEAF–WRAPPED SALMON
WITH SERRANO-SCALLION SAUCE

SERVES **4**

TIME **45 min**

16 large jarred grape leaves, drained and patted dry

1 cup orange or yellow grape tomatoes, halved

5 scallions, julienned, plus 2 Tbsp. minced scallion

3 serrano chiles with seeds, halved and thinly sliced

Kosher salt and pepper

Four 6-oz. skinless salmon fillets

2 Tbsp. unsalted butter

¼ cup Champagne vinegar

½ cup heavy cream

F&W's Justin Chapple wraps salmon fillets in tangy brined grape leaves, which perfume the fish and keep them moist as they roast. While the salmon cooks, he makes a quick, creamy sauce spiced with hot serrano chiles to drizzle on top.

1 Preheat the oven to 450° and line a large rimmed baking sheet with parchment paper. Arrange the grape leaves in groups of 4 on a work surface, overlapping them slightly. Mound the tomatoes, three-fourths of the julienned scallions and one-third of the sliced serranos in the center of the grape leaves and season lightly with salt and pepper. Season the salmon fillets with salt and pepper and place them on top, then wrap the grape leaves around the fish. Carefully turn the packets seam side down on the prepared baking sheet and roast for 10 to 12 minutes, until the salmon is medium within. Transfer the packets to plates.

2 Meanwhile, in a small saucepan, melt the butter. Add the minced scallion and cook over moderate heat, stirring, until softened, about 2 minutes. Add the vinegar and bring to a boil. Simmer over moderately high heat until reduced by half, about 3 minutes. Whisk in the cream and bring just to a simmer, then cook over moderately high heat, whisking occasionally, until slightly thickened, about 2 minutes. Stir in the remaining serranos and season the sauce with salt and pepper.

3 Cut open the salmon packets and drizzle the sauce over the fish. Garnish with the remaining julienned scallions and serve right away. —*Justin Chapple*

WINE

Vivid, crisp Austrian Riesling.

BAKED SHRIMP RISOTTO

SERVES **4**

TIME **Active 10 min; Total 30 min**

2 Tbsp. extra-virgin olive oil

5 garlic cloves, thinly sliced

1 cup arborio rice

3½ cups low-sodium chicken broth

½ cup freshly grated Parmigiano-Reggiano cheese, plus more for garnish

20 cooked shelled large shrimp

1 Tbsp. unsalted butter

1 Tbsp. fresh lemon juice

Kosher salt

Pesto, for serving

In her clever cheater's risotto, F&W's Kay Chun doesn't bother with stirring; instead, she bakes the rice in the oven, then adds shrimp and cheese at the very end.

1 Preheat the oven to 400°. In a medium enameled cast-iron casserole, heat the olive oil. Add the garlic and rice and cook over moderate heat, stirring, until very fragrant, 2 minutes. Stir in the broth and bring to a boil. Cover, transfer to the oven and bake for about 20 minutes, until the rice is tender. Stir in the ½ cup of cheese, the shrimp, butter and lemon juice; season with salt. Serve, drizzled with pesto and garnished with cheese. —*Kay Chun*

WINE

Minerally, sea-spray-scented white, such as Santorini.

"I make this when I want the comfort of risotto without having to stand over the stove and stir forever. It's the perfect 'set it and forget it' dish. It's great with a traditional basil pesto, but it also works well with olive tapenade or a sun-dried tomato pesto."

—EMILY TYLMAN, TEST KITCHEN ASSISTANT

COCKLES WITH BEANS AND CHERRY TOMATOES
IN GARLIC BROTH

SERVES 4

TIME Active 30 min; Total 1 hr 15 min

- 1 cup dried cranberry or borlotti beans (6 oz.)
- 2 Tbsp. extra-virgin olive oil
- 7 garlic cloves, thinly sliced
- 2 shallots, finely chopped
- ½ lb. yellow cherry tomatoes, halved
- Kosher salt and pepper
- ½ cup dry white wine
- 1 cup low-sodium chicken broth
- 3 lbs. cockles, rinsed
- ½ cup coarsely chopped parsley
- ½ cup coarsely chopped tarragon
- Grilled bread, for serving

F&W Test Kitchen senior editor Kay Chun makes this hearty, supereasy seafood stew with small, briny cockles. These are some of the smallest bivalves, but they deliver an enormous amount of flavor. If you can't find them, use scrubbed and debearded mussels or littleneck clams instead.

1 In a large saucepan, cover the beans with 3 inches of water and bring to a boil. Simmer, stirring occasionally, until the beans are tender, about 45 minutes. Drain the beans.

2 In a large enameled cast-iron casserole, heat the olive oil. Add the garlic and shallots and cook over moderate heat, stirring, until fragrant and golden, about 3 minutes. Add the beans and tomatoes and season with salt and pepper. Cook, stirring occasionally, until the tomatoes soften, about 3 minutes. Stir in the wine and cook until almost evaporated, about 1 minute. Add the broth and cockles and bring to a simmer. Cover and cook over low heat until the cockles open, about 3 minutes. Discard any unopened cockles. Stir in the parsley and tarragon and serve with grilled bread. —*Kay Chun*

MAKE AHEAD

The cooked beans can be refrigerated for up to 2 days.

WINE

Fresh and minerally Picpoul de Pinet, a white wine from France's Languedoc region, offers fantastic value, and it's great with seafood.

> "This recipe is one of my favorite date-night meals: You can serve the mussels in the same pot that you made them in, and you have to get in there and eat with your hands, leaving no time to be shy. The only thing missing? A good loaf of crusty bread and a nice bottle of wine." —JULIA HEFFELFINGER, ASSISTANT FOOD EDITOR

MUSSELS WITH PANCETTA AND CRÈME FRAÎCHE

SERVES **2**

TIME **45 min**

- **2 Tbsp. extra-virgin olive oil**
- **4 oz. pancetta or bacon, finely chopped**
- **½ red onion, finely chopped**
- **1 celery rib, finely chopped**
- **½ fennel bulb, chopped**
- **4 garlic cloves, thinly sliced**
- **¾ cup dry white wine**
- **4 dozen mussels, scrubbed**
- **1¼ cups fish stock, or ¾ cup clam juice plus ½ cup water**
- **½ cup crème fraîche**
- **2 Tbsp. fresh lemon juice**
- **½ cup packed parsley leaves**
- **2 Tbsp. marjoram leaves**
- **Pinch of crushed red pepper**
- **Kosher salt**
- **Crusty bread, for serving**

This recipe is from chef Jimmy Bannos, Jr., of The Purple Pig in Chicago. The luscious broth is creamy, tangy and lightly scented with fresh marjoram.

1 In a large enameled cast-iron casserole, heat the olive oil. Add the pancetta and cook over moderately low heat until crisp, about 5 minutes. Add the onion, celery, fennel and garlic and cook, stirring, until softened, about 7 minutes. Stir in the wine and simmer over moderately high heat until almost all of the liquid has evaporated, about 3 minutes. Add the mussels and stock and bring to a simmer; cover and cook until the mussels open, about 4 minutes. Discard any unopened mussels. Stir in the crème fraîche.

2 Off the heat, stir in the lemon juice, parsley, marjoram and crushed red pepper. Season with salt and transfer to bowls. Serve with crusty bread.
—*Jimmy Bannos, Jr.*

WINE

Brisk Italian white, such as Verdicchio.

CHICKEN IN AN HERB GARDEN

SERVES **4**

TIME **Active 30 min; Total 3 hr 30 min**

4 skinless, boneless chicken breast halves (2 lbs.), pounded ¼ inch thick

Kosher salt and pepper

2½ cups white wine vinegar

1 cup extra-virgin olive oil

1 cup finely chopped mixed herbs, such as parsley, tarragon, basil, thyme, rosemary, sage and mint

Crusty bread, for serving

For this light, summery make-ahead dish, Katie Caldesi poaches rolled chicken breasts in vinegar before marinating them in olive oil with plenty of fresh herbs. The recipe is from her cookbook *Rome: Centuries in an Italian Kitchen*.

1 Season the chicken breasts with salt and pepper. Tightly roll them up lengthwise and secure with toothpicks at 1-inch intervals.

2 In a large saucepan, combine the vinegar, ¾ cup of water and a pinch of salt and bring to a gentle simmer. Add the chicken and cook over low heat until just white throughout, 10 to 12 minutes. Transfer the chicken to a work surface and let cool slightly. Discard the toothpicks. Slice the chicken crosswise into 1-inch-thick rounds.

3 In a large bowl, whisk the olive oil with the mixed herbs and season with salt and pepper. Add the chicken, turning to coat in the herb oil. Let cool to room temperature, about 30 minutes. Cover and refrigerate for at least 2 hours or overnight. Bring to room temperature and serve with crusty bread.
—*Katie Caldesi*

WINE

Lively, zesty Italian white, such as Vermentino.

"I don't mean to be negative, but poached chicken breasts? Yuck. But this is one of my all-time favorite recipes! The magic here is poaching with vinegar, then allowing the chicken to sit in a super-herby olive oil mixture until it's silky, deeply flavorful and utterly delicious." —KATE HEDDINGS, FOOD DIRECTOR

ZESTY BRAISED CHICKEN
WITH LEMON AND CAPERS

SERVES **4**

TIME **Active 25 min; Total 1 hr 30 min**

Eight 6-oz. chicken thighs

Kosher salt and pepper

All-purpose flour, for dusting

2 **Tbsp. unsalted butter**

2 **Tbsp. extra-virgin olive oil**

4 **large garlic cloves, peeled**

1½ **cups Sauvignon Blanc**

1½ **cups chicken stock or low-sodium broth**

Four 1-inch strips of lemon zest

4 **thyme sprigs**

1 **Tbsp. drained capers**

1 **bay leaf**

"I've always braised chicken in a covered pan," says cookbook author and former F&W Test Kitchen senior editor Grace Parisi. "And the result has always been the same: flabby skin that needs crisping and a watery sauce that needs reducing." Parisi's easy fix is to braise with the lid off. She cooks the chicken in Sauvignon Blanc, which adds zip to the braising liquid in this bright update on coq au vin.

1 Preheat the oven to 350°. Season the chicken with salt and pepper and dust with flour. In a large ovenproof skillet, melt the butter in the oil. Add the chicken skin side down and cook over high heat, turning once, until browned, 12 to 14 minutes. Transfer the chicken to a large plate and pour off all but 1 tablespoon of the fat from the skillet.

2 Add the garlic to the skillet and cook over low heat until softened, about 5 minutes. Add the wine and boil over high heat until reduced by half, about 5 minutes. Add the stock, lemon zest, thyme, capers and bay leaf and bring to a boil. Return the chicken to the skillet, skin side up. Transfer to the oven and braise for about 45 minutes, until the meat is tender.

3 Return the skillet to the stove and boil until the sauce is slightly reduced, about 5 minutes. Discard the thyme, bay leaf and lemon zest, if desired, before serving. —*Grace Parisi*

WINE

Chablis or a comparable minerally style of Chardonnay.

> "I love the kick of heat Peppadew peppers give this dish (which is great with just about any kind of southern Italian red wine, by the way). This recipe is speedy enough for a post-work dinner, and the leftovers taste great in a sandwich."
>
> —RAY ISLE, EXECUTIVE WINE EDITOR

CHICKEN SCARPARIELLO

SERVES **4**

TIME **40 min**

- **8 small skinless, boneless chicken thighs (2 lbs.)**
- **Kosher salt and pepper**
- **All-purpose flour, for dusting**
- **½ cup extra-virgin olive oil**
- **8 garlic cloves, halved lengthwise and lightly smashed**
- **4 large rosemary sprigs, broken into 2-inch pieces**
- **2 cups chicken stock or low-sodium broth**
- **2 Tbsp. fresh lemon juice**
- **2 Tbsp. unsalted butter**
- **½ cup Peppadew peppers or other pickled peppers, sliced**

The traditional method for making the southern Italian dish scarpariello—chicken sautéed in a tangy lemon glaze with bell pepper—calls for a whole chicken cut into pieces and cooked on the stove for hours. Grace Parisi opts for faster-cooking boneless thighs and skips the bell pepper in favor of jarred Peppadews, sweet-spicy pickled peppers from South Africa, sold in many US supermarkets.

1 Season the chicken with salt and pepper and dust with flour. In a large skillet, heat the oil until shimmering. Add the chicken and cook over high heat, turning once, until browned and crusty on both sides, about 10 minutes. Add the garlic and rosemary and cook for about 3 minutes, until the garlic is lightly browned. Transfer the chicken to a platter, leaving the rosemary and garlic in the skillet.

2 Add the stock to the skillet and cook over high heat, scraping up any browned bits, until reduced by half, about 5 minutes. Add the lemon juice and butter and swirl until emulsified. Return the chicken and any accumulated juices to the skillet. Add the peppers and cook, turning the chicken until coated in the sauce, about 3 minutes. Transfer the chicken and sauce to the platter and serve. —*Grace Parisi*

SERVE WITH

Crusty bread.

WINE

Fruity Nero d'Avola from Sicily.

"This French bistro classic is typically prepared with a cut-up whole chicken, but using only chicken thighs makes it much easier to manage. It's a great sweet and tangy dish to serve at a dinner party because you can make most of it ahead and finish it at the last minute." —TINA UJLAKI, EXECUTIVE FOOD EDITOR

CHICKEN IN RED WINE VINEGAR

SERVES **4**

TIME **Active 30 min; Total 1 hr 15 min**

14 **Tbsp. red wine vinegar**
½ **cup low-sodium chicken broth**
1 **Tbsp. honey**
1 **Tbsp. tomato paste**
2 **Tbsp. unsalted butter**
8 **large chicken thighs**
  Kosher salt and pepper
4 **garlic cloves, thinly sliced**
3 **large shallots, thinly sliced**
¾ **cup dry white wine**
2 **Tbsp. crème fraîche**
3 **Tbsp. chopped tarragon**

For legendary cookbook author Paula Wolfert, this rustic Lyonnais dish is the ultimate comfort food. Slow cooking transforms red wine vinegar, tomato, shallots, garlic and a touch of honey into a perfectly balanced sauce for chicken.

1 In a medium saucepan, bring the vinegar, broth, honey and tomato paste to a boil, stirring well. Simmer the vinegar sauce until reduced to ½ cup, about 8 minutes.

2 In a large, heavy skillet, heat the butter. Season the chicken thighs with salt and pepper and add half of them to the skillet, skin side down. Cook over moderate heat, turning once, until browned, about 10 minutes. Transfer to a plate. Repeat with the remaining thighs.

3 Add the garlic and shallots to the skillet and cook over low heat for 5 minutes. Add the wine and boil until reduced to ¼ cup, about 3 minutes. Add the vinegar sauce and bring to a simmer.

4 Return the chicken to the skillet, skin side up. Cover and simmer over low heat until cooked through, about 20 minutes. Transfer the chicken to plates.

5 Add the crème fraîche to the skillet and boil for 3 minutes. Add the tarragon and season with salt and pepper. Pour the sauce over the chicken and serve.
—*Paula Wolfert*

WINE

Red-cherry-rich Beaujolais from France's Burgundy region.

CAST-IRON ROAST CHICKEN WITH LENTILS
AND WALNUT VINAIGRETTE

SERVES **4**

TIME **1 hr**

LENTILS
- ½ cup walnuts
- 1 Tbsp. extra-virgin olive oil
- 1 small red onion, thinly sliced
- 1 cup black beluga lentils
- 1 bay leaf
- ½ cup balsamic vinegar
- 3 Tbsp. unsalted butter
- 1 Tbsp. Dijon mustard
- Kosher salt and pepper

CHICKEN
- 2 Tbsp. extra-virgin olive oil
- One 4-lb. chicken, backbone removed, chicken halved
- Kosher salt and pepper
- 1 Tbsp. unsalted butter

WALNUT VINAIGRETTE
- ¼ cup toasted walnut oil
- 2 Tbsp. sherry vinegar
- 1 Tbsp. chopped parsley
- Kosher salt and pepper

This bistro-inspired meal is from Ryan Angulo, the chef at Brooklyn's French Louie. He weighs down luscious roast chicken in a cast-iron skillet so the skin gets extra-crispy.

1 MAKE THE LENTILS In a medium saucepan, toast the walnuts over moderate heat until lightly golden, about 5 minutes. Chop the nuts and transfer to a small bowl. In the same saucepan, heat the olive oil. Add the onion and cook over moderate heat, stirring occasionally, until golden, about 3 minutes. Add the lentils, bay leaf, balsamic vinegar and 1½ cups of water and bring to a simmer. Cover and cook over low heat for 15 minutes. Uncover and cook, stirring occasionally, until the liquid is absorbed and the lentils are just tender, 15 minutes longer. Stir in the butter and mustard and season with salt and pepper. Keep warm.

2 MEANWHILE, MAKE THE CHICKEN Preheat the oven to 400°. In a large cast-iron skillet, heat the olive oil. Season the chicken with salt and pepper and set breast side down in the skillet. Cover with foil and another large cast-iron skillet. Cook the chicken over moderate heat until golden, 8 to 10 minutes. Flip the chicken halves and roast in the oven, uncovered, until golden and an instant-read thermometer inserted in an inner thigh registers 165°, about 30 minutes. Transfer the chicken to a cutting board and let rest for 5 minutes. Whisk the butter into the pan juices and season with salt and pepper. Strain the jus and keep warm.

3 MAKE THE VINAIGRETTE In a small bowl, whisk the walnut oil with the sherry vinegar and parsley. Season with salt and pepper.

4 Carve the chicken. Stir the toasted walnuts into the lentils and spoon onto plates. Top with the chicken. Drizzle with the vinaigrette and serve the chicken jus on the side. —*Ryan Angulo*

MAKE AHEAD

The lentils (without the walnuts) can be refrigerated overnight. Rewarm them before serving.

WINE

This bird is tangy, nutty and earthy. Red blends from the Côtes du Rhône can perfectly handle all of these flavor components.

BUTTER-ROASTED CHICKEN
WITH SOY-GARLIC GLAZE

SERVES 4

TIME Active 40 min; Total 1 hr 45 min

- 5 whole cloves
- 5 star anise pods
- 4 Tbsp. unsalted butter, at room temperature
- Kosher salt and pepper
- ½ cup low-sodium soy sauce
- 2 Tbsp. distilled white vinegar
- One 2-inch piece of ginger, thinly sliced
- 3 garlic cloves, crushed
- 1½ Tbsp. sugar
- One 3½- to 4-lb. chicken
- 2 Tbsp. canola oil
- 1 cup all-purpose flour, plus more for dusting
- ⅓ cup plus 1 Tbsp. boiling water
- Toasted sesame oil, for brushing
- Sliced cucumbers, sliced scallions, sliced chiles and hoisin sauce, for serving

F&W Test Kitchen senior editor Kay Chun rubs an Asian-spiced butter under chicken skin before roasting. The result: an incredibly juicy and flavorful bird.

1 Preheat the oven to 450°. Finely grind the cloves and 3 of the star anise pods in a spice grinder and transfer to a small bowl. Mix in the butter and season with salt and pepper.

2 In a small saucepan, combine the soy sauce, vinegar, ginger, garlic, sugar and the remaining 2 star anise pods. Cook over moderate heat, stirring occasionally, until the glaze thickens, about 10 minutes.

3 Place the chicken on a rack set over a baking sheet. Beginning at the top of the breast, gently separate the chicken skin from the breast and thighs. Season the chicken cavity with salt and pepper. Rub the spiced butter under the skin, spreading it over the breast and thighs. Rub the canola oil all over the outside of the chicken and season with salt and pepper. Roast the chicken for 50 to 60 minutes, until golden brown and an instant-read thermometer inserted into the thickest part of a thigh registers 165°. Brush the chicken all over with the soy glaze and let rest for 15 minutes.

4 Meanwhile, in a small bowl, using a wooden spoon, stir the 1 cup of flour and the boiling water until a shaggy dough forms. Turn the dough out onto a lightly floured surface and knead until smooth, about 5 minutes. Cut into 8 even pieces and roll into balls; keep covered with a damp paper towel. Using a lightly floured rolling pin, roll each piece of dough into an ⅛-inch-thick round.

5 Heat a griddle and brush it with sesame oil. Cook the pancakes, turning once, until golden in spots and cooked through, about 2 minutes. Transfer the pancakes to a plate and cover to keep warm.

6 Carve the chicken and serve with the warm pancakes, cucumbers, scallions, chiles and hoisin sauce. —*Kay Chun*

MAKE AHEAD

The pancakes can be refrigerated overnight and rewarmed before serving.

WINE

Chardonnay is made in many different styles, but in Burgundy, it tends to have focused and firm fruit, without an abundance of oak. This makes it great with chicken. Try a simple version, such as Bourgogne Blanc or Mâcon-Villages.

CHICKEN CHILE VERDE

SERVES **4**

TIME **1 hr**

2 **poblano chiles**

1 **lb. tomatillos—husked, rinsed and quartered**

1 **large jalapeño, chopped**

2 **garlic cloves**

1 **white onion, minced**

1 **cup cilantro leaves**

Kosher salt and pepper

2 **Tbsp. vegetable oil**

1½ **lbs. skinless, boneless chicken thighs, cut into ½-inch pieces**

Steamed rice, chopped avocado and sour cream, for serving

The secret to this tangy and spicy stew from Deborah Schneider, chef at Sol Cocina in Newport Beach, California, is the warm tomatillo and chile sauce; topped with creamy avocado and cool sour cream, the dish is a perfect meal. Schneider sometimes swaps pork, cubed tofu or vegetables like zucchini or mushrooms for the chicken.

1 Roast the poblanos directly over a gas flame or under the broiler, turning, until charred all over. Transfer to a bowl, cover with plastic wrap and let cool. Peel, stem and seed the poblanos, then cut into ½-inch dice.

2 Meanwhile, in a medium saucepan, combine the tomatillos, jalapeño, garlic and half of the onion with 3 cups of water and bring to a boil. Simmer over moderately high heat until softened, 5 to 7 minutes. Drain the vegetables, reserving ½ cup of the cooking liquid.

3 In a blender, combine the boiled vegetables with the cilantro and reserved cooking liquid and puree until smooth. Season the sauce with salt and pepper.

4 In a large, deep skillet, heat the oil. Season the chicken with salt and pepper and cook over moderately high heat for 5 minutes, stirring occasionally. Add the remaining onion and the poblanos and cook, stirring occasionally, until the onion is just starting to brown, 5 to 7 minutes. Stir in the sauce and bring to a boil, then simmer over moderate heat until slightly thickened, about 5 minutes. Serve the chile verde with rice, avocado and sour cream.
—*Deborah Schneider*

MAKE AHEAD

The chicken chile verde can be refrigerated overnight. Reheat gently, adding tablespoons of water if it seems too thick.

WINE

Zesty, herbal-tinged Sauvignon Blanc.

"When we made this stew in the Test Kitchen, it was so popular that we were elbowing each other out of the way to get more. Chicken thighs always work nicely in stews, but they're especially good in this very bright and tangy sauce. I'd double this to save for leftovers." —KATE HEDDINGS, FOOD DIRECTOR

EXTRA-CRISPY FRIED CHICKEN

SERVES **6 to 8**

TIME **Active 1 hr 15 min;**
Total 4 hr 30 min

¼ **cup plus 2 Tbsp. kosher salt**

¼ **cup freshly ground pepper**

¼ **cup extra-virgin olive oil**

1½ **Tbsp. minced rosemary plus**
4 medium sprigs

1½ **Tbsp. minced thyme plus**
4 sprigs

1½ **Tbsp. minced sage plus 4 sprigs**

5 **minced bay leaves, preferably**
fresh, plus 5 whole leaves

3 **garlic cloves, minced, plus 1 head**
broken into cloves

Two 3-lb. chickens

1 **quart buttermilk**

1 **Tbsp. hot sauce, such as Tabasco**

1 **tsp. sugar**

Grapeseed or vegetable oil,
for frying

2 **cups all-purpose flour**

½ **cup rice flour**

¼ **cup garlic powder**

¼ **cup onion powder**

Flaky sea salt, for sprinkling

Lemon wedges, for serving

To make his phenomenal fried chicken, star chef Tyler Florence first bakes it low and slow, so it's juicy. Then he coats the chicken pieces in seasoned flour and fries them in oil that's been flavored with garlic and herbs.

1 Preheat the oven to 200°. In a small bowl, whisk 3 tablespoons of the kosher salt with 2 tablespoons of the pepper, the olive oil and the minced rosemary, thyme, sage, bay leaves and garlic. Rub the mixture all over the chickens and set them in a roasting pan. Roast for about 2½ hours, until an instant-read thermometer inserted in the inner thighs registers 150°. Let the chickens cool, then cut each into 10 pieces. (You should have 4 drumsticks, 4 thighs, 4 wings and 8 breast quarters.)

2 In a very large bowl, whisk the buttermilk with the hot sauce and sugar. Add the chicken pieces and toss well. Cover and refrigerate for 1 hour.

3 In a large saucepan, heat 2 inches of grapeseed oil to 375° with the rosemary, thyme and sage sprigs, the 5 whole bay leaves and the head of garlic. When the herbs are crispy and the garlic is golden, transfer to a paper towel–lined plate using a slotted spoon.

4 Meanwhile, in a large bowl, whisk the all-purpose and rice flours with the garlic and onion powders. Whisk in the remaining 3 tablespoons of kosher salt and 2 tablespoons of pepper.

5 Remove half of the chicken pieces from the buttermilk, letting the excess drip back into the bowl. Dredge the chicken in the seasoned flour, patting it on lightly so it adheres. In the large saucepan, bring the oil back to 375° and fry the chicken over high heat, turning occasionally, until golden and an instant-read thermometer inserted in the thickest part of each piece registers 160°, about 6 minutes for the breasts and 8 minutes for the wings, thighs and drumsticks. Transfer the fried chicken to a paper towel–lined baking sheet to drain. Let the oil return to 375° before you coat and fry the remaining chicken. Transfer the fried chicken to a platter and garnish with the fried garlic and herbs. Sprinkle with flaky sea salt and serve right away, with lemon wedges.
—*Tyler Florence*

WINE

Fresh, berry-rich Italian sparkling red wine, such as Lambrusco.

"This has become one of my tried-and-true Sunday-dinner dishes, especially when I want to keep it casual and give friends something familiar but different. Sometimes I buy extra caperberries and use them to garnish martinis before dinner, too!"

—KATE HEDDINGS, FOOD DIRECTOR

CHICKEN ROASTED ON BREAD WITH CAPERBERRIES AND CHARRED LEMONS

SERVES **4**

TIME **Active 20 min; Total 1 hr**

- ½ **lb. sourdough bread, torn into bite-size pieces**
- 4 **large shallots, quartered lengthwise**
- ¾ **cup drained caperberries (see Note)**
- 2 **lemons, scrubbed and quartered lengthwise**
- ¼ **cup extra-virgin olive oil, plus more for brushing**
  Kosher salt and pepper
  Four 12-oz. whole chicken legs

NOTE

Capers are the brined or pickled buds of the caper plant; when the buds aren't picked from the plant, they blossom into seed-filled caperberries. These bigger, grape-size berries taste milder than caper buds; they're sold in jars at specialty markets.

In this supersimple dish from F&W Test Kitchen senior editor Justin Chapple, chicken legs roast on top of torn pieces of bread that absorb the rich and tangy juices, becoming delectably crisp and chewy.

1 Preheat the oven to 400°. On a large rimmed baking sheet, toss the bread with the shallots, caperberries, lemons and the ¼ cup of olive oil; season with salt and pepper. Brush the chicken legs with oil and season with salt and pepper. Arrange the chicken on the bread and roast for about 50 minutes, until the bread is crisp and an instant-read thermometer inserted in the thighs registers 160°. Transfer the chicken, bread and vegetables to plates and serve.
—*Justin Chapple*

WINE

Savory, full-bodied white Burgundy.

ROAST CHICKEN CACCIATORE
WITH RED WINE BUTTER

SERVES **4**

TIME **Active 1 hr; Total 2 hr 45 min plus overnight curing**

One 3½-lb. chicken

Kosher salt

5 thyme sprigs

1 cup red wine

2 Tbsp. tomato paste

2 Tbsp. unsalted butter, softened

4 basil sprigs, plus leaves for garnish

4 oregano sprigs

3 garlic cloves, crushed

1 small fennel bulb, cut into ¾-inch wedges through the core

1 cup cherry tomatoes

¾ cup pearl onions

8 jarred sweet Peppadew peppers, halved

6 baby bell peppers, halved lengthwise and seeded

1 Tbsp. extra-virgin olive oil

½ cup chicken stock or low-sodium broth

½ cup Castelvetrano olives, pitted and chopped

Food Network star Giada De Laurentiis has been making variations of chicken cacciatore for years. For this exceptional oven-roasted version, she cooks a whole bird with red wine butter on a bed of fennel, cherry tomatoes and Peppadew peppers.

1 Season the chicken with 2 teaspoons of salt and stuff the thyme sprigs in the cavity. Transfer the chicken to a bowl, cover with plastic wrap and poke holes in the top; refrigerate overnight.

2 In a small saucepan, boil the wine over moderately high heat until reduced to 2 tablespoons, about 7 minutes. Off the heat, whisk in the tomato paste, butter and 1 teaspoon of salt. Let cool slightly.

3 Preheat the oven to 400°. Loosen the breast and thigh skin of the chicken and spread three-fourths of the red wine butter under the skin. Stuff the basil sprigs, oregano sprigs and garlic into the cavity and tie the legs with string. Rub the remaining butter over the chicken and let stand for 30 minutes.

4 Meanwhile, in a large, deep ovenproof skillet, toss the fennel, tomatoes, onions and both peppers with the olive oil; season with salt. Set the chicken in the center of the vegetables. Pour in the stock. Roast for 1 hour and 10 minutes, until an instant-read thermometer inserted in an inner thigh registers 155°. Transfer to a carving board and let rest for 15 minutes.

5 Simmer the broth over moderately high heat until slightly reduced, about 3 minutes. Stir in the olives and transfer to a platter. Carve the chicken and arrange on the platter. Garnish with basil leaves and serve.
—*Giada De Laurentiis*

WINE

Young, brambly-fruited Barbera from Piedmont.

> "I'm a sucker for one-pot meals, especially when they're simple and serve a crowd. I make this a lot for Sunday dinners in colder months (it's excellent football-watching food)." —KATE HEDDINGS, FOOD DIRECTOR

CHICKEN-CHILI TAMALE PIE

SERVES **8**

TIME **Active 30 min; Total 1 hr 30 min**

CHILI

- ⅓ cup vegetable oil
- 1 large onion, chopped
- 2 garlic cloves, minced
- 1 large jalapeño, seeded and minced
- 1 cup fresh or frozen corn kernels
- 2 Tbsp. New Mexico chile powder (see Note)
- 1 Tbsp. ground cumin
  Kosher salt
- 3 Tbsp. tomato paste
- 5 cups shredded skinned chicken from 2 rotisserie chickens
- 3 cups low-sodium chicken broth
- 2 Tbsp. chopped cilantro

CORN BREAD TOPPING

- 1½ cups coarse cornmeal
- 1 cup plus 2 Tbsp. all-purpose flour
- 3 Tbsp. sugar
- 2 tsp. baking powder
- 1 tsp. kosher salt
- 6 oz. cheddar cheese, shredded
- 1 cup plus 2 Tbsp. milk
- ¼ cup plus 2 Tbsp. vegetable oil
- 3 large eggs

NOTE

New Mexico chile powder has a mild, fruity flavor. It is available from amazon.com. Ancho chile powder is a good substitute.

This recipe combines two Southern comfort foods in one savory pie: chicken-jalapeño chili and a cheesy corn bread. Using rotisserie chicken and a ceramic baking dish that goes from oven to table makes this a supereasy dish to serve a group.

1 MAKE THE CHILI Preheat the oven to 350°. In a large skillet, heat the oil. Add the onion, garlic, jalapeño and corn and cook over moderate heat until softened, about 6 minutes. Stir in the chile powder and cumin, season with salt and cook for 1 minute. Stir in the tomato paste, then add the chicken and broth and bring to a boil. Simmer over moderate heat until thickened, about 5 minutes. Stir in the cilantro. Pour the chili into a 9-by-13-inch ceramic baking dish.

2 MAKE THE CORN BREAD In a medium bowl, whisk the cornmeal, flour, sugar, baking powder and salt. Stir in three-fourths of the cheese. In a glass measuring cup, whisk the milk with the vegetable oil and eggs, then stir into the dry ingredients until evenly moistened.

3 Spread the corn bread batter over the chili and sprinkle the remaining cheese on top. Bake in the center of the oven for about 45 minutes, until the corn bread is golden. Let the tamale pie rest for 10 minutes before serving.
—Grace Parisi

MAKE AHEAD

The chicken chili can be refrigerated for up to 3 days.

WINE

Rich California Chardonnay.

GRILLED CHICKEN WITH
SPICY-SWEET CHILE OIL

SERVES **2 to 4**

TIME **Active 30 min; Total 1 hr plus overnight salting and 4 hr marinating**

One 3½-lb. chicken, backbone removed, chicken halved

2 tsp. kosher salt

2½ Tbsp. fresh lemon juice

½ cup extra-virgin olive oil

1 Tbsp. piment d'Espelette

1 Fresno chile or red jalapeño, chopped

1½ Tbsp. light brown sugar

2 garlic cloves, thinly sliced

¼ tsp. black pepper

Paul Kahan, whose Chicago restaurant empire includes The Publican, uses a few powerhouse ingredients to flavor the oil for his chicken: garlic, lemon juice, chile and the mildly spicy Basque red pepper piment d'Espelette (available at specialty food stores). He marinates the chicken in half of the seasoned oil; the rest gets served on the side.

1 Place the chicken halves skin side up on a baking sheet. Season all over with the salt, cover and refrigerate overnight.

2 In a medium bowl, combine all of the remaining ingredients and mix well. Pour half of the chile oil into a large bowl, add the chicken and turn to coat; refrigerate for 4 hours. Reserve the remaining chile oil for serving.

3 Light a grill and set it up for indirect grilling. Alternatively, preheat the broiler and position the rack 8 to 10 inches from the heat. Remove the chicken from the bowl; reserve any chile oil remaining. Grill the chicken skin side down over indirect heat until lightly golden, about 20 minutes. Alternatively, broil the chicken skin side up on a rack set over a baking sheet for 20 minutes. Baste the chicken with any chile oil remaining in the large bowl and continue grilling or broiling for 15 minutes longer; if grilling, turn occasionally. The chicken is done when the skin is deep golden and an instant-read thermometer inserted in an inner thigh registers 165°. Let the chicken rest for 10 minutes. Carve into 8 pieces and serve with the reserved chile oil. —*Paul Kahan*

SERVE WITH

French fries.

WINE

Juicy, medium-bodied Garnacha from Spain.

TURMERIC CHICKEN AND RICE

SERVES **4**

TIME **Active 35 min; Total 1 hr 10 min**

One 4½-lb. chicken, cut into 8 pieces

Kosher salt and pepper

2 **Tbsp. unsalted butter**

1½ **tsp. ground turmeric**

1 **small onion, chopped**

1 **Tbsp. finely chopped peeled fresh ginger**

4 **garlic cloves, minced**

2 **plum tomatoes, chopped**

2 **tsp. curry powder**

½ **tsp. cinnamon**

½ **tsp. ground cumin**

2 **cups jasmine rice**

3 **bay leaves**

1½ **Tbsp. Asian fish sauce**

3 **cups chicken stock or low-sodium broth**

Plain whole-milk yogurt, sliced cucumbers, mint leaves and lime wedges, for serving

"This is an easy one-pot chicken-and-rice dish, but the turmeric adds color, spice and flavor," says Edward Lee, the chef at 610 Magnolia in Louisville, Kentucky. "That makes it a winner in my house." He recommends using a whole organic chicken so you know exactly where the bird came from and serving the dish family-style.

1 Season the chicken with salt and pepper. In a large enameled cast-iron casserole or Dutch oven, melt the butter and sprinkle with the turmeric. Add the chicken skin side down and cook over moderately high heat, turning once, until browned on both sides, about 8 minutes. Transfer the chicken to a plate.

2 Add the onion, ginger and garlic to the casserole and cook, stirring occasionally, until starting to brown, about 5 minutes. Add the tomatoes, curry powder, cinnamon, cumin and rice and stir constantly until fragrant, about 1 minute. Return the chicken to the pot, skin side up. Add the bay leaves, fish sauce and chicken stock and bring to a boil over high heat.

3 Cover the casserole and simmer over low heat for 10 minutes. Adjust the lid to cover partially and simmer until the rice is cooked, 10 to 15 minutes longer. Remove from the heat, uncover and let stand for 5 minutes. Serve with yogurt, cucumbers, mint and lime wedges. —*Edward Lee*

WINE

A bold, lime-scented dry Riesling from Australia is perfect for spice blends like the one used in this dish.

"Edward Lee draws on Southeast Asian, Indian and who knows what other influences for this crazily good one-pot dish. It calls for a cut-up whole chicken, but boneless thighs work very well, too."

—RAY ISLE, EXECUTIVE WINE EDITOR

JULIA'S FAVORITE ROAST CHICKEN

SERVES 4

TIME Active 30 min; Total 2 hr 15 min

2½ Tbsp. unsalted butter

⅓ cup finely diced carrots plus ½ cup sliced carrots

⅓ cup finely diced onion plus ½ cup sliced onion

⅓ cup finely diced celery

1 tsp. chopped thyme, savory or mixed herbs, or 2 thyme or savory sprigs

One 3½- to 4-lb. chicken

Salt and pepper

Parsley stems

Celery leaves

Six ⅛-inch-thick lemon slices

1 Tbsp. fresh lemon juice

¾ cup chicken stock or low-sodium broth

Julia Child seasoned this roast chicken inside and out by packing sautéed vegetables, lemon slices and fresh herbs into the cavity, then rubbing the skin with butter. In typical French fashion, she trussed the bird to promote even cooking.

1 Preheat the oven to 425°. Melt 1 tablespoon of the butter in a medium skillet. Add the diced carrots, onion and celery and cook over moderate heat until softened. Stir in the herbs.

2 Wash the chicken rapidly inside and out with hot water and pat thoroughly dry. For easier carving, cut out and discard the wishbone. Pull the neck skin up over the breast and secure it to the back with a toothpick. Salt and pepper the cavity and spoon in the cooked vegetables, a handful of parsley stems and celery leaves and the lemon slices. Massage the chicken all over with 1 tablespoon of the butter, then truss it. Alternatively, tie the ends of the drumsticks together and tuck the wings under the body.

3 Choose a flameproof roasting pan that is about 1 inch larger than the chicken. Salt the chicken all over and set it breast up on a rack in the pan. (Thoroughly wash all surfaces and utensils that have been in contact with the raw chicken.)

4 Roast the chicken in the oven for about 1 hour and 15 minutes, as follows:
AT 15 MINUTES Brush the chicken with the remaining ½ tablespoon of butter. Scatter the sliced onion and carrots all around the chicken. Reduce the oven temperature to 350°.
AT 45 MINUTES Brush the lemon juice over the chicken. If necessary, add ½ cup of water to the vegetables to prevent burning.
AT 60 MINUTES Baste with the pan juices. Test for doneness: The drumsticks should move easily in their sockets; their flesh should feel somewhat soft. If not, continue roasting, basting and testing every 7 to 8 minutes, until an instant-read thermometer registers 165°.

5 Spear the chicken through the shoulders and lift it up to drain; if the last of the juices run clear yellow, the chicken is done. Let rest on a carving board for 15 minutes; discard the string.

6 Spoon all but 1 tablespoon of fat from the juices in the pan. Add the stock and boil until lightly syrupy, 5 minutes. Strain the juices; you will have just enough to bathe each serving with a fragrant spoonful. —*Julia Child*

WINE

Minerally, full-bodied Loire Valley white, such as Cour-Cheverny.

EASY TURKEY CHILI

SERVES **8**

TIME **Active 30 min; Total 1 hr 30 min**

- ¼ cup extra-virgin olive oil
- 1 bunch of scallions, sliced ½ inch thick
- 1 medium red bell pepper, finely diced
- 1 large poblano, finely diced
- 2 garlic cloves, minced
  Kosher salt and pepper
- 3 lbs. ground turkey
- ⅓ cup pure ancho chile powder
- 3 Tbsp. ground cumin
  One 28-oz. can tomato sauce (3 cups)
- 5 thyme sprigs
- 2 canned chipotle chiles in adobo, stemmed and minced
- 2 Tbsp. stone-ground cornmeal
- 2 imported bay leaves
- 1 tsp. dried oregano, crumbled
  Two 15-oz. cans black beans or pink beans, drained (3 cups)
  Shredded cheddar cheese, chopped cilantro, sour cream and warm corn tortillas, for serving

This flavor-packed turkey-and-bean chili is super-versatile. You can serve it over rice or egg noodles, with crusty bread or crispy tortillas, or even scooped over nachos.

1 In a large, heavy casserole, heat 1½ tablespoons of the olive oil. Add the scallions, bell pepper, poblano and garlic, season with salt and pepper and cook over moderately high heat, stirring, until softened, about 5 minutes. Scrape the vegetables onto a plate.

2 Add the remaining 2½ tablespoons of olive oil to the casserole. Add the turkey, season with salt and pepper and cook, stirring to break up the meat, until nearly cooked but still slightly pink, about 4 minutes. Add the chile powder and cumin and cook until the liquid evaporates, about 5 minutes longer. Add 3 cups of water and the tomato sauce, thyme, chipotles, cornmeal, bay leaves, oregano and cooked vegetables and bring to a boil. Cover partially and cook over moderately low heat, stirring occasionally, until the sauce is slightly reduced and the meat is tender, about 45 minutes. Add the beans, season with salt and pepper and simmer 10 minutes longer. Remove the bay leaves. Serve the chili in deep bowls, passing cheese, cilantro, sour cream and tortillas on the side. —*Tina Ujlaki*

WINE

Medium-bodied, spice-driven red, such as Zinfandel.

"This is my go-to chili. The secret, I've discovered, is the one-two punch of ancho chile powder and chipotles, which add incredible depth and flavor. The other secret: A little ground cornmeal gives the chili a thick, hearty texture."
—KATE HEDDINGS, FOOD DIRECTOR

CHIPOTLE-BUTTER TURKEY

SERVES **10 to 12**

TIME **Active 40 min; Total 3 hr 30 min**

One 12- to 14-lb. turkey, rinsed and patted dry

Kosher salt and black pepper

2 **sticks unsalted butter**

½ **cup distilled white vinegar**

⅓ **cup minced chipotle chiles in adobo**

2 **Tbsp. minced garlic**

1 **Tbsp. dried oregano**

1 **Tbsp. chopped thyme plus 4 sprigs**

1 **head of garlic, halved crosswise**

1 **lime, quartered**

4 **oregano sprigs**

3 **cups chicken stock or low-sodium broth**

Justin Chapple, star of F&W's Mad Genius Tips videos, shares his method for making an effortlessly juicy bird. His basting trick: Soak a cheesecloth in melted chipotle-spiked butter, then drape it over the turkey before roasting. The bird will become moist and flavorful.

1 Season the turkey inside and out with salt and pepper. Transfer to a rack set in a roasting pan and let come to room temperature.

2 Meanwhile, preheat the oven to 400°. In a medium saucepan, melt the butter. Whisk in the vinegar, chipotles, minced garlic, dried oregano and chopped thyme; let cool slightly. Transfer half of the chipotle butter to a small bowl and refrigerate until spreadable, about 20 minutes.

3 Run your fingers under the turkey breast and thigh skin to loosen it, then spread the chilled butter under the skin and over the breast and thighs. Stuff the turkey cavity with the head of garlic, the lime wedges and the thyme and oregano sprigs. Dampen an 18-by-18-inch double-layer piece of cheesecloth with water and squeeze dry. Soak the cheesecloth in the remaining chipotle butter and drape it over the breast and legs; pour any remaining butter on top.

4 Roast the turkey for about 30 minutes. Add the stock to the roasting pan and continue to roast for about 1 hour and 45 minutes longer, rotating the pan a few times, until an instant-read thermometer inserted in an inner thigh registers 165°.

5 Carefully peel the cheesecloth off the turkey. Transfer the turkey to a cutting board and let rest for 30 minutes. Skim the fat off the pan juices and transfer to a gravy bowl. Carve the turkey and serve with the pan juices.
—*Justin Chapple*

WINE

Rhône-inspired white, such as Roussanne or Marsanne.

DUCK BREASTS WITH
DULCE DE LECHE CHILE SAUCE

SERVES **6 to 8**

TIME **1 hr**

- **4 ancho chiles, stemmed and seeded**
- **½ cup fresh orange juice**
- **½ cup chicken stock or low-sodium broth**
- **¼ cup dulce de leche**
- **3 garlic cloves, chopped**
- **Four 12-oz. Muscovy duck breast halves, excess fat removed, skin scored**
- **Kosher salt and pepper**
- **1 chile de árbol**
- **1 thyme sprig**
- **3 Tbsp. unsalted butter, cut into cubes**
- **2 Tbsp. fresh lemon juice**
- **2 Tbsp. chopped cilantro, plus small sprigs for serving**

Dulce de leche makes a brilliant addition to the spicy sauce that Food Network star Aarón Sánchez serves alongside crispy pan-seared duck breasts. "I like to use dulce de leche in sauces as a substitute for honey," he says. "It adds sweetness, but because it's creamy, it also adds a stealth layer of richness."

1 In a large skillet, toast the ancho chiles over moderately high heat, turning, until fragrant and pliable, about 1 minute. Transfer to a heatproof bowl, cover with 2 cups of hot water and let stand until softened, about 20 minutes. Drain, reserving the soaking liquid.

2 In a small saucepan, simmer the orange juice over moderately high heat until reduced by half, 3 to 5 minutes. Transfer to a blender and add the stock, dulce de leche, anchos, 1 cup of the chile soaking liquid and one-third of the garlic. Puree until smooth.

3 Heat the large skillet. Season the duck breasts with salt and pepper and add to the skillet skin side down. Cook over moderate heat, spooning off the fat, until golden and crisp, about 10 minutes. Turn the duck skin side up and add the árbol chile, thyme, 2 tablespoons of the butter, the lemon juice and the remaining garlic to the skillet. Cook, basting the duck occasionally, until medium within, about 8 minutes. Transfer the duck to a carving board and let rest for 5 minutes.

4 Pour off all but 2 tablespoons of fat from the skillet. Add the chile mixture and bring to a boil. Simmer over moderately high heat, stirring frequently, until just thickened, about 5 minutes. Off the heat, whisk in the remaining 1 tablespoon of butter and the chopped cilantro. Discard the árbol chile and thyme; season the sauce with salt and pepper. Thinly slice the duck across the grain and serve with the sauce and cilantro sprigs. —*Aarón Sánchez*

SERVE WITH

Sautéed spinach.

WINE

Lively, red-berried Spanish red, such as Mencía.

GRILLED PORK WITH COCONUT RICE AND LEMONGRASS SAMBAL

SERVES **6**

TIME **2 hr plus 6 hr soaking**

PORK

- 1 **cup packed cilantro leaves**
- 2 **garlic cloves, crushed**
- 2 **jalapeños, seeded and chopped**
- ¼ **cup extra-virgin olive oil**
- **Two 1-lb. pork tenderloins**
- ½ **cup roasted peanuts**
- 2 **stalks of fresh lemongrass, tender inner white parts only, thinly sliced**
- 2 **fresh kaffir lime leaves, thinly sliced**
- 2 **Thai bird chiles, thinly sliced**
- 4 **shallots, very thinly sliced and separated into rings**
- 1 **Tbsp. finely grated peeled fresh ginger**
- ¼ **cup fresh lime juice**
- ½ **cup grapeseed or canola oil**
- **Kosher salt**

RICE

- 2 **cups jasmine rice**
- **One 13.5-oz. can unsweetened coconut milk**
- 2 **oz. grated palm sugar (⅓ cup) or ¼ cup granulated sugar**
- **Kosher salt**
- 2 **heads of baby bok choy, halved and thinly sliced through the core**
- 2 **scallions, thinly sliced**

This recipe is from F&W Best New Chef 1999 Suzanne Goin of Lucques in Los Angeles. After eating sambal (an Asian, chile-spiked condiment) in Bali, Goin created a version to serve with pork that's fragrant with lemongrass and kaffir lime.

1 PREPARE THE PORK In a food processor, combine ¾ cup of the cilantro with the garlic and jalapeños. With the machine on, drizzle in the olive oil until a loose paste forms. Coat the pork evenly with the cilantro paste and refrigerate for at least 4 hours or overnight.

2 Meanwhile, preheat the oven to 350°. Toast the peanuts in a pie plate for about 5 minutes, until fragrant. Finely chop the peanuts. In a small bowl, combine the lemongrass, lime leaves, chiles, shallots, ginger, lime juice and grapeseed oil. Season the sambal with salt.

3 PREPARE THE RICE In a medium bowl, cover the rice with water and let soak for 6 hours. Drain and rinse 3 times, until the water runs clear.

4 Bring a few inches of water to a boil in a pot and line a vegetable steamer insert with a double layer of cheesecloth. Evenly spread the rice on the cheesecloth. Set the steamer 3 inches over the boiling water. Cover and steam the rice until almost tender, about 45 minutes. Add water to the pot if necessary.

5 In a small saucepan, cook the coconut milk and sugar over moderate heat, stirring, until the sugar is dissolved. Remove the steamer insert from the pot and drain off the water. Spread the steamed rice evenly in the pot. Pour the hot coconut milk evenly over the rice; do not stir. Cover and let stand for 10 minutes. Stir and season with salt.

6 Light a grill; lightly oil the grate. Wipe off most of the marinade from the pork. Grill over moderate heat for 20 minutes, turning, until an instant-read thermometer inserted in the center registers 140°. Let rest for 15 minutes.

7 Toss the bok choy with half of the sambal, the remaining ¼ cup of cilantro and the scallions. Spoon the coconut rice onto a platter and scatter the bok choy on top. Thinly slice the pork and arrange on the rice with the remaining sambal. Garnish with the peanuts and serve. —*Suzanne Goin*

WINE

Peach-scented Chenin Blanc, such as Montlouis or Vouvray.

> "I love the juicy texture you get from following the age-old technique of cooking this large, tough cut of meat in milk. This pork-and-fennel variation begs to be served with mashed potatoes for soaking up the garlicky cream sauce."
>
> —JULIA HEFFELFINGER, ASSISTANT FOOD EDITOR

PORK ROAST WITH GARLIC-PARMESAN CREAM

SERVES **8**

TIME **Active 30 min; Total 4 hr 45 min**

- 1 **quart heavy cream**
- 2 **cups buttermilk**
- 4 **Tbsp. unsalted butter**
- 3 **heads of garlic, top ½ inch cut off**

   One 3-oz. Parmigiano-Reggiano cheese rind

- 2 **small sage sprigs**

   One 5-lb. boneless pork shoulder roast

   Kosher salt and pepper

- ¼ **cup fresh lemon juice**
- 4 **medium fennel bulbs (3 lbs.), trimmed and cut into wedges**
- ¼ **cup extra-virgin olive oil**

   Chopped parsley, for garnish

F&W Test Kitchen senior editor Kay Chun poaches pork in garlic-and-Parmesan-infused cream, which helps it develop a savory glaze while it roasts. Reduced, the cream becomes a lovely sauce.

1 In a pot just large enough to hold the pork, combine the cream with the buttermilk, butter, garlic, cheese rind and 1 sage sprig. Season the pork with salt and pepper and add to the pot. Bring just to a simmer. Cover, leaving it open just a crack, and cook over low heat for about 3½ hours, until very tender. Transfer the pork and garlic to a large plate; discard the cheese rind.

2 Boil the poaching liquid over moderately high heat, whisking occasionally, until thickened, about 20 minutes. Strain the sauce into a bowl. Whisk in the lemon juice and season with salt and pepper; keep warm.

3 Meanwhile, preheat the oven to 450°. On a large baking sheet, toss the fennel and the remaining sage sprig with the olive oil and season with salt and pepper. Arrange the fennel in a single layer. Place the pork on top of the fennel and roast until the pork is deeply golden and the fennel is tender, about 20 minutes. Transfer the pork to a cutting board and let rest for 15 minutes.

4 Thinly slice the pork. Arrange the fennel and garlic on a platter and top with the pork. Garnish with parsley and serve the sauce on the side. —*Kay Chun*

WINE

Slightly herbal Tuscan red.

KOREAN GARLIC AND CHILE PORK

SERVES **4 to 6**

TIME **30 min plus overnight marinating**

¼ cup gochujang (Korean red pepper paste)

3 Tbsp. sugar

3 Tbsp. minced garlic

1 Tbsp. minced peeled fresh ginger

1 Tbsp. dry sake

1 Tbsp. mirin

2 Tbsp. toasted sesame oil

2 Tbsp. gochugaru (Korean red pepper flakes)

½ small onion, thinly sliced

2 lbs. pork shoulder or pork belly, cut into 4-by-⅛-inch strips

Canola oil, for frying

Thinly sliced scallions, for garnish

Lettuce leaves and steamed short-grain rice, for serving

Hooni Kim, the chef at Danji and Hanjan in New York City, sautés strips of pork marinated in a sweet-and-spicy sauce. The pork is delicious in lettuce wraps or soft steamed Asian buns.

1 In a large bowl, combine all of the ingredients except the pork, canola oil, scallions, lettuce and rice. Add the pork and turn to coat. Cover with plastic wrap and refrigerate overnight.

2 In a large nonstick skillet, heat 1 tablespoon of canola oil. Add the pork in batches, taking care not to crowd the pan, and stir-fry over moderately high heat until cooked through and browned in spots, about 2 minutes per batch. Add more oil to the skillet as necessary.

3 Transfer the pork to a platter and garnish with scallions. Serve with lettuce leaves and steamed rice. —*Hooni Kim*

WINE

Slightly off-dry German Riesling.

"This recipe is a supereasy way to DIY Korean barbecue at home. For a shortcut, I buy presliced pork from the Korean market. They're practically paper-thin, so you get more caramelized edges, which are really the best parts." —SUSAN CHOUNG, BOOKS EDITOR

TACOS AL PASTOR

SERVES **8**

TIME **1 hr 15 min plus overnight marinating**

- 1 Tbsp. canola oil, plus more for brushing
- 3 garlic cloves
- 1 tsp. dried oregano
- ½ tsp. ground cumin
- ½ tsp. pepper
- ¼ tsp. ground cloves
- 4 guajillo chiles—stemmed, seeded and cut into 2-inch pieces
- ⅓ cup pineapple juice
- ¼ cup distilled white vinegar
- 2 Tbsp. achiote paste
  Sea salt
- 2 lbs. boneless pork shoulder, sliced ¼ inch thick
- ½ medium pineapple, peeled and sliced ½ inch thick
- 1 medium red onion, sliced crosswise ½ inch thick
  Warm corn tortillas, chopped cilantro and lime wedges, for serving

This supersmart hack of the classic Mexican recipe gives you all the flavor without all the fuss. Rather than marinating pork shoulder for days and then spit-roasting, Courtney Contos, founder of Chef Contos Kitchen & Store in Shelburne, Vermont, marinates pork slices overnight, then grills them for less than five minutes.

1 In a medium saucepan, heat the 1 tablespoon of oil. Add the garlic and cook over moderately high heat, turning occasionally, until lightly browned, about 1 minute. Stir in the oregano, cumin, pepper and cloves and cook until fragrant, about 1 minute. Add the chiles and cook, stirring, until blistered in spots, about 30 seconds. Add the pineapple juice, vinegar and achiote paste and bring to a boil. Remove from the heat and let stand for 5 minutes.

2 Transfer the chile mixture to a blender and puree until smooth. Season with salt. Scrape the marinade into a large, sturdy plastic bag. Add the pork and turn to coat. Set the bag in a small baking dish and refrigerate overnight.

3 Light a grill or heat a grill pan. Brush the pineapple and onion with oil. Grill over high heat, turning once, until lightly charred and softened, 3 to 5 minutes. Transfer to a carving board and tent with foil.

4 Remove the pork from the marinade. Grill over high heat until lightly charred and just cooked through, 2 to 4 minutes. Transfer to the carving board and let rest for 5 minutes.

5 Cut the pineapple, onion and pork into thin strips and transfer to a bowl. Season with salt. Serve with corn tortillas, chopped cilantro and lime wedges. —*Courtney Contos*

WINE OR BEER

Sweet, tangy pineapple is tough to pair with wine. Try a light, floral red, such as a Loire Valley Gamay. Alternatively, have these tasty tacos with a crisp, lightly malty beer, like an amber ale.

PORK MEAT LOAF
WITH TOMATO-CHICKPEA SAUCE

SERVES **8**

TIME **Active 30 min; Total 1 hr 15 min**

Four 1-inch-thick slices of Italian bread, crusts removed, bread soaked in 1 cup of milk and squeezed dry

4 oz. sliced bacon

4 oz. sliced prosciutto

1 medium onion, thinly sliced

2 garlic cloves, very finely chopped

4 oil-packed sun-dried tomatoes

1 roasted red pepper from a jar

2 large eggs

2 Tbsp. chopped flat-leaf parsley

1 tsp. chopped thyme

1 tsp. crushed red pepper

½ tsp. dried oregano

Kosher salt and black pepper

2½ lbs. lean ground pork

1 Tbsp. extra-virgin olive oil, plus more for brushing

1 cup tomato puree

1 cup chicken stock or low-sodium broth

½ cup prepared plain hummus

Andrew Carmellini, the chef at Locanda Verde in New York City and an F&W Best New Chef 2000, mixes ground pork loin and jowl with pancetta and nearly 20 other ingredients to make juicy meatballs, which he then braises in a spicy tomato-chickpea sauce. This streamlined recipe omits the pork jowl (and about a dozen other ingredients) and calls for shaping the meat into loaves rather than time-consuming meatballs. Prepared hummus stands in for chickpeas in the sauce.

1 In a food processor, pulse the bread, bacon and prosciutto. Add the onion, garlic, sun-dried tomatoes, roasted pepper and eggs; process to a paste. Pulse in the parsley, thyme, crushed red pepper, oregano and 1 teaspoon each of salt and black pepper. Transfer to a bowl and knead in the pork.

2 Preheat the broiler. Pat the pork mixture into two 8-inch-long loaves. In a large nonstick roasting pan, heat the 1 tablespoon of oil. Add the loaves and cook over moderate heat until the bottoms are browned, about 6 minutes. Brush the tops with oil, transfer to the broiler and broil until slightly browned. Turn the oven temperature to 350°.

3 In a small bowl, combine the tomato puree, stock and hummus. Pour the mixture into the roasting pan and bake for 30 minutes, until an instant-read thermometer inserted into the center of a loaf registers 180°.

4 Turn on the broiler. Spoon some of the sauce over the loaves and broil until browned. Transfer to a platter and serve with the gravy. —*Andrew Carmellini*

SERVE WITH

Mashed or roasted potatoes.

WINE

Robust and smoky Italian red, such as Aglianico.

PORK-AND-RICOTTA MEATBALLS
IN PARMESAN BROTH

SERVES 6

TIME Active 30 min; Total 50 min

- 1 cup fresh ricotta cheese (8 oz.)
- ¼ cup freshly grated Parmigiano-Reggiano cheese, plus more for garnish
- 1 large egg
- ½ cup dry breadcrumbs
- ½ tsp. freshly grated nutmeg
  Kosher salt and pepper
- 1¼ lbs. ground pork
- 2 Tbsp. extra-virgin olive oil
- 1 quart low-sodium chicken broth
  One 3-by-1-inch piece of Parmigiano-Reggiano cheese
- 1 cup thawed frozen peas
- 2 cups baby spinach
  Cooked egg noodles, for serving

To make these pork meatballs incredibly tender, F&W Test Kitchen senior editor Kay Chun mixes a generous amount of fresh ricotta into the meat.

1 In a large bowl, stir the ricotta and ¼ cup of grated Parmigiano with the egg, breadcrumbs, nutmeg, 1 teaspoon of salt, ½ teaspoon of pepper and ¼ cup of water. Add the pork and combine. Form into 12 meatballs.

2 In a large enameled cast-iron casserole, heat the olive oil. Add the meatballs and cook over moderate heat, turning, until golden all over, about 10 minutes. Stir in the broth and the piece of cheese. Cover and simmer gently over moderate heat, stirring occasionally, until the meatballs are cooked through and the broth is slightly reduced, about 20 minutes. Stir in the peas and spinach, season with salt and pepper and simmer until the peas are warmed through.

3 In shallow bowls, spoon the meatballs and broth over egg noodles. Garnish with grated Parmigiano and serve. —*Kay Chun*

WINE

Fresh, minerally Alpine white: Pinot Bianco from Alto Adige.

MAPO TOFU

SERVES 4

TIME 15 min

1 tsp. canola oil

½ lb. ground beef chuck (85% lean)

½ lb. ground pork

Kosher salt

2 Tbsp. chile-bean sauce, preferably toban djan

2 Tbsp. hoisin sauce or tenmenjan (soybean paste)

1 Tbsp. soy sauce

One 14-oz. package soft tofu, finely diced

1½ tsp. cornstarch

3 scallions, finely chopped

Steamed white rice, for serving

"I'm sure Chinese people wouldn't call this mapo tofu!" says L.A. chef Kuniko Yagi about her inauthentic, meat-heavy version. Jarred toban djan gives the dish its signature heat and deeply savory flavor, but any other chile-bean sauce is a fine substitute.

1 Heat a large skillet until hot. Add the oil, then the beef and pork. Season with salt and cook over high heat, stirring and breaking up the meat, until crumbly and lightly browned, about 3 minutes.

2 Stir the chile-bean sauce, hoisin and soy sauce into the skillet and cook, stirring, for 3 minutes. Gently fold in the tofu. In a small bowl, whisk the cornstarch into ½ cup of water. Add to the skillet and simmer until the sauce thickens, about 2 minutes. Stir in the scallions and serve with rice. —*Kuniko Yagi*

WINE

German Riesling goes great with dishes that combine savory, sweet and umami flavors.

"This is my absolute favorite weeknight meal because it's superfast. I only ever need to pick up some ground meat and tofu; for me, everything else is a pantry staple. If you can find Sichuan peppercorns, they are a wonderful addition here."

—JUSTIN CHAPPLE, TEST KITCHEN SENIOR EDITOR

RICE CONGEE WITH PORK MEATBALLS

SERVES 4 to 6

TIME 45 min

½ lb. ground pork

2 Tbsp. Asian fish sauce, plus more for serving

1 Tbsp. soy sauce

Freshly ground white pepper

8 cups chicken stock or low-sodium broth

1 cup jasmine rice

1 stalk of fresh lemongrass, cut into three 3-inch pieces and crushed

5 dried Thai bird chiles, stemmed, or 1 Tbsp. crushed dried Thai chile

¼ cup vegetable oil

5 garlic cloves, thinly sliced

1 serrano chile, seeded and minced

¼ cup distilled white vinegar

½ tsp. sugar

Lime wedges, sliced scallions and chopped cilantro, for serving

F&W Best New Chef 2010 James Syhabout of Commis in Oakland, California, flavors his meatballs with just fish sauce and soy sauce. He serves them in a soothing congee (rice porridge) with an array of bright condiments, including cilantro, garlic oil and chile vinegar.

1 In a medium bowl, combine the pork with the 2 tablespoons of fish sauce, the soy sauce and a pinch of white pepper. Let stand for 10 to 30 minutes.

2 In a large enameled cast-iron casserole, combine the chicken stock, rice and lemongrass and bring to a boil over moderately high heat. Reduce the heat to low, cover partially and simmer until the rice is soft, about 25 minutes. Discard the lemongrass.

3 Meanwhile, in a small skillet, toast the dried chiles over moderate heat until lightly browned and fragrant, about 3 minutes. Transfer to a spice grinder and grind to a coarse powder; some seeds will remain. Transfer to a small bowl and wipe out the skillet.

4 Heat the oil in the skillet. Add the garlic and cook over low heat until caramelized, about 10 minutes. Scrape the garlic oil into another small bowl. In a third small bowl, combine the serrano, vinegar and sugar and stir until the sugar is dissolved.

5 Using a small ice cream scoop, make generous 1-inch meatballs with the ground pork. Drop into the rice and broth in the casserole. Cover and simmer over moderately high heat, stirring occasionally, until the meatballs are cooked through, about 10 minutes.

6 Ladle the congee into bowls. Serve with little bowls of the toasted chile powder, fried garlic oil, chile vinegar, lime wedges, scallions, cilantro, white pepper and fish sauce. —*James Syhabout*

MAKE AHEAD

The uncooked meatballs can be refrigerated overnight.

WINE

Vibrant South African Chenin Blanc.

SWEET SAUSAGES STEWED
IN FENNEL-TOMATO SAUCE

SERVES **8**

TIME **Active 30 min; Total 1 hr 30 min**

¼ **cup extra-virgin olive oil**

12 **sweet Italian sausages (4½ lbs.)**

3 **fennel bulbs—trimmed, each bulb cut into 8 wedges, fronds chopped**

1 **medium onion, chopped**

4 **garlic cloves, minced**

½ **tsp. fennel seeds, crushed**

Kosher salt

One 28-oz. can San Marzano whole tomatoes, crushed by hand, juices reserved

1 **cup dry white wine**

3 **pequin chiles (see Note) or 2 chiles de árbol**

Creamy polenta, for serving

NOTE

Small, spicy dried red Mexican pequin chiles are available at Latin American markets and specialty food stores.

A big pot of simmering red sauce makes New York City chef April Bloomfield think of the home kitchen of her former boss Ruth Rogers, of London's River Café. This is Bloomfield's version of the sauce, with sausage and wedges of fresh fennel. "I just love slow-cooked fennel," she says. "It gives the dish a nice, soft creaminess with the slightly bouncy sausage."

1 In a large enameled cast-iron casserole, heat the olive oil. Add half of the sausages and cook over moderate heat, turning, until browned all over, about 5 minutes. Transfer to a plate; repeat with the remaining sausages.

2 Add the fennel wedges to the casserole and cook over moderate heat, stirring, until golden, about 5 minutes. Add the onion, garlic, fennel seeds and 1 teaspoon of salt and cook, stirring, until the fennel is lightly browned, about 3 minutes. Add the tomatoes and their juices, the wine and chiles. Tuck the sausages into the sauce. Cover and cook over low heat for 15 minutes. Uncover and simmer until the sausages are cooked through and the sauce is thickened, about 45 minutes longer. Garnish the stew with fennel fronds and serve over polenta.
—*April Bloomfield*

MAKE AHEAD

The stewed sausages can be refrigerated for up to 2 days; rewarm before serving.

WINE

For these sausages, look for a wine that has a lot of juicy red fruit but not a lot of tannins, like Frappato from Sicily.

"I'm firmly in the thin double-patty camp for burgers, and this one is my ultimate version. The key is to press them firmly with your hands before grilling. Definitely don't do this on the grill with your spatula or you'll lose all of those amazing juices (and you'll have committed a serious grilling crime)."

—JULIA HEFFELFINGER, ASSISTANT FOOD EDITOR

BACON-AND-KIMCHI BURGERS

SERVES **4**

TIME **30 min**

¼ cup **sambal oelek**

¼ cup **mayonnaise**

¼ cup **ketchup**

4 slices of **thick-cut bacon**

1¼ lbs. **ground beef chuck**

Kosher salt

4 slices of **American cheese**

4 **potato buns, toasted**

1 cup **chopped drained cabbage kimchi (6 oz.)**

These over-the-top Shake Shack–inspired burgers are from Wesley Genovart, chef and co-owner of SoLo Farm & Table in South Londonderry, Vermont. He makes them with two superthin stacked patties, thick-cut bacon, kimchi and a spicy take on Shack sauce.

1 In a small bowl, combine the sambal with the mayonnaise and ketchup and mix well.

2 Light a grill or heat a grill pan. Grill the bacon over moderate heat, turning, until golden and crisp, about 5 minutes. Drain on paper towels.

3 Form the beef into eight ¼-inch-thick burgers and season with salt. Grill over high heat, turning, until browned, 1 minute per side. Make 4 stacks of 2 burgers each on the grill and spoon 1 tablespoon of the sambal mayo over each stack. Top with the cheese, cover and grill over high heat just until the cheese is melted, about 1 minute.

4 Spread the remaining sambal mayo on the bottom buns. Top with the burgers, bacon and kimchi, close and serve. —*Wesley Genovart*

BEER

Hoppy but balanced New England IPA.

TUSCAN-STYLE SPARERIBS
WITH BALSAMIC GLAZE

SERVES **6**

TIME **Active 20 min; Total 4 hr 30 min**

- 2 Tbsp. extra-virgin olive oil
- 2 Tbsp. chopped rosemary
- 1½ Tbsp. kosher salt
- 1½ Tbsp. fennel seeds
- 2 tsp. freshly ground black pepper
- 2 tsp. chopped sage
- 2 tsp. chopped thyme
- 2 tsp. sweet paprika
- 1 tsp. crushed red pepper
- 1 tsp. ground coriander
- ½ tsp. ground allspice
- 6 lbs. pork spareribs
- 3 Tbsp. balsamic vinegar, preferably one aged for at least 5 years

Bruce Aidells, author of *Bruce Aidells's Complete Book of Pork*, loves to barbecue spareribs, but his favorite way to prepare them is to generously season the ribs with a mix of aromatic herbs and spices and slow-roast them until tender and crisp. Like his favorite Tuscan cooks, he finishes the ribs with a tangy-sweet balsamic glaze.

1 In a small bowl, combine the olive oil, rosemary, salt, fennel, black pepper, sage, thyme, paprika, crushed red pepper, coriander and allspice. Rub the spice paste all over the spareribs and let stand at room temperature for 2 hours or refrigerate overnight.

2 Preheat the oven to 325°. Arrange the ribs meaty side up on a large rimmed baking sheet or roasting pan and roast for 2 hours, until tender.

3 Preheat the broiler. Brush the meaty side of the ribs with the balsamic vinegar and broil 6 inches from the heat until browned, about 2 minutes. Let stand for 5 minutes, then cut between the ribs and serve. —*Bruce Aidells*

WINE

Slightly spicy, medium-bodied red like Chianti.

FARRO WITH SPANISH CHORIZO, FETA AND DILL

SERVES **4**

TIME **45 min**

- 2 **cups farro (12 oz.)**
  Kosher salt
- 2 **tsp. extra-virgin olive oil**
- 8 **oz. dry Spanish chorizo, very thinly sliced**
- 2 **medium shallots, minced**
- ½ **cup minced celery**
- 1 **cup chicken stock or low-sodium broth**
- 2 **Tbsp. unsalted butter**
- ½ **cup chopped parsley**
- 4 **oz. feta cheese, crumbled (½ cup)**
- ¼ **cup chopped dill**

Most cooks use farro for side dishes, but F&W Best New Chef 2002 Hugh Acheson of Five & Ten in Athens, Georgia, turns it into an easy main course. He tosses the chewy, nutty grains with the unusual combination of feta, chorizo and dill.

1 In a medium saucepan, cover the farro with water and bring to a boil. Add a generous pinch of salt and simmer over moderate heat, stirring occasionally, until al dente, about 25 minutes; drain well.

2 In a large, deep skillet, heat the olive oil. Add the chorizo and cook over moderate heat, stirring occasionally, until just starting to brown, about 5 minutes. Add the shallots and celery and cook, stirring, until softened, about 4 minutes. Stir in the drained farro and the chicken stock and cook, stirring, until most of the stock is absorbed, about 3 minutes. Stir in the butter and parsley and season lightly with salt. Transfer the farro to shallow bowls, scatter the feta and dill on top and serve. —*Hugh Acheson*

WINE

Bright, aromatic Spanish white, such as Albariño.

"I am always looking for smart and delicious ways to use farro, which is one of my favorite grains. It's no surprise that the brilliant chef Hugh Acheson gave us one of the best recipes for it, ever. You would never know by eating this dish just how simple it is."

—KATE HEDDINGS, FOOD DIRECTOR

GRILLED APPLE-MARINATED SHORT RIBS

SERVES **4**

TIME **1 hr plus 4 hr marinating**

RIBS

1¼ cups apple juice

⅓ cup soy sauce

¼ cup fresh lemon juice

4 scallions, thinly sliced

3 garlic cloves, minced

1 Tbsp. minced peeled fresh ginger

1 Tbsp. toasted sesame oil

4 meaty, boneless beef short ribs

SAUCE

1 tsp. canola oil

2 shallots, thinly sliced

Kosher salt

3 garlic cloves, crushed

2 scallions, thinly sliced

⅓ cup red miso

2½ Tbsp. gochujang (Korean red pepper paste)

2 Tbsp. unseasoned rice vinegar

2 Tbsp. toasted sesame oil

2 Tbsp. sugar

1 Granny Smith apple, cored and very thinly sliced

Instead of braising short ribs, L.A. chef Kuniko Yagi marinates the meat in a mix of apple juice, lemon juice and soy sauce. She then grills the short ribs until they're charred on the outside and medium-rare within.

1 PREPARE THE RIBS In a medium bowl, combine the apple juice, soy sauce, lemon juice, scallions, garlic, ginger and sesame oil. Put the short ribs in a large, sturdy, resealable plastic bag and pour in the marinade. Seal the bag, set it in a baking dish and refrigerate for at least 4 hours and up to 24 hours. An hour before cooking, remove the marinated ribs from the refrigerator and let stand at room temperature.

2 MAKE THE SAUCE In a small skillet, heat the canola oil. Add the shallots, season with salt and cook over moderately high heat, stirring a few times, until lightly golden and softened, about 5 minutes. Transfer to a blender or mini food processor and let cool slightly. Add the garlic, scallions, miso, gochujang, vinegar, sesame oil and sugar and process to a smooth puree. Season the sauce with salt and transfer to a small bowl.

3 Light a grill or heat a grill pan. Remove the ribs from the marinade, scraping off any excess. Grill the ribs over moderately high heat, turning occasionally, until medium-rare, about 20 minutes. Let rest for 10 minutes, then thinly slice across the grain. Serve the ribs with the sauce and the sliced apple.
—Kuniko Yagi

WINE

Syrah's generous fruit is sublime with these ribs. Try one from Santa Barbara in California's Central Coast.

> "The bagna cauda butter is so good on the steak and almost everything else. I always double the batch and keep extra in the freezer. It's wonderful tossed with roasted vegetables or grated over baked fish."
> —JUSTIN CHAPPLE, TEST KITCHEN SENIOR EDITOR

RIB EYE AND RADISHES IN
BAGNA CAUDA BUTTER

SERVES **4**

TIME **1 hr**

- 1 **stick unsalted butter, at room temperature**
- 5 **oil-packed anchovies, minced**
- 1 **large garlic clove, minced**
- ¼ **cup chopped parsley**
   Kosher salt and pepper
- 1 **Tbsp. extra-virgin olive oil**
   One 1¾-lb. bone-in rib eye steak (2 inches thick), at room temperature for 1 hour
- 2 **rosemary sprigs**
- 2 **bunches of radishes**

The trick to this amazingly juicy steak is basting it with garlicky anchovy butter while it roasts.

1 Preheat the oven to 450°. In a medium bowl, stir the butter with the anchovies, garlic and 2 tablespoons of the parsley. Season with salt and pepper and mix well.

2 In a large cast-iron skillet, heat the oil until shimmering. Season the steak with salt and pepper. Add the steak and rosemary to the skillet and sear over moderately high heat until the steak is browned, 2 minutes per side. Add the radishes and half of the bagna cauda butter and roast in the oven for 18 to 20 minutes, basting every 3 minutes, until an instant-read thermometer inserted in the meat registers 125° for medium-rare; transfer to a board to rest for 15 minutes. Discard the rosemary.

3 Thinly slice the steak and transfer to a platter along with the radishes. Sprinkle with the remaining parsley and serve with the remaining bagna cauda butter.
—*Kay Chun*

MAKE AHEAD

The bagna cauda butter can be refrigerated for up to 1 week or frozen for up to 1 month.

WINE

Cassis-scented Cabernet Franc.

SOUTHEAST ASIAN RIB EYE STEAKS

SERVES **4**

TIME **30 min plus 2 hr marinating**

Four 1-inch-thick rib eye steaks (about 3½ lbs.)

Kosher salt

1 **Tbsp. plus 1 tsp. dry mustard**

1 **Tbsp. dark brown sugar**

10 **anchovy fillets, minced**

2 **tsp. onion powder**

2 **tsp. garlic powder**

2 **tsp. ground ginger**

2 **tsp. freshly ground black pepper**

1 **tsp. freshly ground white pepper**

Bryant Ng, the chef at Cassia in L.A. and an F&W Best New Chef 2012, includes anchovies and dry mustard in the marinade for these steaks. This gives the meat a salty, almost umami-like flavor that mimics the taste of dry-aged steaks.

1 Season the steaks with salt and let them stand at room temperature for 10 minutes.

2 In a small bowl, stir the dry mustard and brown sugar with 2 tablespoons of warm water until the sugar is dissolved. Stir in the anchovies, onion powder, garlic powder, ginger, black pepper and white pepper. Spread the paste on both sides of the steaks and refrigerate for 2 hours.

3 Bring the steaks to room temperature. Light a grill. Grill the steaks over moderately high heat for about 3 minutes per side, until nicely charred outside and medium-rare within. Let the steaks rest for 5 minutes before serving. —*Bryant Ng*

SERVE WITH

Sautéed bok choy.

WINE

A juicy, cherry-rich red blend from Napa.

"Who needs to buy dry-aged meat—it's so expensive!—when you can get the same insanely rich flavor with the technique in this recipe?"

—JUSTIN CHAPPLE, TEST KITCHEN SENIOR EDITOR

GRILLED SKIRT STEAK
WITH GREEN SRIRACHA

SERVES **20**

TIME **1 hr**

- 3 **large poblano chiles**
- 2 **serrano chiles, stemmed**
- 3 **large garlic cloves, peeled and smashed**
- ½ **cup thinly sliced peeled fresh ginger**

  One ½-inch piece of fresh turmeric (see Note), sliced, or ½ tsp. ground turmeric
- 1 **cup shredded unsweetened coconut**
- 2 **loose cups basil leaves**
- 2 **loose cups mint leaves**
- 1½ **cups snipped chives**
- ½ **cup chopped cilantro**
- 4 **kaffir lime leaves, shredded**
- 1 **stalk of fresh lemongrass, tender inner white part only, bottom 4 inches peeled and thinly sliced**
- 1 **cup canola oil, plus more for grilling**
- ¼ **cup plus 2 Tbsp. fresh lime juice**

  Kosher salt
- 5 **lbs. skirt steak, cut into 4-inch pieces**

NOTE

Fresh turmeric is available at Indian markets and many Whole Foods stores.

Susan Feniger, the chef at Mud Hen Tavern in Los Angeles, purees poblano chiles, kaffir lime leaves and four kinds of herbs to create a green version of Sriracha to pair with slices of grilled skirt steak.

1 Roast the poblanos directly over a gas flame, turning, until charred and tender. Transfer to a bowl, cover with plastic wrap and let cool. Peel, core and seed the poblanos, then transfer to a blender. Add the serranos, garlic, ginger, turmeric, coconut, basil, mint, chives, cilantro, lime leaves and lemongrass and pulse to chop. With the machine on, add the 1 cup of oil and puree. Add the lime juice and season the green Sriracha with salt.

2 Light a grill and oil the grate. Brush the steak with oil, season with salt and grill in batches over high heat, turning once or twice, until the meat is lightly charred and medium-rare, 5 to 6 minutes. Transfer to a carving board and let rest for 5 minutes before slicing across the grain. Serve the steak with the green Sriracha. —*Susan Feniger*

MAKE AHEAD

The steak can be grilled earlier in the day and refrigerated. The green Sriracha can be refrigerated for up to 3 days.

WINE

Spice-inflected red, such as Rioja.

BARBACOA BEEF TACOS
WITH SALSA VERDE CRUDA

SERVES 6

TIME Active 45 min; Total 4 hr

BARBACOA

- **4 large ancho chiles, stemmed and seeded**
- **4 dried chipotle chiles, stemmed**
- **3 celery ribs, chopped**
- **2 medium carrots, chopped**
- **1 large onion, halved and thinly sliced**
- **15 garlic cloves, crushed and peeled**
- **8 bay leaves**
- **Six 1-lb. English-cut beef short ribs**
- **2 Tbsp. dried oregano**
- **½ tsp. ground cumin**
- **Kosher salt and pepper**

SALSA VERDE CRUDA

- **½ lb. tomatillos—husked, rinsed and quartered**
- **½ cup coarsely chopped cilantro**
- **1 jalapeño, stemmed and chopped**
- **1 garlic clove, crushed and peeled**
- **Kosher salt and pepper**

FOR SERVING

- **Warm corn tortillas, cilantro sprigs, finely chopped white onion and lime wedges**

While most cooks put meat on the grill raw, Roberto Santibañez, the chef at New York City's Fonda restaurants, takes a different tack. He first braises beef short ribs with chiles and spices until they're intensely flavorful and meltingly tender. Then he crisps the meat on the grill before shredding it to serve in corn tortillas with a sauce made from the braising liquid as well as a fresh green salsa.

1 MAKE THE BARBACOA Preheat the oven to 325°. In a medium skillet, toast the ancho chiles over moderate heat, turning, until pliable and charred in spots, about 2 minutes; let cool slightly, then tear into pieces.

2 In a large roasting pan, toss the ancho and chipotle chiles with the celery, carrots, onion, garlic and bay leaves. In a large bowl, toss the short ribs with the oregano, cumin and 2 tablespoons of salt; arrange them on the vegetables. Add 2 cups of water to the pan, cover tightly with foil and braise in the oven for about 3½ hours, until the meat is very tender.

3 MEANWHILE, MAKE THE SALSA VERDE CRUDA In a blender, combine the tomatillos, cilantro, jalapeño and garlic and puree until smooth. Season the salsa with salt and pepper.

4 When the ribs are done, transfer them to a baking sheet. Strain the braising liquid through a colander set over a heatproof bowl; skim off any fat. Discard the bay leaves and return the vegetables and chiles to the braising liquid. Working in batches, puree the vegetables, chiles and liquid in a blender until smooth. Season the chile sauce with salt and pepper.

5 Light a grill or heat a grill pan. Working in batches if necessary, grill the ribs over high heat, turning occasionally, until charred and crisp, about 5 minutes per batch. Transfer to a platter and, using two forks, shred the meat; discard the bones. Serve the barbacoa in warm corn tortillas with the salsa, chile sauce, cilantro, chopped onion and lime wedges. —*Roberto Santibañez*

MAKE AHEAD

The braised short ribs and chile sauce can be refrigerated separately for up to 3 days. Warm the ribs in a low oven before grilling. The salsa can be refrigerated overnight.

BEER

Clean, bright lager, such as pilsner.

BEEF-AND-FARRO SOUP

SERVES **6**

TIME **Active 30 min; Total 2 hr 40 min**

2 Tbsp. canola oil

1½ lbs. beef chuck, cut into 1-inch pieces

Kosher salt and pepper

9 cups chicken stock or low-sodium broth

1 head of garlic, pierced all over with a knife

3 thyme sprigs

3 bay leaves

1 cup farro

2 medium tomatoes, chopped

1 leek, light green and white parts only, thinly sliced

2 celery ribs, thinly sliced

3 small carrots, chopped

1 small bunch of Tuscan kale, chopped (3 cups)

2 Tbsp. shiro (white) miso

1 tsp. smoked paprika

Freshly shaved Parmigiano-Reggiano cheese, for garnish

"You could easily become a well-fed hermit by doubling this recipe and holing up at home," says chef and TV personality Hugh Acheson. The key to the soup's exceptionally savory flavor is miso.

1 In a large enameled cast-iron casserole, heat the oil. Season the meat with salt and pepper, add half to the casserole and cook over moderate heat, turning, until browned, about 5 minutes; using a slotted spoon, transfer to a large plate. Repeat with the remaining meat.

2 Pour off all of the oil from the casserole. Add 1 cup of the stock and stir, scraping up any browned bits. Add the remaining 8 cups of stock along with the meat, garlic, thyme and bay leaves and bring to a simmer. Cover and cook over low heat, stirring occasionally, until the meat is tender, about 1½ hours.

3 Stir in the farro and bring to a simmer. Cover and cook over moderate heat until the farro is almost tender, 20 minutes. Stir in the tomatoes, leek, celery, carrots, kale, miso and paprika. Cover and cook until the vegetables are tender, about 10 minutes. Discard the garlic, thyme sprigs and bay leaves. Season with salt and pepper. Ladle the soup into bowls, garnish with cheese and serve. —*Hugh Acheson*

WINE

Fresh, berry-scented Italian red, such as Dolcetto d'Alba.

"A big pot of this soup simmering on the stove is one of my winter comforts. It's lighter than a beef stew but still has plenty of deep flavor that warms you to the bone. I love the chewy grains of farro and the touch of smoke from the paprika."

—SUSAN CHOUNG, BOOKS EDITOR

> "This is one of the best beef stews we've ever made at F&W. The succulent meat falls off the bone in a rich broth. But it also has incredible layers of spice, heat and tang from ginger, star anise, five-spice powder and fish sauce. I also love the spinach, which brightens it even more." —KATE HEDDINGS, FOOD DIRECTOR

ASIAN BEEF STEW

SERVES **4**

TIME **Active 45 min; Total 3 hr 30 min**

- 2 **Tbsp. coconut oil**
- 5 **lbs. English-cut beef short ribs**
  Sea salt and pepper
- 1 **red onion, finely chopped**
- 3 **garlic cloves, finely chopped**
- 3 **Tbsp. finely chopped peeled fresh ginger**
- 1 **tsp. Chinese five-spice powder**
- 3 **star anise pods**
- 3 **large carrots, peeled and cut into 2-inch pieces**
- 2 **celery ribs, cut into 1-inch pieces**
- 3 **Tbsp. Asian fish sauce**
  One 14.5-oz. can crushed tomatoes
- 2 **cups beef stock or broth**
- 4 **cups stemmed curly spinach (4 oz.)**
- 1 **Tbsp. fresh lemon juice**
  Chopped cilantro, for garnish

Jasmine and Melissa Hemsley, the British sisters behind the Hemsley + Hemsley wellness blog, invigorate this stew with fish sauce, Asian spices and lemon juice. "We both just love sour flavors," says Jasmine. "It's our Filipino mum's influence."

1 In a large enameled cast-iron casserole, heat the coconut oil. Season the ribs with salt and pepper. Working in 2 batches, brown the ribs over moderately high heat, turning, 4 to 5 minutes per batch. Transfer the ribs to a large plate. Add the onion, garlic and ginger to the casserole and cook over moderate heat, stirring, until golden, about 3 minutes. Stir in the five-spice powder, then add the star anise, carrots, celery and fish sauce and cook, stirring, for 1 minute. Add the tomatoes, stock and short ribs to the casserole and bring to a simmer. Cover and cook over moderately low heat, turning the ribs every hour, until they are very tender, about 2½ hours.

2 Discard the star anise. Stir the spinach and lemon juice into the casserole and season with salt and pepper. Ladle the stew into bowls and garnish with cilantro. —*Jasmine and Melissa Hemsley*

MAKE AHEAD

The stew can be refrigerated for up to 3 days.

WINE

Peppery, fruit-dense California Syrah.

BEEF STEW IN RED WINE SAUCE

SERVES **4**

TIME **Active 1 hr; Total 2 hr 40 min**

- **1 Tbsp. unsalted butter**
- **2 Tbsp. olive oil**
- **2 lbs. trimmed beef flatiron steak or chuck, cut into 8 pieces**
- **Kosher salt and pepper**
- **1 cup finely chopped onion**
- **1 Tbsp. finely chopped garlic**
- **1 Tbsp. all-purpose flour**
- **One 750-ml bottle dry red wine**
- **2 bay leaves**
- **1 thyme sprig**
- **One 5-oz. piece of pancetta**
- **15 pearl or small cipollini onions, peeled**
- **15 cremini mushrooms**
- **15 baby carrots, peeled**
- **Sugar**
- **Chopped parsley, for garnish**

This is the quintessential beef stew. Master chef Jacques Pépin's mother served it at her restaurant, Le Pelican, where she made it with tough cuts of meat that required a long braise. Jacques likes the flatiron—a long, narrow cut that's extremely lean, tender and moist. He doesn't use stock, demiglace or even water in his stew, relying on robust red wine for the deep-flavored sauce.

1 Preheat the oven to 350°. In a large enameled cast-iron casserole, melt the butter in 1 tablespoon of the olive oil. Arrange the meat in the casserole in a single layer and season with salt and pepper. Cook over moderately high heat, turning occasionally, until browned on all sides, about 8 minutes. Add the chopped onion and garlic and cook over moderate heat, stirring occasionally, until the onion is softened, about 5 minutes. Add the flour and stir to coat the meat. Add the wine, bay leaves and thyme, season with salt and pepper and bring to a boil, stirring to dissolve any brown bits stuck to the bottom of the pot.

2 Cover the casserole and transfer it to the oven. Cook the stew for 1½ hours, until the meat is very tender and the sauce is flavorful.

3 Meanwhile, in a saucepan, cover the pancetta with 2 cups of water and bring to a boil. Reduce the heat and simmer for 30 minutes. Drain the pancetta and slice it ½ inch thick, then cut the slices into 1-inch-wide lardons.

4 In a large skillet, combine the lardons, pearl onions, mushrooms and carrots. Add the remaining 1 tablespoon of olive oil, ¼ cup of water and a large pinch each of sugar, salt and pepper. Bring to a boil, cover and simmer until almost all of the water has evaporated, 15 minutes. Uncover and cook over high heat, tossing, until the vegetables are tender and nicely browned, about 4 minutes.

5 To serve, stir some of the vegetables and lardons into the stew and scatter the rest on top as a garnish. Top with a little chopped parsley and serve.
—*Jacques Pépin*

WINE

Though Jacques's hearty stew is inspired by boeuf bourguignon, classically flavored with red Burgundy, he prepares his version with the rich red wines of the southern Rhône, particularly those made from the wild herb–scented Carignan grape.

MOROCCAN LAMB BURGERS
WITH MINT-YOGURT SAUCE

SERVES **4**

TIME **40 min**

1 cup plain whole-milk yogurt

¼ cup chopped mint

1 garlic clove, minced

1 Tbsp. plus 1 tsp. fresh
  lemon juice

  Kosher salt and pepper

2 Tbsp. dried currants

2 Tbsp. pine nuts

2 Tbsp. coarsely chopped
  flat-leaf parsley

1 tsp. finely grated lemon zest

½ tsp. ground cumin

½ tsp. ground coriander

½ tsp. cinnamon

1¾ lbs. ground lamb

  Vegetable oil, for the grill

4 hamburger buns or kaiser rolls,
  split

These plump, Moroccan-style lamb burgers from Australian chef Sally James get phenomenal flavor from dried currants, pine nuts and herbs. The only condiment you'll want is the tangy yogurt sauce spiked with garlic and mint.

1 In a small bowl, mix the yogurt with the mint, garlic and 1 tablespoon of the lemon juice. Season the yogurt sauce with salt and pepper and refrigerate.

2 In a mini food processor, combine the currants, pine nuts, parsley, lemon zest, cumin, coriander and cinnamon with 1 teaspoon of salt and the remaining 1 teaspoon of lemon juice. Process until a coarse paste forms.

3 Scrape the currant–pine nut paste into a large bowl and add the ground lamb. Using your hands, gently mix the ground meat thoroughly with the seasonings and pat into 4 plump burgers. Set the burgers on a plate, cover them with plastic wrap and refrigerate for 15 minutes.

4 Light a grill or heat a grill pan and lightly brush with oil. Grill the burgers over moderately high heat for 6 minutes per side for medium-rare. Grill the buns cut side down until toasted. Set the burgers on the buns and serve with the mint-yogurt sauce. —*Sally James*

MAKE AHEAD

The yogurt sauce and burger patties can be refrigerated overnight. Let the burgers stand at room temperature for 15 minutes before grilling.

WINE

Spice-and-herb-inflected red, such as Greek Agiorgitiko.

"My wife prefers lamb to beef, so we make this when we're in a burger mood. Of the many lamb burgers in the world, this one is my favorite–the currant-pine nut-parsley paste mingles throughout every bite of the burger in a great way." —RAY ISLE, EXECUTIVE WINE EDITOR

LAMB SHANK POSOLE

SERVES **8**

TIME **Active 1 hr; Total 3 hr 30 min**

¼ cup canola oil

8 lamb shanks (about 8 lbs.)

Kosher salt and pepper

1 head of garlic, halved crosswise

1 large red onion, diced

3 celery ribs, diced

2 medium carrots, diced

One 2-inch cinnamon stick

2 Tbsp. chopped oregano

2 tsp. ground cumin

8 dried guajillo chiles, stemmed, 4 chopped

3 quarts chicken stock or low-sodium broth

¼ cup extra-virgin olive oil

1 tsp. ground coriander

Two 15-oz. cans hominy, rinsed and drained

One 15-oz. can pinto beans, rinsed and drained

2 Tbsp. fresh lime juice

Cilantro, diced avocado and lime wedges, for serving

Chef Hugh Acheson of Five & Ten in Athens, Georgia, creates a luxurious version of posole. The classic Mexican stew usually involves shredded pork, but lamb shanks are more impressive, and the bones help flavor the broth.

1 Preheat the oven to 375°. In a large enameled cast-iron casserole, heat 2 tablespoons of the canola oil. Season the lamb shanks with salt and pepper. Add 4 shanks to the casserole and cook over moderately high heat, turning, until browned all over, 7 to 8 minutes; transfer to a baking sheet. Repeat with the remaining canola oil and lamb shanks.

2 Add the garlic and half each of the onion, celery and carrots to the casserole; cook, stirring occasionally, until golden, about 5 minutes. Stir in the cinnamon, oregano, 1 teaspoon of the cumin and the chopped chiles. Add the lamb and any juices. Add the stock and bring to a boil. Cover and braise in the oven for 2 hours, until the lamb is very tender.

3 Meanwhile, in a heatproof bowl, cover the remaining chiles with 2 cups of boiling water; soak for 30 minutes. Transfer the chiles and 1 cup of the liquid to a blender; puree until smooth.

4 Transfer the lamb to a baking sheet and loosely tent with foil. Strain the broth into a large bowl, discarding the solids. Skim off the fat. Wipe out the casserole.

5 Heat the olive oil in the casserole. Add the remaining onion, celery and carrots and cook over moderate heat, stirring occasionally, until golden, about 5 minutes. Stir in the chile puree, the coriander, hominy, pinto beans and the remaining 1 teaspoon of cumin and cook for 2 minutes. Add the strained broth and simmer for 10 minutes. Stir in the lime juice and season the posole with salt and pepper. Add the lamb shanks to the casserole and cook just until heated through. Serve the posole in bowls, passing cilantro, avocado and lime wedges at the table. —*Hugh Acheson*

WINE

Juicy, medium-bodied Spanish Garnacha.

SLOW-ROASTED LAMB SHOULDER
WITH HOMEMADE HARISSA

SERVES **6**

TIME **Active 30 min; Total 8 hr**

¼ tsp. caraway seeds

¼ tsp. coriander seeds

¼ tsp. cumin seeds

2 oz. ancho chiles (about 4), stemmed and seeded

1 Tbsp. smoked sweet paprika

1 Tbsp. fresh lemon juice

3 large garlic cloves, 1 clove mashed to a paste

¼ cup extra-virgin olive oil

Kosher salt and pepper

One 3-lb. lamb shoulder roast on the bone

1 cup plain Greek yogurt

2 Tbsp. chopped cilantro

Lettuce leaves and warm naan, for serving

Peter Hoffman believes in eating with your hands so much, his menu at Back Forty West in Manhattan has a section called "Hands." When he makes his sensational harissa-coated lamb—meant to be torn apart and eaten in flatbread or lettuce wraps—he roasts it slowly for 10 hours. In this quicker version, the lamb cooks at higher heat for half the time: five hours. It's still falling-apart tender.

1 In a spice grinder, finely grind the caraway, coriander and cumin seeds. In a microwave-safe bowl, cover the ancho chiles with water and microwave at high power for 2 minutes. Let cool slightly, then transfer the softened chiles and 2 tablespoons of the soaking liquid to a blender. Add the ground spices, paprika, lemon juice, the 2 whole garlic cloves, 2 tablespoons of the olive oil and 1 tablespoon of salt. Puree the harissa until smooth.

2 Set the lamb in a medium roasting pan and rub ½ cup of the harissa all over the meat; let stand at room temperature for 2 hours or refrigerate overnight.

3 Preheat the oven to 325°. Add ½ cup of water to the roasting pan and cover the pan loosely with foil. Roast the lamb for 2½ hours, adding water to the pan a few times to prevent scorching. Remove the foil and roast for about 2½ hours longer, until the lamb is very brown and tender; occasionally spoon the pan juices on top. Let stand for 20 minutes.

4 Meanwhile, in a small bowl, combine the yogurt with the cilantro, mashed garlic clove and the remaining 2 tablespoons of olive oil. Season the yogurt sauce with salt and pepper.

5 Using forks or tongs, pull the lamb off the bone in large chunks. Using your fingers, pull the meat into smaller shreds and serve with the yogurt sauce, lettuce leaves, naan and the remaining harissa. —*Peter Hoffman*

MAKE AHEAD

The harissa can be refrigerated for up to 1 week. The whole roasted lamb shoulder can be refrigerated overnight; rewarm before serving.

WINE

Meaty, red-berried Australian Shiraz.

GREEN-OLIVE-AND-LEMON-CRUSTED LEG OF LAMB

SERVES 10

TIME Active 25 min; Total 1 hr 30 min

4 **anchovy fillets**

4 **garlic cloves, thinly sliced**

Finely grated zest of 2 lemons

1 **Tbsp. chopped marjoram**

1 **tsp. freshly ground pepper**

1 **cup pitted green olives, such as Picholine**

⅓ **cup extra-virgin olive oil**

One 7-lb. bone-in leg of lamb

Meat guru Bruce Aidells's inspiration for this roasted leg of lamb was a dish he tried during the annual sheep festival in St-Rémy, Provence. During the festival, legs of lamb are strung up and cooked over an open fire, then served with a green olive tapenade; that tapenade became the basis for the lemon-scented crust here. "You can also use the crust as a stuffing in a boneless leg of lamb," Aidells says.

1 Preheat the oven to 450°. In a food processor, combine the anchovies, garlic, lemon zest, marjoram and pepper and pulse until finely chopped. Add the olives and pulse until finely chopped. With the machine on, add the olive oil and process to a coarse paste.

2 Place a rack in a roasting pan and set the lamb on top. Slather the lamb with the olive paste and roast on the lowest rack of the oven for 20 minutes. Reduce the temperature to 350° and roast the lamb for about 1 hour and 10 minutes longer, until an instant-read thermometer inserted into the thickest part of the meat registers 125°. Let rest for 15 minutes before carving. Pour any juices into a bowl and serve with the lamb. —*Bruce Aidells*

WINE

In keeping with the inspiration for this dish, try a savory, full-bodied Mourvèdre-based red from the Bandol region of Provence.

brunch

We're obsessed with brunch because we love breakfast food any time of day. Plus, when we're feeling indecisive, it's easy to mix sweet and savory dishes to get the best of both.

BACK-TO-SCHOOL RASPBERRY GRANOLA BARS

MAKES **16**

TIME **Active 15 min; Total 1 hr plus 3 hr cooling**

1½ sticks unsalted butter, melted, plus more for greasing

1 cup pecans, coarsely chopped

1½ cups all-purpose flour

1¼ cups old-fashioned rolled oats

⅓ cup granulated sugar

⅓ cup packed dark brown sugar

1 tsp. kosher salt

½ tsp. baking soda

1 cup raspberry preserves

New York City pastry chef Karen DeMasco's crumbly soft, jammy-sweet bars travel well, so they're ideal for school bake sales. She says, "They're quick to put together with pantry staples, and everyone seems to love them." The bars are delicious made with any flavor of jam as well as the raspberry preserves called for here.

1 Preheat the oven to 350°. Butter an 8-inch square baking pan and line the bottom and sides with parchment paper. Spread the chopped pecans in a pie plate and toast in the oven for about 5 minutes, until lightly browned and fragrant. Let cool.

2 In a large bowl, whisk the flour with the rolled oats, granulated sugar, brown sugar, salt, baking soda and toasted pecans. Using a wooden spoon, stir in the melted butter until the oat mixture is thoroughly combined.

3 Press two-thirds of the oat mixture in an even layer on the bottom of the prepared baking pan and top with the raspberry preserves. Sprinkle the preserves with the remaining oat mixture.

4 Bake the bars for about 45 minutes, rotating the pan halfway through baking, until the top is golden brown. Transfer the pan to a wire rack and let the granola bars cool completely, about 3 hours. Cut into squares and serve.
—*Karen DeMasco*

MAKE AHEAD

The bars can be kept in an airtight container for up to 1 week.

> "I love the slightly chewy texture of this granola, especially the unexpected combination of dried cherries and crystallized ginger. The food stylist at the photo shoot handed me a bag of it, and I've been making weekly batches ever since."
> —SUZIE MYERS, STYLE EDITOR

CANDIED GINGER, COCONUT AND QUINOA GRANOLA

MAKES **About 5½ cups**

TIME **Active 15 min; Total 45 min plus cooling**

- ¾ cup rolled oats
- ½ cup quinoa, rinsed and drained
- ⅓ cup pumpkin seeds
- ⅓ cup sliced almonds
- ⅓ cup sweetened shredded coconut
- ¼ cup light brown sugar
- 1 tsp. cinnamon
- 1 tsp. ground ginger
- 1 tsp. kosher salt
- ½ cup applesauce
- ¼ cup honey
- 2 Tbsp. coconut oil
- ¼ cup each dried cranberries and halved dried cherries
- ¼ cup crystallized ginger, finely chopped

"Quinoa gives granola a nice little crunch," says Amanda Rockman, pastry chef at South Congress Hotel in Austin. "It's an unconventional crunch."

1 Preheat the oven to 325°. In a medium bowl, combine the oats, quinoa, pumpkin seeds, almonds, coconut, brown sugar, cinnamon, ground ginger and salt. In a small bowl, whisk the applesauce with the honey and coconut oil. Add the applesauce mixture to the dry ingredients and toss to coat. Scatter the granola in an even layer on a parchment paper–lined baking sheet and bake for 30 minutes, stirring occasionally, until golden brown and crisp. Let the granola cool completely.

2 Transfer the granola to a bowl and stir in the dried cranberries and cherries and the crystallized ginger. —*Amanda Rockman*

SERVE WITH

Fresh ricotta cheese or plain Greek yogurt and mixed berries.

CREAMY STEEL-CUT OATS
WITH DRIED CHERRIES AND ALMONDS

SERVES **4 to 6**

TIME **30 min**

½ cup dried sour cherries

1 cup whole milk or cream

1 cup unsweetened, unflavored almond milk

1 cup steel-cut oats

1 tsp. cinnamon

1 tsp. ground ginger

¼ tsp. ground allspice

Kosher salt

1 Tbsp. pure maple syrup, plus more for drizzling

¼ cup sliced almonds, plus more for topping

Steel-cut oats are simply chopped whole oats; they're super-nutritious and have a great chew. Marco Canora, chef at Hearth in New York City, likes to simmer the oats in whole milk or cream and almond milk with sweet spices for a breakfast with staying power.

1 In a small bowl, cover the dried sour cherries with warm water and let stand until plumped and softened, about 15 minutes. Drain the cherries and discard the soaking water.

2 Meanwhile, in a medium saucepan, combine the whole milk, almond milk and 1 cup of water and bring to a boil. Stir in the oats, cinnamon, ginger, allspice and ¼ teaspoon of salt. Cover and cook over low heat, stirring occasionally, until the oats are al dente and the porridge is creamy, about 20 minutes.

3 Stir in the cherries, 1 tablespoon of maple syrup and ¼ cup of almonds and season with salt. Serve topped with more maple syrup and almonds.
—Marco Canora

MAKE AHEAD

The porridge can be refrigerated for up to 2 days. Reheat gently with more milk or cream to loosen as necessary.

"I've always cooked my steel-cut oats in water, so this method of using whole milk and almond milk was a total revelation. I love the cherry-almond combo, but of course you can substitute any fruit and nut combination you like." —TINA UJLAKI, EXECUTIVE FOOD EDITOR

BREAKFAST BISCUIT SANDWICHES

MAKES **10**

TIME **1 hr**

- 4 **cups all-purpose flour, plus more for dusting**
- 2 **Tbsp. kosher salt**
- 1½ **Tbsp. baking powder**
- 1 **tsp. baking soda**
- 2 **sticks unsalted butter, cubed and chilled, plus more for spreading**
- 1½ **cups buttermilk**
- 10 **oz. sliced country ham, 10 oz. sliced cheddar cheese and 10 fried eggs, for serving**

  Raspberry jam, for serving (optional)

New York City husband-and-wife chef duo Preston Madson and Ginger Pierce make a breakfast sandwich that's a giant step up from fast-food versions: tender buttermilk biscuits filled with eggs, cheese and country ham (jam is optional). The biscuits have a salty edge; if you like, decrease the amount of salt in the recipe to 1½ tablespoons.

1 Preheat the oven to 400° and position racks in the upper and lower thirds. Line 2 baking sheets with parchment paper. In a large bowl, whisk the 4 cups of flour with the salt, baking powder and baking soda. Using a pastry blender or two knives, cut in the 2 sticks of butter until it is the size of small peas. Add the buttermilk and stir until a shaggy dough forms.

2 Turn the dough out onto a floured work surface; knead until it comes together. Pat the dough ¾ inch thick. Using a 3½-inch round cutter, stamp out as many biscuits as possible. Reroll the scraps and stamp out more biscuits. You should have 10.

3 Transfer the biscuits to the baking sheets and bake for about 30 minutes, until golden and risen, shifting the pans halfway through baking. Let the biscuits cool.

4 Split the biscuits and spread with butter. Preheat a griddle and cook the biscuits, cut side down, until golden. Fill the biscuits with ham, cheddar and fried eggs. Spread with raspberry jam, if desired. Close and serve.
—*Preston Madson and Ginger Pierce*

MAKE AHEAD

The biscuits can be made up to 1 day ahead and kept in an airtight container before proceeding with Step 4.

BACON, TOMATO AND CHEDDAR
BREAKFAST BAKE WITH EGGS

SERVES **8**

TIME **Active 30 min; Total 2 hr**

- 1 **lb. bakery white bread, cut into 1-inch cubes (16 cups)**
- ¼ **cup extra-virgin olive oil**
- 1 **lb. sliced applewood-smoked bacon, cut into ½-inch pieces**
- 1 **large onion, halved and thinly sliced**
-    **One 28-oz. can whole peeled tomatoes—drained, chopped and patted dry**
- ½ **tsp. crushed red pepper**
- ½ **lb. extra-sharp cheddar cheese, shredded (about 2 cups)**
- ½ **lb. Monterey Jack cheese, shredded (about 2 cups)**
- 2 **Tbsp. snipped chives**
- 1¾ **cups low-sodium chicken broth**
-    **Kosher salt**
- 8 **large eggs**
-    **Hot sauce, for serving**

This breakfast bake is from cookbook author and former F&W Test Kitchen senior editor Grace Parisi. Topped with runny eggs, it develops a terrific texture as it cooks slowly in a glass dish (which makes it easy to see when the bottom is perfectly browned). As one F&W editor remarked on tasting it, "I worship the crisp bottom and the chewy, moist bread."

1 Preheat the oven to 350°. Lightly oil a 9-by-13-inch glass baking dish. In a large bowl, toss the bread with the olive oil and spread on a large rimmed baking sheet. Bake for about 20 minutes, tossing once or twice, until the bread is golden and lightly crisp.

2 Meanwhile, in a large skillet, cook the bacon over moderately high heat, stirring occasionally, until crisp, about 8 minutes. Transfer the bacon to paper towels to drain; reserve 2 tablespoons of the fat in the skillet.

3 Add the onion to the skillet and cook over moderate heat, stirring occasionally, until softened, about 5 minutes. Add the tomatoes and crushed red pepper and cook until any liquid has evaporated, about 3 minutes.

4 Return the toasted bread cubes to the bowl. Add the contents of the skillet along with the bacon, shredded cheeses, chives and broth. Stir until the bread is evenly moistened. Season with salt. Spread the mixture in the prepared baking dish and cover with lightly oiled foil.

5 Bake the bread mixture in the center of the oven for 30 minutes. Remove the foil and bake until the top is crispy, about 15 minutes longer. Carefully remove the baking dish from the oven and, using a ladle or spoon, make 8 wells in the bread mixture. Crack an egg into each well. Return the dish to the oven and bake for about 15 minutes, until the egg whites are set but the yolks are still runny. Serve the breakfast bake right away, with hot sauce. —*Grace Parisi*

MAKE AHEAD

The recipe can be prepared through Step 4 and refrigerated overnight.

WINE

Fresh, fruity sparkling wine, like Prosecco.

SMOTHERED CAULIFLOWER
WITH EGGS

SERVES **4**

TIME **40 min**

One 10-oz. head of cauliflower, leaves removed, head cut into slabs

½ **cup all-purpose flour**

¼ **cup extra-virgin olive oil**

1 **lb. yellow tomatoes, cored and finely chopped (3 cups)**

¼ **tsp. crushed red pepper**

½ **tsp. finely grated lemon zest**

Kosher salt

2 **Tbsp. sliced almonds**

4 **large eggs**

Marjoram leaves and herb flowers, for garnish (optional)

Heidi Swanson, the author of *Super Natural Every Day* and the blogger behind 101 Cookbooks, creates a stunning twist on the Italian breakfast dish called Eggs in Purgatory: She poaches eggs in a yellow-tomato sauce simmered with sweet, caramelized cauliflower steaks.

1 In a large saucepan of salted boiling water, cook the cauliflower until crisp-tender, about 3 minutes. Drain and pat dry. Transfer to a bowl and toss with the flour, tapping off the excess.

2 In a large, deep skillet, heat the oil until shimmering. Add the cauliflower and cook over moderately high heat, turning, until browned. Add the tomatoes, crushed red pepper and lemon zest and season with salt. Cook over moderate heat until the tomatoes have broken down, about 5 minutes.

3 Meanwhile, in a small dry skillet, toast the almonds over moderate heat, stirring, until lightly browned, about 5 minutes. Let cool.

4 Using a ladle or spoon, make 4 wells in the tomato sauce. Crack the eggs into the wells, cover and cook over moderately low heat until the eggs are just set, about 3 minutes. Garnish the eggs with the almonds, marjoram leaves and flowers and serve right away. —*Heidi Swanson*

SERVE WITH

Crusty bread.

WINE

This dish goes with a full-bodied, fruity white. Pour a Pinot Gris from Oregon's Willamette Valley.

OVER-THE-TOP MUSHROOM QUICHE

SERVES 12

TIME   Active 1 hr 30 min;
       Total 5 hr 30 min

BUTTERY PASTRY SHELL

- 2 **cups all-purpose flour, sifted, plus more for dusting**
- 1 **tsp. kosher salt**
- 2 **sticks chilled unsalted butter, cut into ¼-inch dice**
- ¼ **cup ice water**
  Canola oil, for brushing

FILLING

- 1 **Tbsp. vegetable oil**
- 1 **lb. oyster mushrooms, stems trimmed, large caps halved or quartered**
- 1 **lb. white mushrooms, thinly sliced**
  Kosher salt and white pepper
- 1 **Tbsp. unsalted butter**
- 2 **small shallots, minced**
- 1 **Tbsp. thyme, chopped**
- ¾ **cup shredded Comté or Emmental cheese (2½ oz.)**
- 2 **cups milk**
- 2 **cups heavy cream**
- 6 **large eggs, lightly beaten**
  Freshly grated nutmeg

"I love quiche, but it has to be several inches high and made right," says star chef Thomas Keller. This high-rising version, which is adapted from a recipe in his *Bouchon* cookbook, just might be the perfect one.

1 MAKE THE BUTTERY PASTRY SHELL In a stand mixer fitted with the paddle, mix 1 cup of the flour with the salt. At low speed, add the butter pieces a handful at a time. Increase the speed to medium and mix until the butter is completely incorporated. Reduce the speed to low and add the remaining 1 cup of flour just until blended. Mix in the water just until thoroughly incorporated. Flatten the pastry into an 8-inch disk, wrap in plastic and refrigerate until chilled, at least 1 hour or overnight.

2 Set the ring of a 9-inch springform pan on a rimmed baking sheet lined with parchment paper, leaving the hinge open. Brush the inside of the ring with oil.

3 Dust the pastry on both sides with flour. On a lightly floured work surface, roll out the pastry to a 16-inch round, about ³⁄₁₆ inch thick. Carefully roll the pastry around the rolling pin and transfer to the prepared ring, pressing it into the corners. Trim the overhang to 1 inch and press it firmly against the outside of the ring. Use the trimmings to fill any cracks. Refrigerate for 20 minutes.

4 Preheat the oven to 375°. Line the pastry shell with a 14-inch round of parchment paper; fill the shell with pie weights. Bake until the edge of the pastry is lightly browned, about 40 minutes. Remove the parchment and weights and continue baking the pastry for about 15 minutes longer, until richly browned on the bottom. Transfer the baking sheet to a rack and let cool.

5 MAKE THE FILLING Lower the oven temperature to 325°. In a very large skillet, heat the oil. Add the mushrooms, season with salt and pepper and cook over high heat, stirring, until starting to soften, about 5 minutes. Reduce the heat to moderate. Add the butter, shallots and thyme and cook, stirring often, until the mushrooms are tender, about 12 minutes longer. Season with salt and pepper and let cool.

6 Scatter ¼ cup of the cheese and half of the mushrooms evenly over the bottom of the pastry shell. In a blender, mix half each of the milk, cream and eggs with 1½ teaspoons of salt, ⅛ teaspoon of pepper and a pinch of nutmeg. Blend at high speed until frothy, about 1 minute. Pour the custard into the pastry shell. Top with another ¼ cup of cheese and the remaining mushrooms. Make a second batch of custard with the remaining milk, cream and eggs plus the same amount of salt, pepper and nutmeg and pour into the shell. Scatter the remaining ¼ cup of cheese on top. Bake the quiche for 1½ hours, until richly browned on top and the custard is barely set in the center. Let cool in the pan until very warm. Using a serrated knife, cut the pastry shell flush with the top of the pan. Carefully lift the springform pan ring off the quiche. Cut the quiche into wedges, transfer to plates and serve warm. —*Thomas Keller*

HAM AND SAUSAGE STRATA

SERVES 12

TIME Active 1 hr; Total 2 hr plus 4 hr refrigerating

- Two ½-lb. baguettes, cut into ½-inch dice
- 2 Tbsp. unsalted butter, plus more for greasing
- 2 Tbsp. extra-virgin olive oil
- 1 large onion, finely chopped
- 3 celery ribs, peeled and cut into ½-inch pieces
- 1 jalapeño, seeded and minced
- ¾ lb. sweet Italian sausages (about 4), casings removed
- 1 lb. smoked baked ham, cut into ⅓-inch pieces
- 1 andouille sausage (about 4 oz.), finely diced
- 1 Tbsp. thyme leaves
- 1 Tbsp. kosher salt
- ½ tsp. pepper
- ½ lb. Gruyère cheese, cut into ⅓-inch pieces
- ½ cup freshly grated Parmesan cheese
- 2 large eggs, lightly beaten
- 4 cups chicken stock or low-sodium broth
- 1½ cups half-and-half or whole milk

This layered casserole needs to be refrigerated for at least four hours before baking, so plan accordingly.

1 Preheat the oven to 375°. Spread the bread on 2 large baking sheets and bake in the upper and lower thirds of the oven until golden and crisp, about 10 minutes; shift the pans from top to bottom and front to back halfway through.

2 In a large enameled cast-iron casserole, melt the 2 tablespoons of butter in the olive oil. Add the onion, celery and jalapeño and cook over moderate heat, stirring, until softened, about 6 minutes. Add the Italian sausages and cook, breaking up any large pieces, until no longer pink, about 8 minutes. Stir in the ham, andouille, thyme, salt and pepper. Transfer to a large bowl and let cool.

3 Add the Gruyère, Parmesan and bread to the meat. In another bowl, whisk the eggs, stock and half-and-half and add to the meat and bread mixture; toss until evenly mixed and moistened. Cover the strata with plastic and refrigerate for at least 4 hours or overnight.

4 Preheat the oven to 350°. Butter a 4-quart glass or ceramic baking dish. Transfer the strata to the prepared baking dish and smooth the surface. Butter a large sheet of foil and cover the baking dish with it. Bake the strata in the center of the oven for 30 minutes, until barely set. Remove the foil and bake for 45 minutes longer, until the strata is bubbling and the top is golden and crusty. Let cool for 15 minutes before serving. —*Grace Parisi*

MAKE AHEAD

The baked strata can be kept at room temperature for up to 4 hours. Reheat before serving.

"This breakfast strata will wow your brunch guests and make your life easy because it's simple to prep the night before. It's unapologetically hearty and rich, but it's just so good." —KATE HEDDINGS, FOOD DIRECTOR

CHRISTMAS-MORNING CASSEROLE

SERVES **8**

TIME **Active 40 min; Total 1 hr 40 min plus overnight soaking**

Butter, for greasing

2 Tbsp. extra-virgin olive oil

½ cup finely diced pepperoni (2 oz.)

½ lb. shiitake mushrooms, stems discarded, caps cut into ¾-inch pieces

1 medium onion, minced

1 red bell pepper, cut into ½-inch pieces

Kosher salt

8 large eggs

3 cups whole milk

1 Tbsp. Dijon mustard

1 Tbsp. soy sauce

½ tsp. pepper

¾ lb. day-old challah, sliced 1 inch thick and cut into 1-inch dice (10 cups)

6 oz. Black Forest ham, finely diced (1¼ cups)

1 cup shredded Monterey Jack cheese (¼ lb.)

1 cup shredded aged white cheddar cheese (¼ lb.)

½ cup finely chopped scallions, plus thinly sliced scallions for garnish

Hot sauce, for serving

Bryan Voltaggio, chef at Volt in Frederick, Maryland, shares his mom Sharon's recipe for this make-ahead dish: a classic baked bread-and-egg casserole with bites of pepperoni, mushrooms and gooey cheese. "Christmas is crazy when you have three kids," Sharon says, "so I would set the casserole up the night before, and in the morning, when all the chaos was happening, I'd pop it in the oven and they'd have something to eat. At other times of the year, I come across the recipe and think, I should make that. It would be a great dinner."

1 Butter a 9-by-13-inch baking dish. In a large skillet, heat the olive oil. Add the pepperoni and cook over moderate heat until the fat is rendered, about 3 minutes. Add the shiitake and cook until lightly browned and tender, about 5 minutes. Add the onion, bell pepper and a generous pinch of salt and cook, stirring occasionally, until softened and browned, about 7 minutes; let the vegetable mixture cool completely.

2 In a large bowl, beat the eggs with the milk, mustard, soy sauce, pepper and 2 teaspoons of salt. Add the cooled vegetable mixture, the challah, ham, both cheeses and the chopped scallions and mix well. Scrape the mixture into the prepared baking dish, cover with plastic wrap and refrigerate overnight.

3 Preheat the oven to 350°. Uncover the casserole and bake for about 50 minutes, until just set and browned on top. Let stand for 10 minutes, then garnish with thinly sliced scallions and serve with hot sauce. —*Bryan Voltaggio*

VARIATION

Switch up the cheeses and the other add-ins as you wish.

KAISERSCHMARRN
WITH PEACHES

SERVES **6**

TIME **30 min**

- **4 Tbsp. unsalted butter**
- **3 firm, ripe medium peaches—peeled, quartered and sliced ¼ inch thick**
- **¼ cup granulated sugar**
- **1 Tbsp. fresh lemon juice**
- **1 cup all-purpose flour**
- **1 cup milk**
- **4 large eggs, separated**
- **1 tsp. finely grated lemon zest**
- **Pinch of kosher salt**
- **⅓ cup confectioners' sugar, plus more for dusting**
- **1 pint blackberries**

Kaiserschmarrn is a popular Austrian dessert that can also be eaten for breakfast or brunch. It's a light pancake, cut up while it's frying and topped with fruit and confectioners' sugar. To make it extra-special (and even more delicious), toss it with warm peaches and fresh blackberries.

1 In a 12-inch nonstick skillet, melt ½ tablespoon of the butter. Add the peaches, 1 tablespoon of the granulated sugar and the lemon juice and cook over high heat, stirring occasionally, until the peaches are tender and lightly browned, about 5 minutes. Transfer the peaches to a plate and clean the skillet.

2 In a large bowl, whisk the flour, milk, egg yolks, lemon zest and 2 tablespoons of the granulated sugar until smooth. In another bowl, using a hand mixer, beat the egg whites with the salt at high speed until soft peaks form. Beat in the remaining 1 tablespoon of granulated sugar until the whites are glossy. Fold the whites into the batter until no streaks remain.

3 In the skillet, melt 1 tablespoon of the butter. Add the batter, cover and cook over moderately low heat until the bottom is golden and the top is beginning to set, 4 to 5 minutes. Slide the pancake onto a large plate. Carefully invert the skillet over the pancake. Using oven mitts, flip the skillet and the plate to return the pancake to the pan. Cook until the underside of the pancake is set and lightly browned, about 2 minutes.

4 Using a wooden or heatproof plastic spatula, cut the pancake in the skillet into 2-inch squares. Dot with the remaining 2½ tablespoons of butter, sprinkle with the ⅓ cup of confectioners' sugar and top with the peaches. Cook, tossing, until the pancake is caramelized, about 5 minutes. Add the blackberries and toss until heated through, about 1 minute. Transfer the kaiserschmarrn to a platter, sprinkle with confectioners' sugar and serve. —*Grace Parisi*

VARIATION

Swap in raspberries, blueberries or sliced strawberries for the blackberries.

RICOTTA PANCAKES
WITH ORANGE SYRUP

SERVES **6**

TIME **1 hr**

ORANGE SYRUP

- **1 orange**
- **1 cup fresh orange juice**
- **1 cup sugar**

RICOTTA TOPPING

- **1½ cups fresh ricotta cheese**
- **1½ Tbsp. sugar**
- **¾ tsp. finely grated lemon zest**
- **Seeds scraped from ½ vanilla bean**

PANCAKES

- **1½ cups all-purpose flour**
- **¼ cup fine white cornmeal**
- **2 Tbsp. sugar**
- **½ tsp. salt**
- **½ tsp. baking powder**
- **½ tsp. baking soda**
- **2 cups buttermilk**
- **2 large eggs, separated**
- **½ cup fresh ricotta cheese**
- **Vegetable oil, for frying**
- **Toasted almond slices, for serving**

April Bloomfield, chef at The Breslin in New York City, adds fresh ricotta to the batter to make these cornmeal pancakes supermoist. They're exquisite with the soft ricotta topping, crunchy sliced almonds and ingeniously vibrant (and neon-bright) orange syrup.

1 MAKE THE ORANGE SYRUP Peel the zest from the orange in long strips and julienne. In a small saucepan of boiling water, blanch the zest for 30 seconds. Drain and repeat. Return the julienned zest to the saucepan. Add the orange juice, sugar and 1 cup of water and simmer until syrupy, about 10 minutes. Let cool.

2 MAKE THE RICOTTA TOPPING In a medium bowl, mix together the ricotta, sugar, lemon zest and vanilla bean seeds.

3 MAKE THE PANCAKES In a large bowl, whisk the flour, cornmeal, sugar, salt, baking powder and baking soda. In another large bowl, whisk the buttermilk, egg yolks and ricotta. Fold the wet ingredients into the dry ingredients. In a large, clean stainless steel bowl, beat the egg whites until stiff but not dry; fold them into the batter.

4 In a large cast-iron skillet, heat a thin film of vegetable oil. Drop in ¼-cup dollops of batter and cook over moderately high heat for about 2 minutes per side, until golden and fluffy. Serve about 3 pancakes per person. Pass the orange syrup, ricotta topping and toasted almonds at the table.
—*April Bloomfield*

> "A former F&W colleague and I used to talk about this recipe like an old friend. It's reliable and always there for you when you have overripe bananas and a craving for something sweet. It freezes really well, so you can double the recipe and save a loaf for another time."
>
> —JAMES MAIKOWSKI, ART DIRECTOR

BANANA BREAD

MAKES One 9-by-5-inch loaf

TIME Active 15 min;
Total 1 hr 30 min

- ½ cup canola oil, plus more for greasing
- 4 medium overripe bananas, the blacker the better
- 1 cup sugar
- 2 large eggs, at room temperature
- 1 tsp. pure vanilla extract
- 1½ cups all-purpose flour
- 1½ tsp. baking soda
- ½ tsp. kosher salt
- ½ cup or more chopped nuts, raisins or chocolate chips (optional)

F&W executive food editor Tina Ujlaki has made this recipe at least 300 times in all kinds of pans: loaf, square, round, muffin. It's based on one from Sally Sampson's *The Bake Sale Cookbook,* which calls for butter and 1¼ cups of sugar. Ujlaki prefers it with just 1 cup of sugar, and she uses oil instead of butter. "I've added everything from nuts, raisins, dates and dried cherries to chocolate chips and cut-up Snickers bars to the batter," she says. "I've turned it into birthday cake and into a base for ice cream sundaes with caramel or hot fudge sauce. It never disappoints."

1 Preheat the oven to 350°. Grease a 9-by-5-by-3-inch loaf pan. In a medium bowl, mash the bananas with the sugar, then mash in the ½ cup of oil. Beat in the eggs and vanilla. In another medium bowl, mix the flour with the baking soda and salt, then add to the banana mixture. Mix just until the ingredients are blended. Fold in the nuts, raisins or chocolate chips, if using. Scrape the batter into the prepared loaf pan and bake until the banana bread is well browned and a cake tester inserted in the center comes out clean, about 1 hour. Let cool for 10 minutes, then unmold and let cool to warm before eating. —*Tina Ujlaki*

dessert

When we're tasting recipes in the
F&W Test Kitchen for a giant dessert story,
we wake up happy—then put on our
loosest pants to get ready for the day.

MAPLE-APPLE UPSIDE-DOWN CAKE

SERVES **12**

TIME **Active 25 min; Total 3 hr**

1½ **sticks unsalted butter, softened, plus more for greasing**

2 **cups all-purpose flour, plus more for dusting**

1 **cup pure maple syrup**

3 **Granny Smith apples—peeled, cored and cut into eighths**

1 **tsp. baking powder**

1 **tsp. salt**

½ **tsp. baking soda**

3 **large eggs**

¾ **cup buttermilk**

1 **Tbsp. pure vanilla extract**

1⅓ **cups sugar**

Crème fraîche, for serving

Joanne Chang, pastry chef at Flour Bakery + Cafe in Boston, created one of the best upside-down cakes ever. Maple syrup infuses both the apples and the cake, making the dessert taste like a stack of apple pancakes.

1 Preheat the oven to 350°. Butter and flour a 10-inch round cake pan. In a large saucepan, bring the maple syrup to a boil over high heat, then simmer over low heat until very thick and reduced to ¾ cup, about 20 minutes. Pour the thickened syrup into the prepared cake pan. Arrange the apples in the pan in 2 concentric circles, overlapping them slightly.

2 In a medium bowl, whisk the 2 cups of flour with the baking powder, salt and baking soda. In a glass measuring cup, whisk the eggs with the buttermilk and vanilla. In a stand mixer fitted with the paddle, beat the 1½ sticks of butter with the sugar at medium speed until fluffy, about 3 minutes. Beat in the dry and wet ingredients in 3 alternating batches until the batter is smooth; scrape down the side of the bowl.

3 Scrape the batter over the apples and spread it in an even layer. Bake the cake for about 1½ hours, until golden on top and a toothpick inserted in the center comes out clean. Let the cake cool on a rack for 45 minutes.

4 Place a plate on top of the cake and invert the cake onto the plate; tap lightly to release the cake. Remove the pan. Let the cake cool slightly, then cut into wedges and serve with crème fraîche. —*Joanne Chang*

VARIATION

This cake is also wonderful made with a mix of sliced pears and apples, or served with softened vanilla ice cream instead of crème fraîche.

BUTTERMILK CAKE WITH
BLACKBERRIES

MAKES	One 9-inch cake
TIME	Active 20 min; Total 1 hr plus cooling

4 Tbsp. unsalted butter, softened, plus more for greasing

1 cup all-purpose flour

½ tsp. baking powder

½ tsp. baking soda

¼ tsp. salt

⅔ cup plus 1½ Tbsp. sugar

1 large egg, at room temperature

1 tsp. pure vanilla extract

½ cup buttermilk, at room temperature

1¼ cups blackberries, plus more for serving

Sweetened whipped cream, for serving

This light and moist buttermilk cake with an irresistible crispy top is from Nico and Amelia Monday, chefs at The Market Restaurant in Gloucester, Massachusetts. With sweet-tart berries in every bite and taking just 20 minutes to prep, it will become your go-to cake whenever blackberries (or even raspberries) are in season.

1 Preheat the oven to 400°. Butter a 9-inch round cake pan and line the bottom with parchment paper. Butter the paper.

2 In a small bowl, whisk the flour, baking powder, baking soda and salt. In a large bowl, using a hand mixer, beat the 4 tablespoons of butter with ⅔ cup of the sugar at medium-high speed until fluffy, about 3 minutes. Beat in the egg and vanilla. At low speed, beat in the buttermilk and dry ingredients in 3 alternating batches, ending with the dry ingredients; do not overbeat. Gently fold the batter just until blended, then scrape into the prepared pan and smooth the top.

3 Scatter the 1¼ cups of blackberries over the batter; lightly press them in. Sprinkle the remaining 1½ tablespoons of sugar over the cake. Bake for about 30 minutes, until a cake tester inserted in the center comes out clean.

4 Transfer the cake to a rack to cool for 10 minutes, then turn out the cake and remove the paper. Turn the cake right side up and let cool completely. Serve with whipped cream and more blackberries. —*Nico and Amelia Monday*

SKILLET GRAHAM CAKE WITH PEACHES AND BLUEBERRIES

SERVES **10**

TIME **Active 1 hr; Total 2 hr 30 min plus cooling**

STREUSEL

- ¾ cup graham cracker crumbs
- ¾ cup all-purpose flour
- ½ cup light brown sugar
- 1 stick unsalted butter, softened
- ½ tsp. kosher salt

FRUIT

- 3 large peaches, each cut into 1-inch wedges
- ¾ cup blueberries
- ½ cup granulated sugar
- 3 Tbsp. fresh lemon juice
- 1 Tbsp. cornstarch
- 1 Tbsp. unsalted butter

CAKE

- 1½ cups all-purpose flour
- ½ cup whole-wheat flour
- ½ cup fine graham cracker crumbs
- 2 tsp. baking powder
- 1½ tsp. kosher salt
- 1 stick plus 3 Tbsp. unsalted butter, softened
- 1¼ cups light brown sugar
- ¼ cup granulated sugar
- 3 Tbsp. honey
- 4 large eggs
- 1¼ cups buttermilk
- ⅓ cup canola oil
- 1 Tbsp. pure vanilla extract

For outdoor parties, F&W Best New Chef 2011 Stephanie Izard of Chicago's Girl & the Goat bakes her skillet cake on the grill. It gets amazing flavor from graham crackers mixed into both the batter and the crumbly streusel topping. The cake can also be baked in a 300° oven for the same amount of time.

1 MAKE THE STREUSEL In a stand mixer fitted with the paddle, beat all of the ingredients together at medium speed until crumbs form. Transfer the crumbs to a bowl and press into clumps. Refrigerate until chilled, about 15 minutes.

2 MEANWHILE, PREPARE THE FRUIT Set up a gas grill for indirect grilling, then heat to 300°. In a medium bowl, toss the peaches with the blueberries, sugar, lemon juice and cornstarch. In a 12-inch cast-iron skillet, melt the butter over low heat. Remove from the heat. Scrape the fruit and any juices into the skillet.

3 MAKE THE CAKE In a medium bowl, whisk both flours with the graham cracker crumbs, baking powder and salt. In a stand mixer fitted with the paddle, beat the butter with both sugars and the honey at medium speed until fluffy. Beat in the eggs one at a time, then beat in the buttermilk, oil and vanilla. Scrape down the side of the bowl and beat in the dry ingredients until just smooth. Spread the batter over the fruit in an even layer. Scatter the streusel evenly on top.

4 Set the skillet on the grill over indirect heat. Close the grill and bake for about 1½ hours, rotating the skillet every 20 minutes, until a toothpick inserted in the cake comes out clean; keep an eye on the heat to maintain the grill temperature. Let the cake cool for 1 hour before cutting into wedges and serving. —*Stephanie Izard*

SERVE WITH

Vanilla ice cream.

BEER

Fruit desserts pair best with fruity sour beers. Izard loves this cake with St. Louis brewery Side Project's Fuzzy, a peach-scented sour beer aged in Chardonnay barrels.

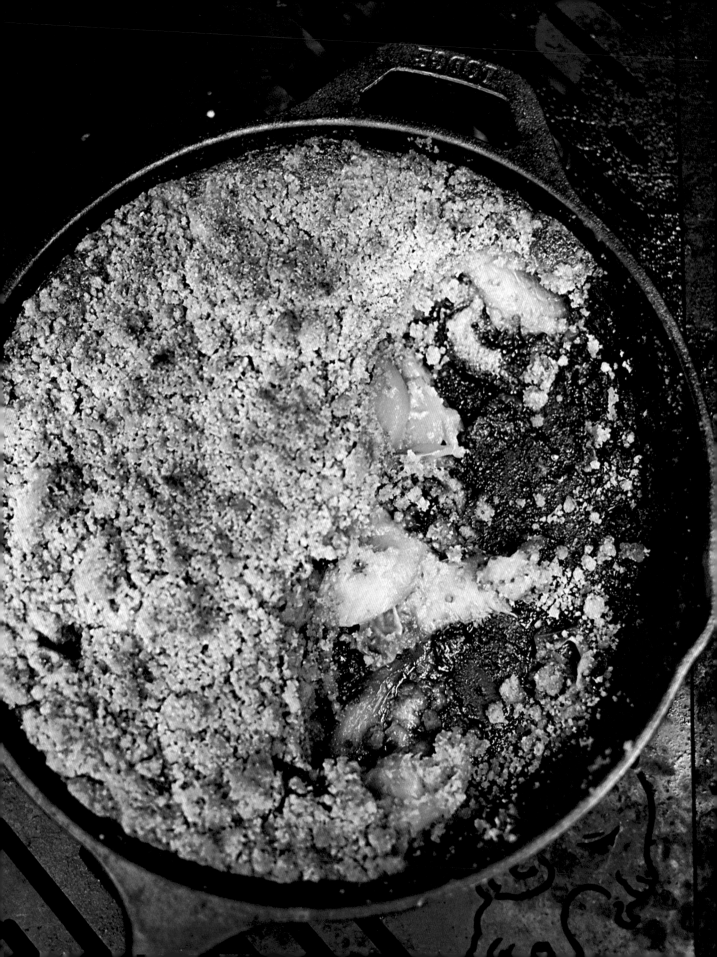

RIESLING-POACHED PEACHES
WITH TARRAGON AND SALTED SOUR CREAM

SERVES 4

TIME **30 min plus chilling**

2½ cups semidry Riesling

¼ cup sugar

½ vanilla bean, split lengthwise, seeds scraped

5 tarragon sprigs

4 ripe but firm freestone peaches, halved and pitted

⅔ cup sour cream

  Kosher salt

Justin Chapple, star of F&W's Mad Genius Tips videos, poaches peaches with the skin on to give them a rosy blush. He likes to reduce any of the fragrant poaching liquid left over into a syrup for drizzling over cake, melon or ice cream; mixing with sparkling wine or water; or stirring into fruit salad.

1 In a medium saucepan, combine the wine, sugar, vanilla bean and seeds and 1 tarragon sprig and bring just to a boil. Add the peach halves and simmer over moderate heat, turning occasionally, until tender, about 10 minutes. Let cool completely, then refrigerate until chilled, at least 1 hour.

2 In a medium bowl, whisk the sour cream with a big pinch of salt. Dollop the cream in bowls and top with the peach halves and some of their poaching liquid. Garnish each plate with a tarragon sprig and serve. —*Justin Chapple*

MAKE AHEAD

The peaches can be refrigerated in their poaching liquid for up to 3 days.

"I'm that person who goes overboard buying peaches at the farmers' market in the summer. I can't help myself! They have such an alluring color and fragrance, which are both accentuated in this chic dessert. It's like a less-sweet, grown-up version of canned peaches in syrup." —SUSAN CHOUNG, BOOKS EDITOR

TRIPLE-LAYER SOUR CREAM CHOCOLATE CAKE

SERVES **12**

TIME **Active 1 hr 15 min; Total 2 hr 45 min**

CAKE

Unsalted butter, for greasing

3 cups **cake flour, plus more for dusting**

9 oz. **unsweetened chocolate, finely chopped**

2 cups **hot brewed coffee**

1 Tbsp. **pure vanilla extract**

4 **large eggs, at room temperature**

1 cup **canola oil**

1 cup **sour cream, at room temperature**

3 cups **sugar**

1½ tsp. **baking soda**

1 tsp. **cinnamon**

1 tsp. **fine sea salt**

GANACHE

1½ cups **heavy cream**

1½ **sticks unsalted butter, cut into 1-inch pieces**

½ cup **sugar**

½ tsp. **fine sea salt**

1½ lbs. **semisweet chocolate, finely chopped**

⅓ cup **hot brewed coffee**

1½ tsp. **pure vanilla extract**

Sugared cranberries, for garnish (see Note)

NOTE

Toss fresh cranberries in simple syrup, drain and chill. Roll the cranberries in sugar and spread on a plate; chill for about 1 hour before serving.

This magnificent cake is from Cheryl and Griffith Day, owners of Back in the Day Bakery in Savannah, Georgia. It has three layers of moist, coffee-laced chocolate with a hint of cinnamon and a silky chocolate ganache.

1 MAKE THE CAKE Preheat the oven to 350° and position racks in the middle and lower thirds. Butter three 9-by-2-inch round cake pans and line with parchment paper. Butter the paper and dust the pans with flour, tapping out the excess.

2 In a medium bowl, combine the chocolate with the coffee and vanilla and let stand for 2 minutes, then stir until the chocolate is melted. In another medium bowl, whisk the eggs with the oil until pale yellow, then whisk in the sour cream. Gradually whisk in the melted chocolate mixture until smooth.

3 In a stand mixer fitted with the paddle, combine the 3 cups of flour with the sugar, baking soda, cinnamon and salt and mix well. At medium speed, beat in the wet ingredients in 3 batches until just incorporated. Scrape down the bowl and beat until the batter is smooth.

4 Pour the batter evenly into the prepared cake pans. Gently tap the pans on the counter to release any air bubbles. Bake for about 35 minutes, until a toothpick inserted in the center of each cake comes out clean; shift the pans halfway through baking. Let the cakes cool completely, then carefully invert them onto a rack and peel off the parchment.

5 MEANWHILE, MAKE THE GANACHE In a medium saucepan, bring the cream, butter, sugar and salt just to a simmer over moderate heat, stirring to dissolve the sugar. Remove from the heat and add the chocolate. Let stand for 2 minutes, then stir until smooth. Stir in the coffee and vanilla. Let cool completely, stirring occasionally.

6 Transfer 1 cake to a plate. Spoon one-fourth of the ganache on top and spread in an even layer. Top with another cake and one-fourth of the ganache. Cover with the third cake and spread the remaining ganache over the top and side of the cake; decoratively swirl the ganache on top. Top the cake with sugared cranberries, cut into wedges and serve. —*Cheryl and Griffith Day*

MAKE AHEAD

The frosted cake can be stored in an airtight container for up to 3 days.

STICKY TOFFEE PUDDING CAKE

MAKES   **One 10-inch cake**

TIME   **Active 45 min;
Total 1 hr 30 min**

CAKE

Nonstick spray

1½ cups **chopped pitted dates
(9 oz.)**

1 tsp. **baking soda**

1½ cups **all-purpose flour**

1 tsp. **baking powder**

½ tsp. **kosher salt**

4 Tbsp. **unsalted butter, at room
temperature**

1 cup **granulated sugar**

2 **large eggs**

1 tsp. **pure vanilla extract**

SAUCE

1¼ cups **dark brown sugar**

1 stick **unsalted butter, cubed**

½ cup **heavy cream**

2 tsp. **brandy**

1 tsp. **pure vanilla extract**

½ tsp. **kosher salt**

Rich and buttery, this killer sticky toffee cake from Abigail Quinn of Proof Bakeshop in Atlanta soaks up great flavor from a brandy-spiked caramel sauce.

1 MAKE THE CAKE Preheat the oven to 350°. Coat a 10-inch round cake pan with nonstick spray and line with parchment paper. In a small saucepan, cover the dates with 1 cup of water and bring to a boil. Remove from the heat and whisk in the baking soda; it will foam up. Let cool slightly.

2 In a medium bowl, sift the flour with the baking powder and salt. In a stand mixer fitted with the paddle, beat the butter with the granulated sugar at medium speed until light and fluffy, 1 to 2 minutes. Beat in the eggs and vanilla. In 2 alternating batches, beat in the dry ingredients and the date mixture until just incorporated. Scrape the batter into the prepared pan and bake for 35 to 40 minutes, until a toothpick inserted in the center comes out clean. Let the cake cool in the pan for 10 minutes.

3 MEANWHILE, MAKE THE SAUCE In a medium saucepan, bring the brown sugar, butter and heavy cream to a boil over moderate heat, whisking to dissolve the sugar. Simmer over moderately low heat, whisking, for 2 minutes. Remove from the heat; whisk in the brandy, vanilla and salt. Keep warm.

4 Turn the cake out onto a rack and peel off the parchment. Carefully return the cake, top side down, to the pan. Using a skewer, poke 15 to 20 holes in it. Pour half of the warm sauce over the cake and let stand until absorbed, about 5 minutes. Invert onto a platter and poke another 15 to 20 holes in the top. Pour the remaining sauce over the top. Serve warm. —*Abigail Quinn*

SERVE WITH

Vanilla ice cream or crème fraîche.

> "This olive oil cake is dead simple to make but never fails to impress. I actually make it in a loaf pan and like to slice either thick wedges (for breakfast) or the thinnest of thin slices (delicious with ice cream and berries). It gets better over a few days' time! Everyone always asks for this recipe." —SARA PARKS, PHOTO EDITOR

OLIVE OIL BUNDT CAKE

SERVES **12**

TIME **Active 15 min; Total 1 hr 15 min plus cooling**

Butter, for greasing

2 **cups cake flour, plus more for dusting**

5 **large eggs, at room temperature**

1¼ **cups sugar**

1 **Tbsp. finely grated orange zest**

1 **cup extra-virgin olive oil**

1¼ **tsp. baking powder**

1 **tsp. fine sea salt**

New York City chef Will Prunty created this not-too-sweet olive oil cake recipe to showcase the delicious fruitiness of extra-virgin olive oil from Sicily.

1 Preheat the oven to 325° and butter and flour a 10-cup bundt pan. In a large bowl, using a hand mixer, beat the eggs with the sugar and orange zest at medium-high speed until smooth. Gradually beat in the olive oil until creamy, about 2 minutes. In a small bowl, whisk the 2 cups of cake flour with the baking powder and salt. Add the dry ingredients to the egg mixture in 3 batches, beating at medium speed between additions.

2 Scrape the batter into the prepared pan and bake in the middle of the oven for about 1 hour, until a toothpick inserted in the center of the cake comes out clean. Let cool in the pan for 15 minutes, then invert onto a rack. Let the cake cool completely before cutting into slices and serving. —*Will Prunty*

MAKE AHEAD

The olive oil cake can be kept in an airtight container at room temperature for up to 4 days.

DOUBLE DARK CHOCOLATE CUPCAKES
WITH PEANUT BUTTER FILLING

MAKES **24**

TIME **Active 45 min; Total 3 hr**

¾ cup plus 2 Tbsp. cocoa powder (not Dutch process)

½ cup boiling water

1 cup buttermilk

1¾ cups all-purpose flour

1¼ tsp. baking soda

¼ tsp. baking powder

¼ tsp. salt

1½ sticks plus 3 Tbsp. unsalted butter, softened

1½ cups granulated sugar

2 large eggs, at room temperature

1 tsp. pure vanilla extract

1 cup creamy peanut butter

⅔ cup confectioners' sugar

1 cup heavy cream

8 oz. semisweet chocolate, chopped

NOTE

If you don't have a pastry bag with a fitted tip, you can fill these cupcakes by carving a hole in the center (from the top) with a sharp paring knife. Put the filling in a resealable plastic bag and snip off one of the corners. Pipe the filling directly into the hole.

Cookbook author Peggy Cullen fills her tender chocolate cupcakes with a creamy, salty peanut butter mixture, then dips the tops twice in a rich, silky chocolate ganache frosting. "For some reason, most bakers don't fill their cupcakes," says Cullen, "but taking that extra step is no big deal." All you need to do is poke a hole into the top and squeeze in the ultrasimple blend of peanut butter, sugar and butter.

1 Preheat the oven to 350° and position racks in the middle and lower thirds. Line 24 muffin cups with paper or foil liners.

2 Put the cocoa powder in a medium heatproof bowl. Add the boiling water and whisk until a smooth paste forms. Whisk in the buttermilk until combined. In a medium bowl, sift the flour with the baking soda, baking powder and salt. In a large bowl, using a hand mixer, beat 1½ sticks of the butter with the granulated sugar until light and fluffy, about 3 minutes. Beat in the eggs and vanilla, then beat in the dry ingredients in 2 batches, alternating with the cocoa mixture. Carefully spoon the cupcake batter into the lined muffin cups, filling them about two-thirds full. Bake for 20 to 22 minutes, until the cupcakes are springy. Let the cupcakes cool in the pans for 5 minutes, then transfer them to wire racks to cool completely.

3 In a medium bowl, beat the peanut butter with the remaining 3 tablespoons of butter until creamy. Sift the confectioners' sugar into the bowl and beat until light and fluffy, about 2 minutes. Spoon all but 3 tablespoons of the peanut butter filling into a pastry bag fitted with a ¼-inch star tip. Holding a cupcake in your hand, plunge the tip into the top of the cake, pushing it about ¾ inch deep. Gently squeeze the pastry bag to fill the cupcake, withdrawing it slowly as you squeeze; you will feel the cupcake expand slightly as you fill it. Scrape any filling from the top of the cupcake and repeat until all of the cupcakes are filled.

4 In a small saucepan, bring the heavy cream to a simmer. Off the heat, add the semisweet chocolate to the cream and let stand for 5 minutes, then whisk the melted chocolate into the cream until smooth. Let the chocolate icing stand until slightly cooled and thickened, about 15 minutes. Dip the tops of the cupcakes into the icing, letting the excess drip back into the pan. Transfer the cupcakes to racks and let stand for 5 minutes. Dip the tops of the cupcakes again and transfer them to racks. Spoon the remaining 3 tablespoons of peanut butter filling into the pastry bag and pipe tiny rosettes on the tops of the cupcakes. —*Peggy Cullen*

MAKE AHEAD

The cupcakes are best served the day they are made, but they can be refrigerated overnight in an airtight container.

> "I love the fact that you can whip this crumble up at any time because you always have the ingredients on hand. The ground granola gives it a lovely texture and flavor; either with or without nuts is fine, but don't use granola with dried fruit, or it will end up too hard to eat." —TINA UJLAKI, EXECUTIVE FOOD EDITOR

OATY MIXED BERRY CRUMBLE

SERVES **4 to 6**

TIME **Active 20 min; Total 1 hr 15 min**

TOPPING

¾ **cup all-purpose flour**

¾ **cup old-fashioned rolled oats**

1¼ **cups plain granola**

½ **cup sugar**

1½ **sticks chilled unsalted butter, cut into cubes**

FILLING

¾ **cup sugar**

Finely grated zest of 1 lemon

½ **tsp. cinnamon**

¼ **tsp. ground allspice**

¼ **tsp. freshly grated nutmeg**

1 **lb. blackberries**

¾ **lb. blueberries**

¾ **lb. raspberries**

2 **Tbsp. unsalted butter, cut into small pieces**

Devonshire cream, vanilla ice cream or lightly whipped cream, for serving

Scottish celebrity chef Nick Nairn likes using finely cut oats in this crumble topping, but you can also grind rolled oats in the food processor to achieve the same texture. A generous amount of butter mixed into the oats makes the crumble especially light and crisp.

1 MAKE THE TOPPING Preheat the oven to 400°. In a food processor, combine the flour with the oats, granola and sugar and pulse until the ingredients are coarsely ground. Add the chilled butter and pulse until the mixture resembles fine meal.

2 MAKE THE FILLING In a large bowl, toss the sugar with the lemon zest, cinnamon, allspice and nutmeg. Add the blackberries, blueberries and raspberries and toss well. Carefully spread the berries in a 9-by-13-inch glass or ceramic baking dish and dot with the butter. Spoon the crumble topping over the berries and bake for 40 to 45 minutes, until the fruit is bubbling and the topping is browned. Let the crumble cool slightly and serve warm with Devonshire cream, ice cream or whipped cream. —*Nick Nairn*

MAKE AHEAD

The berry crumble can be made up to 4 hours ahead. Reheat gently before serving.

"Think of this as a giant rustic almond cookie for sharing. For a party, it's fun to bring it to the table whole and let your friends break off pieces; it's killer with espresso or a Cognac after dinner. Also, it's not too sweet, so it's great for breakfast with yogurt or fruit salad." —TINA UJLAKI, EXECUTIVE FOOD EDITOR

TORTA SBRISOLONA

SERVES 12

TIME Active 20 min; Total 1 hr plus cooling

- 7 Tbsp. cold unsalted butter, cut into ½-inch pieces, plus more for greasing
- ¾ cup almonds (4 oz.)
- 1 large egg yolk
- 1 Tbsp. finely grated orange zest
- ¼ tsp. pure almond extract
- ¼ tsp. pure vanilla extract
- 1 cup plus 2 Tbsp. all-purpose flour
- ¼ cup plus 2 Tbsp. fine cornmeal
- ½ tsp. kosher salt
- ⅓ cup granulated sugar
- 3 Tbsp. brown sugar

Suzanne Goin, chef at Lucques in L.A., thinks of this crumbly, buttery, nutty dessert from the Lombardy region of Italy as a cross between biscotti and shortbread. She recommends dipping chunks of it into Champagne-spiked sabayon, an airy dessert sauce made with whipped egg yolks, and serving it with roasted red grapes.

1 Preheat the oven to 350°. Butter a 9-inch springform pan. Spread the almonds on a baking sheet and toast until golden, about 10 minutes. Let cool slightly, then coarsely chop the almonds. Leave the oven on.

2 In a small bowl, mix the egg yolk with the orange zest and the extracts. In a medium bowl, mix the flour, cornmeal and salt. Cut in the 7 tablespoons of butter with a pastry blender or rub it in with your fingers until the mixture resembles coarse meal. Stir in the granulated sugar, brown sugar and toasted almonds. Gently work in the egg yolk mixture with your hands; the dough should be crumbly.

3 Transfer the dough to the prepared pan and lightly press the crumbs; the surface should be uneven. Bake for 40 minutes, until deep golden brown. Transfer to a rack and let cool completely before unmolding. Break the torta into large pieces and serve. —Suzanne Goin

MAKE AHEAD

The torta can be stored in an airtight container for up to 2 days.

APPLE PIE BARS

MAKES **4 dozen 2-inch bars**

TIME **Active 1 hr; Total 2 hr plus cooling**

CRUST

3 sticks unsalted butter, softened
¾ cup sugar
3 cups all-purpose flour
½ tsp. kosher salt

FILLING

6 Tbsp. unsalted butter
½ cup light brown sugar
12 Granny Smith apples (about 6 lbs.)—peeled, cored and thinly sliced
1 Tbsp. cinnamon
¼ tsp. freshly grated nutmeg

TOPPING

¾ cup walnuts
3 cups quick-cooking oats
2 cups all-purpose flour
1½ cups light brown sugar
1¼ tsp. cinnamon
½ tsp. baking soda
½ tsp. kosher salt
3 sticks unsalted butter, cut into ½-inch cubes and chilled

Apple pie morphs into apple bars when the filling is sandwiched between a flaky shortbread crust and crunchy streusel topping. The recipe is from Cathy Johnson, sister of Mary Odson of Big Sugar Bakeshop in Los Angeles.

1 MAKE THE CRUST Preheat the oven to 375°. Line a 15-by-17-inch rimmed baking sheet or jelly roll pan with parchment paper. In a stand mixer fitted with the paddle, beat the butter with the sugar at medium speed until light and fluffy, about 2 minutes. At low speed, beat in the flour and salt until a soft dough forms. Press the dough over the bottom of the prepared pan and ½ inch up the side in an even layer. Bake in the center of the oven for about 20 minutes, until the crust is golden and set. Let cool on a rack.

2 MEANWHILE, MAKE THE FILLING In each of 2 large skillets, melt 3 tablespoons of the butter with ¼ cup of the light brown sugar. Add the apples to the skillets and cook over high heat, stirring occasionally, until softened, about 10 minutes. Stir half of the cinnamon and nutmeg into each skillet. Cook until the apples are caramelized and very tender and the liquid has evaporated, about 10 minutes longer; scrape up any bits stuck to the bottom of the skillets and add up to ½ cup of water to each pan to prevent scorching. Let cool.

3 MAKE THE TOPPING Spread the walnuts in a pie plate and toast until golden and fragrant, about 8 minutes. Let cool, then coarsely chop the walnuts. In a large bowl, mix the oats with the flour, light brown sugar, cinnamon, baking soda and salt. Using a pastry blender or two knives, cut in the butter until the mixture resembles coarse meal. Stir in the walnuts and press the mixture into clumps.

4 Spread the apple filling over the crust. Scatter the crumbs on top, pressing them lightly into an even layer. Bake in the middle of the oven for 1 hour, until the topping is golden; rotate the pan halfway through baking. Let cool completely on a rack before cutting into 2-inch bars. —*Cathy Johnson*

MAKE AHEAD

The bars can be stored in an airtight container at room temperature for up to 4 days or frozen for up to a month.

DEEP-DISH APPLE PIE WITH A CHEDDAR CRUST

MAKES Two 9-inch pies

TIME Active 1 hr; Total 3 hr plus cooling

PIE SHELL

- **3 cups all-purpose flour**
- **½ lb. sharp cheddar cheese, grated**
- **½ tsp. kosher salt**
- **2 sticks cold unsalted butter, cut into tablespoons**
- **2 eggs, slightly beaten**

FILLING

- **5 lbs. Golden Delicious apples (about 12)—peeled, cored and sliced ¼ inch thick**
- **Juice of 1 large lemon**
- **1½ cups light brown sugar**
- **¼ cup all-purpose flour**
- **1 tsp. kosher salt**

This recipe celebrates fall ingredients from the Hudson Valley. It's from chef Waldy Malouf of the Culinary Institute of America in Hyde Park, New York.

1 MAKE THE PIE SHELL In a food processor, pulse the flour, cheese and salt to mix. Add the butter and pulse until the mixture resembles coarse meal. Transfer the mixture to a large bowl and make a well in the center. Stir in the eggs and work the dough into a ball.

2 Divide the dough into quarters and flatten into disks. Roll out each disk to a thin 11-inch round between 2 sheets of wax paper. Remove the wax paper and line two 9-inch pie pans with a dough round. Refrigerate the lined pans and the 2 dough rounds, covered, until thoroughly chilled, about 1 hour.

3 MAKE THE FILLING Preheat the oven to 375°. In a large bowl, toss the apples with the lemon juice. Sprinkle on the brown sugar, flour and salt and toss well. Divide the apples between the lined pie pans. Moisten the pie-shell rims and cover with the dough rounds. Trim any overhang and crimp the edges to seal. Cut 4 steam vents in each pie.

4 Bake the pies on the bottom shelf of the oven for about 1 hour, until golden and bubbly and the apples are tender when pierced; cover the pies with foil halfway through if necessary. Let cool for about 1 hour before serving. —*Waldy Malouf*

MAKE AHEAD

The pies can be made through Step 3, chilled until firm, then wrapped and frozen for up to 2 weeks. Thaw before baking.

"I've been making this fantastic not-too-sweet apple pie ever since the recipe ran in 1996. If you're unsure about swapping your plain crust for a cheesy one, start with a mild cheddar. I worked my way up to extra-sharp pretty quickly, and you may well, too."
—TINA UJLAKI, EXECUTIVE FOOD EDITOR

STRAWBERRY SLAB PIE

SERVES **6**

TIME **Active 30 min; Total 3 hr plus cooling**

PASTRY

- 2 **cups all-purpose flour, plus more for dusting**
- 4 **tsp. granulated sugar**
- 1 **tsp. kosher salt**
- 2 **sticks plus 2 Tbsp. unsalted butter, cut into tablespoons and chilled**
- 2 **large egg yolks**
- ¼ **cup cold whole milk**
  Baking spray

PIE

- 1½ **lbs. strawberries, hulled and quartered (4 cups)**
- 1 **cup granulated sugar**
- ¼ **cup cornstarch**
- ½ **tsp. finely grated orange zest**
- ¼ **tsp. kosher salt**
- 1 **large egg, beaten**
- 3 **Tbsp. sanding or turbinado sugar**

A slab pie is a shallow pie made in a baking sheet or pan. This one from Joanne Chang of Flour Bakery + Cafe in Boston has a perfectly buttery crust and a sweet jammy filling.

1 MAKE THE PASTRY In a stand mixer fitted with the paddle, combine the 2 cups of flour with the sugar and salt and mix at low speed. Add the butter and mix at medium speed until almost incorporated, with some pecan-size pieces remaining, about 1 minute. In a small bowl, whisk the egg yolks with the milk. With the machine on, drizzle the egg mixture into the flour mixture and mix until the pastry just starts to come together, about 30 seconds; it will be crumbly. Scrape the pastry onto a lightly floured work surface and gather it together. Using the heel of your hand, smear the pastry against the work surface to work in the butter. Form the pastry into a 1-inch-thick disk, cover in plastic wrap and refrigerate until firm, at least 1 hour.

2 Preheat the oven to 350°. Grease an 8-inch square baking pan with baking spray and line with parchment paper, leaving 3 inches of overhang on all sides.

3 Cut one-third of the pastry off the disk. On a lightly floured work surface, using a lightly floured rolling pin, roll out the smaller piece of pastry to an 8-inch square; transfer to a parchment paper–lined baking sheet and refrigerate. Roll out the larger piece of pastry to a 12-inch square, about ¼ inch thick. Ease the pastry into the prepared pan, pressing it into the corners and up the sides; trim the excess pastry, leaving no overhang. Line the pastry with parchment paper and fill with pie weights. Bake for about 30 minutes, until just pale golden and set. Remove the pie weights and parchment paper. Transfer the pan to a rack and let the crust cool completely.

4 MAKE THE PIE In a medium bowl, toss the strawberries with the granulated sugar, cornstarch, orange zest and salt. Spread the filling in the pastry crust. Cover with the chilled piece of pastry crust, gently pressing it down around the edges. Brush the top with the beaten egg and sprinkle with the sanding sugar. Using a sharp paring knife, make six 2-inch-long slits in the top pastry. Bake for about 50 minutes, until the crust is deep golden. Transfer the pan to a rack to cool, at least 3 hours. Carefully lift the pie out of the pan and transfer to a platter before serving. *—Joanne Chang*

FARMER'S CHEESECAKE
WITH STRAWBERRIES

SERVES 8

TIME **Active 40 min; Total 3 hr 15 min**

CRUST

- **5 Tbsp. unsalted butter**
- **3 Tbsp. sugar**
- **1¼ cups packed graham cracker crumbs (10 to 12 whole crackers)**
- **¼ tsp. salt**
- **Pinch of ground ginger**
- **Pinch of cinnamon**

FILLING

- **1 lb. fresh ricotta cheese, at room temperature**
- **½ lb. cream cheese, at room temperature**
- **3 Tbsp. agave nectar**
- **½ tsp. finely grated lemon zest plus 1 Tbsp. fresh lemon juice**
- **¼ tsp. salt**
- **Pinch of ground ginger**

TOPPINGS

- **1 pint strawberries, hulled and sliced ¼ inch thick**
- **¼ cup sugar**
- **1 Tbsp. fresh lemon juice**
- **2 tsp. caraway seeds**
- **½ cup honey**

For this elegant, no-bake cheesecake, chef Nicolaus Balla of Bar Tartine in San Francisco ferments his own farmer's cheese (a kind of cottage cheese). Ricotta mixed with cream cheese makes a fabulous substitute for the filling, which is incredibly light, delicately sweet and wonderful inside the crumbly graham cracker crust.

1 MAKE THE CRUST In a small saucepan, melt the butter with the sugar over moderately low heat, stirring, until the sugar dissolves, about 4 minutes. In a medium bowl, mix the graham cracker crumbs with the salt, ginger and cinnamon. Stir in the melted butter until the crumbs are evenly moistened. Press the crumbs evenly over the bottom and up the side of a 9-inch fluted tart pan. Cover with plastic wrap and refrigerate until well chilled, about 1 hour.

2 MAKE THE FILLING In a large bowl, using a hand mixer, beat the ricotta with the cream cheese, agave nectar, lemon zest, lemon juice, salt and ginger just until smooth. Using a spatula, spread the filling in the chilled crust. Cover with plastic wrap and refrigerate until well chilled, about 2 hours.

3 MEANWHILE, PREPARE THE TOPPINGS In a medium bowl, toss the strawberries with the sugar and lemon juice. Let stand at room temperature, stirring once or twice, until the berries are juicy and slightly softened, about 30 minutes.

4 In a small saucepan, toast the caraway seeds over moderate heat until fragrant, about 1 minute. Transfer to a mortar and lightly crush the seeds. Return the caraway seeds to the saucepan and add the honey. Warm the honey over moderately low heat for 10 minutes. Strain the honey into a bowl, discarding the seeds; let cool.

5 Cut the cheesecake into wedges, top with the strawberries and caraway honey and serve. —*Nicolaus Balla*

MAKE AHEAD

The cheesecake can be refrigerated for up to 2 days. The honey can be stored in an airtight container at room temperature for up to 1 month.

> "Sometimes looks are deceiving. These unassuming cookies appear quite plain but are a buttery mix of crunchy and soft with hits of rosemary and salt. You just can't stop eating them—when I shot it, the crew ate the entire batch in ten minutes. No joke."
>
> —FREDRIKA STJÄRNE, CREATIVE DIRECTOR

ROSEMARY-CORNMEAL SUGAR COOKIES

MAKES **About 6 dozen**

TIME **Active 45 min; Total 1 hr 30 min plus cooling**

1½ cups all-purpose flour

1½ cups fine yellow cornmeal

¼ cup nonfat dry milk powder

¾ tsp. baking powder

¼ tsp. baking soda

4 tsp. finely chopped rosemary

1 tsp. salt

¾ cup fresh or thawed frozen corn kernels

2 tsp. finely grated lemon zest plus 2 tsp. fresh lemon juice

2½ sticks unsalted butter, at room temperature

¾ cup plus 3 Tbsp. sugar

1 large egg

¼ cup sorghum molasses or dark honey

1 tsp. pure vanilla extract

Chef Tim Byres of Smoke in Dallas mixes fresh rosemary into cornmeal cookies, giving them a fabulous savory note. The recipe can be made two ways: as drop cookies or the slice-and-bake kind for a crisper texture.

1 Preheat the oven to 350°. Line 2 large baking sheets with parchment paper. In a medium bowl, whisk the flour, cornmeal, milk powder, baking powder, baking soda, rosemary and ½ teaspoon of the salt.

2 In a food processor, pulse the corn with the lemon zest until very finely chopped. In a stand mixer fitted with the paddle, beat the butter with ¾ cup of the sugar at medium-high speed for 2 minutes, until smooth. Beat in the egg until incorporated. At low speed, beat in the chopped corn mixture, then add the molasses, lemon juice and vanilla. Beat at high speed until pale and fluffy, about 5 minutes. At low speed, beat in the dry ingredients in 3 additions.

3 Working in 2 batches, scoop 1¼-inch mounds of dough onto the prepared baking sheets, about 2 inches apart. With damp fingers, flatten each mound slightly. In a small bowl, mix the remaining 3 tablespoons of sugar and ½ teaspoon of salt and sprinkle half of the mixture on the cookies. Bake in the upper and lower thirds of the oven for 12 to 15 minutes, until golden brown; shift the pans from top to bottom and front to back halfway through. Slide the parchment paper from the baking sheets onto racks. Repeat to bake the remaining dough. —*Tim Byres*

VARIATION

For a slice-and-bake version of these cookies, refrigerate the dough for 30 minutes, until no longer sticky. Form it into 2 logs, 2½ inches in diameter. Wrap tightly in plastic and freeze until firm or for up to 1 month. Slice the logs ¼ inch thick and proceed as above.

CHOCOLATE BROWNIE COOKIES

MAKES	About 3 dozen
TIME	Active 30 min; Total 2 hr 30 min plus cooling

1 lb. semisweet chocolate, chopped

4 Tbsp. unsalted butter

4 large eggs, at room temperature

1½ cups sugar

1 tsp. pure vanilla extract

¼ tsp. salt

½ cup all-purpose flour, sifted

½ tsp. baking powder

One 12-oz. bag semisweet chocolate chips

These double-chocolate cookies are like crispy-chewy brownies in cookie form. Belinda Leong of B. Patisserie in San Francisco freezes the batter before baking to attain that crackly outer layer.

1 In a large bowl set over a saucepan of simmering water, melt the chopped chocolate with the butter, stirring a few times, until smooth, about 7 minutes.

2 In another large bowl, using a hand mixer, beat the eggs with the sugar at medium speed until thick and pale, about 5 minutes. Beat in the vanilla and salt. Using a rubber spatula, fold in the melted chocolate, then fold in the flour and baking powder. Stir in the chocolate chips. Scrape the batter into a shallow baking dish, cover and freeze until well chilled and firm, about 1 hour.

3 Preheat the oven to 350° and line 2 baking sheets with parchment paper. Working in batches, scoop 2-tablespoon-size mounds of dough onto the prepared baking sheets, about 2 inches apart. Bake for about 10 minutes, until the cookies are dry around the edges and cracked on top. Let the cookies cool on the baking sheets for 10 minutes, then transfer to a rack to cool completely before serving. *—Belinda Leong*

MAKE AHEAD

The cookies can be stored in an airtight container at room temperature for up to 4 days.

"If a chocolate bar and a brownie had a baby, it would be one of these cookies. They're dense but chewy and super-chocolaty. The crackled top gives them such a great texture. I credit these cookies with making me a popular houseguest." —CHRISTINE QUINLAN, DEPUTY EDITOR

> "This recipe makes a lot of brownies, but fortunately they freeze very well. Some people even like them better that way–they're like frozen candy bars."
> —TINA UJLAKI, EXECUTIVE FOOD EDITOR

QUADRUPLE CHOCOLATE BROWNIES

MAKES	4 dozen 2-inch brownies
TIME	Active 30 min; Total 1 hr plus cooling

1¼ lbs. (5 sticks) unsalted butter, softened

1 lb. unsweetened chocolate, chopped

5½ cups sugar

16 large eggs

2 Tbsp. pure vanilla extract

1½ tsp. kosher salt

3¾ cups all-purpose flour

½ lb. bittersweet chocolate, chopped into ½-inch pieces

½ lb. white chocolate, chopped into ½-inch pieces

½ lb. milk chocolate, chopped into ½-inch pieces

San Francisco chocolatier Michael Recchiuti of Recchiuti Confections creates all kinds of fun, homey chocolate desserts. This one—with white, milk and bittersweet chocolate mixed into a batter made with unsweetened chocolate, plus more melted and drizzled on top—has "all the chocolates I like in one brownie," he says.

1 Preheat the oven to 300°. Line the bottoms of two 9-by-13-inch baking pans with parchment paper. In a large saucepan, melt the butter with the unsweetened chocolate over low heat, stirring frequently, until melted. In a large bowl, whisk the sugar with the eggs, vanilla and salt. Add the melted chocolate and whisk until smooth. Add the flour and whisk until incorporated. Stir in 5 ounces of each of the chopped chocolates. Spread the batter in the prepared pans.

2 Place the remaining chopped chocolates separately in 3 small microwave-safe bowls and melt. Using a spoon, drizzle the melted chocolates over the batter. Using a table knife, make swirls in the batter for a marbled effect. Bake the brownies for about 35 minutes, rotating the pans halfway through, until the tops are shiny and the brownies are set.

3 Transfer the brownies to a wire rack to cool completely before cutting into squares. —*Michael Recchiuti*

CHOCOLATE SOUFFLÉ SUNDAE

SERVES **8**

TIME **Active 45 min;**
Total 1 hr 30 min

- 6 oz. bittersweet or semisweet chocolate, coarsely chopped
- 6 Tbsp. unsalted butter, cut into pieces
- 4 large eggs, at room temperature, 3 separated
- ²/₃ cup sugar
- 1 tsp. pure vanilla extract
- 1½ pints premium-quality vanilla ice cream

  Caramel Sauce and Bittersweet Chocolate Sauce (recipes below), for serving

NOTE

The chocolate soufflé base can be baked up to 1 day ahead; cover tightly with plastic wrap and let stand at room temperature. The sauces can be refrigerated in airtight containers for up to 1 week.

For this epic dessert, baker and candy maker Peggy Cullen fills a light fallen chocolate soufflé base with vanilla ice cream and tops it with two decadent sauces: dark chocolate and intense caramel. If you can't resist the urge to overindulge, add whipped cream, nuts and a cherry.

1 Preheat the oven to 350°. In a microwave-safe bowl, melt the chocolate in 30-second intervals at high power until melted. Whisk in the butter until fully incorporated; let cool slightly.

2 In a large bowl, whisk the 3 egg yolks with the whole egg and ⅓ cup of the sugar until blended. Whisk in the melted chocolate and vanilla.

3 In a medium bowl, beat the 3 egg whites with a hand mixer until soft peaks form. Add the remaining ⅓ cup of sugar, 1 tablespoon at a time, beating for 10 seconds between additions. Continue beating at medium-high speed until the whites are firm and glossy. Whisk one-fourth of the beaten whites into the chocolate mixture until well blended; gently fold in the remaining whites until incorporated.

4 Scrape the chocolate soufflé mixture into an ungreased 9-inch glass pie plate. Gently shake the pie plate to smooth the surface and bake for about 35 minutes, until the soufflé is cracked and no longer wobbles. Transfer to a rack to cool completely.

5 Meanwhile, line a large plate with plastic wrap and freeze until well chilled. Scoop ice cream balls onto the chilled plate and freeze them.

6 Set the ice cream balls on the soufflé, mounding them in the center. Drizzle with ¼ cup each of Caramel Sauce and Chocolate Sauce, cut into wedges and serve right away. Pass the remaining sauce at the table. —*Peggy Cullen*

CARAMEL SAUCE

In a small saucepan, heat ½ cup **heavy cream** just until small bubbles appear around the edge. In a medium saucepan, cook ½ cup **sugar** with 2 Tbsp. **water** over high heat until the sugar is dissolved, washing down the side of the pan with a wet pastry brush. Continue cooking, without stirring, until a honey-colored caramel forms, about 5 minutes. Remove from the heat and carefully stir in the scalded cream. Let cool for 1 minute, then stir in 1 tsp. **pure vanilla extract.** Serve warm. Makes ½ cup. —*PC*

BITTERSWEET CHOCOLATE SAUCE

In a medium saucepan, heat ½ cup **heavy cream** just until small bubbles appear around the edge. Remove from the heat, add 4 oz. coarsely chopped **bittersweet chocolate** and let stand for 1 minute. Add 1 tsp. **pure vanilla extract** and stir until smooth; serve warm. Makes ¾ cup. —*PC*

GRILLED CHOCOLATE SANDWICHES
WITH CARAMEL SAUCE

SERVES 6

TIME 45 min

DARK CHOCOLATE GANACHE

4½ oz. semisweet chocolate chips
(⅔ cup)

4½ oz. 70% dark chocolate, finely
chopped (1 cup)

¾ cup heavy cream

¼ cup unsweetened cocoa powder

1 Tbsp. sugar

¼ tsp. kosher salt

CARAMEL SAUCE

1 cup heavy cream

¾ cup sugar

2 tsp. unsalted butter, at room
temperature

½ tsp. kosher salt

SANDWICHES

Twelve ¼-inch-thick slices of
white country bread

4 Tbsp. unsalted butter, melted

Autumn Martin of Hot Cakes in Seattle is a master of warm chocolate desserts. Her grilled chocolate sandwiches are crisp, gooey and deliciously messy, especially when they're dipped in a warm caramel sauce.

1 MAKE THE GANACHE In a medium heatproof bowl, combine both chocolates. In a medium saucepan with a candy thermometer attached, combine the cream, cocoa powder, sugar and salt. Cook over moderately low heat, whisking frequently, until the mixture is smooth and thick and registers 165° on the thermometer, 3 to 5 minutes. Pour the cream mixture over the chocolate and stir until smooth. Let cool to room temperature.

2 MEANWHILE, MAKE THE CARAMEL SAUCE In a small saucepan, warm the cream. In a medium saucepan, spread the sugar in an even layer. Cook over moderate heat, without stirring, until the sugar starts to melt around the edge, about 3 minutes. Reduce the heat to low and shake the pan to incorporate the dry sugar into the melted sugar. Continue to cook over low heat, swirling the pan frequently, until a light amber caramel forms, about 3 minutes longer. Slowly drizzle in the warm cream. Cook over moderate heat, whisking occasionally, until the caramel is smooth, about 3 minutes. Whisk in the butter and salt. Transfer the caramel to a small bowl and let cool until warm.

3 MAKE THE SANDWICHES Spread ¼ cup of the ganache onto 6 slices of bread. Top with the remaining 6 slices of bread and butter both sides.

4 Heat a large nonstick skillet. Place 3 sandwiches in the skillet and cook over moderate heat until golden and crisp and the ganache is melted, about 2 minutes per side. Transfer the sandwiches to a platter. Repeat with the remaining sandwiches. Serve the sandwiches with the caramel dipping sauce.
—Autumn Martin

MAKE AHEAD

The ganache and caramel can be refrigerated separately for up to 3 days. Bring to room temperature before using.

SALTED-CARAMEL CREAM PUFFS
WITH WARM CHOCOLATE SAUCE

SERVES 8

TIME Active 45 min; Total 1 hr 15 min plus cooling

CARAMEL CUSTARD
- 1 large egg
- 2 large egg yolks
- ¼ cup cornstarch
- 2 cups whole milk
- 1½ cups sugar
- 2 Tbsp. salted butter
- 1 tsp. pure vanilla extract
- ½ tsp. flaky sea salt

CREAM PUFFS
- 6 Tbsp. unsalted butter, cubed, at room temperature
- 2 tsp. sugar
- ½ tsp. kosher salt
- ¾ cup all-purpose flour
- 3 large eggs, at room temperature

CHOCOLATE SAUCE
- ½ cup half-and-half
- 2 Tbsp. unsweetened Dutch-process cocoa powder
- 2 Tbsp. light corn syrup
- 2 Tbsp. sugar
- ½ Tbsp. salted butter, at room temperature
- 4 oz. bittersweet chocolate, finely chopped
- Sliced almonds, confectioners' sugar or flaky sea salt, for garnish (optional)

NOTE

These cream puffs can also be filled with Boursin or salmon spread for a savory hors d'oeuvre. The caramel custard and chocolate sauce can be refrigerated separately for up to 3 days.

One secret to pastry chef David Lebovitz's insanely addictive cream puffs is the salted butter he uses to make the perfect caramel custard filling.

1 MAKE THE CARAMEL CUSTARD In a medium bowl, whisk the egg with the egg yolks, cornstarch and ½ cup of the milk until smooth. In a small saucepan, heat the remaining 1½ cups of milk over low heat; keep warm.

2 In a medium saucepan, combine the sugar with ¼ cup of water. Cook over moderate heat, swirling the pan and brushing down the side with a wet pastry brush, until the sugar dissolves. Cook undisturbed until a deep amber caramel forms, about 5 minutes. Remove the saucepan from the heat and whisk in the butter; be careful, it will boil vigorously. While whisking constantly, slowly drizzle in the warm milk until blended; the mixture may separate a little. Slowly whisk in the egg mixture and bring to a boil, then cook over moderate heat, stirring, until thickened, about 2 minutes. Stir in the vanilla and sea salt. Strain the caramel custard through a fine sieve into a heatproof bowl. Press a piece of plastic wrap directly onto the surface of the custard and refrigerate until completely chilled.

3 MAKE THE CREAM PUFFS Preheat the oven to 400°. Line a baking sheet with parchment paper or a silicone mat. In a medium saucepan, combine the butter, sugar and salt with ¾ cup of water. Cook over moderate heat for 1 minute, until the butter melts. Add all of the flour at once and stir vigorously with a wooden spoon, then cook until the dough pulls away from the side of the pan, 1 to 2 minutes. Remove the saucepan from the heat and let stand for 2 minutes, stirring a few times to cool down the dough. Add the eggs one at a time, beating constantly and thoroughly with a wooden spoon between additions; the dough should be smooth and shiny.

4 Transfer the dough to a pastry bag fitted with a ½-inch plain tip. Pipe the dough into twenty-four 1½-inch mounds on the prepared baking sheet, spacing them 1 inch apart. Bake for about 25 minutes, until the tops and bottoms are golden. Transfer the baking sheet to a rack. Using a skewer, poke a small hole in the side of each cream puff to allow steam to escape; let cool completely.

5 MAKE THE CHOCOLATE SAUCE In a medium saucepan, combine the half-and-half, cocoa, corn syrup and sugar. Bring to a boil over moderate heat, stirring occasionally. Remove from the heat. Stir in the butter and chocolate until melted and the sauce is smooth.

6 Scrape the custard into a piping bag fitted with a ¼-inch plain tip. Pipe the cream into the hole in the side of each cream puff until full. Drizzle with some of the chocolate sauce, sprinkle with garnishes and serve. —*David Lebovitz*

DOUBLE-CHOCOLATE COOKIE CRUMBLE

MAKES 9 cups

TIME Active 20 min; Total 50 min

½ lb. dark chocolate (72%), coarsely chopped

1¾ cups all-purpose flour

⅓ cup oat flour

¼ cup plus 2 Tbsp. unsweetened cocoa powder

2 tsp. baking soda

1¼ tsp. kosher salt

2 sticks unsalted butter, at room temperature

1 cup turbinado sugar

⅓ cup plus 1 Tbsp. granulated sugar

Vanilla ice cream, for serving

This crisp crumble from San Francisco pastry chef Nicole Krasinski is deeply chocolaty, with a nice saltiness. It's fantastic on ice cream but also extremely good on its own.

1 In a food processor, pulse the chocolate until it is the size of peas. Transfer to a plate and freeze for 30 minutes.

2 Preheat the oven to 325°. Line 2 rimmed baking sheets with parchment paper. In a medium bowl, sift both flours with the cocoa powder, baking soda and salt. In a large bowl, using a hand mixer, beat the butter with both sugars at medium speed until very light and fluffy, 5 minutes. Beat in the flour mixture just until incorporated, then stir in the frozen chocolate.

3 Drop almond-size clumps of the dough in a single layer onto the prepared baking sheets; the dough will look crumbly and uneven. Bake for 8 to 10 minutes, until the top is dry but the crumble is still soft. Let the crumble cool completely. Serve over ice cream. —*Nicole Krasinski*

MAKE AHEAD

The raw dough can be frozen for up to 1 month. The baked crumble can be frozen in a resealable plastic bag for up to 1 month.

"I try not to keep too much of this crumble on hand because the first time I tried it, I couldn't stop eating it. It's perfectly balanced–not too sweet. The unbaked dough crisps up nicely on top of a pan of brownies and the baked crumble adds awesome texture when blended into milkshakes."

—EMILY TYLMAN, TEST KITCHEN ASSISTANT

COCONUT ARBORIO RICE PUDDING

SERVES **6**

TIME **45 min**

1 **quart whole milk**
1 **cup arborio rice (about 8 oz.)**
½ **cup sugar**
   One 14-oz. can unsweetened coconut milk
½ **cup coarsely shredded unsweetened coconut**

Most rice puddings call for medium-grain or basmati rice; this recipe from Stephanie Prida, the pastry chef at Manresa in Los Gatos, California, calls for arborio, commonly used in risotto. The plump grains give the coconut-infused pudding a supercreamy texture while staying perfectly firm and chewy.

1 In a large saucepan, combine the milk, rice and sugar with 2 cups of water and bring to a boil. Simmer over moderate heat, stirring frequently, until the rice is tender and suspended in a thick, creamy sauce, about 30 minutes. Stir in the coconut milk and simmer, stirring occasionally, until the rice is very tender and the liquid is thickened, about 10 minutes. Let cool slightly.

2 Meanwhile, in a medium saucepan, toast the coconut over moderate heat, stirring constantly, until fragrant and golden, about 4 minutes. Transfer to a plate to cool.

3 Spoon the rice pudding into bowls, garnish with the toasted coconut and serve. —*Stephanie Prida*

MAKE AHEAD

The pudding can be refrigerated for up to 4 days. Serve warm or cold.

"There are only five ingredients in this excellent riff on rice pudding, but the flavor is intense thanks to a double dose of coconut. To dress it up, I like putting slices or cubes of juicy ripe mango on top."
—KATE HEDDINGS, FOOD DIRECTOR

PUMPKIN BREAD PUDDING WITH
CARAMEL RUM RAISIN SAUCE

SERVES **8 to 10**

TIME **Active 1 hr;
Total 2 hr 30 min**

PUMPKIN BREAD PUDDING

- 2 **cups milk**
- 1½ **cups heavy cream**
- 3 **cinnamon sticks, crushed**
- **One 2-inch piece of fresh ginger, coarsely chopped**
- 1 **vanilla bean, split lengthwise**
- 6 **whole cloves**
- **Butter, for greasing**
- 1 **loaf of brioche (¾ lb.), cut into 1-inch cubes**
- 4 **large eggs**
- 3 **large egg yolks**
- ½ **cup canned unsweetened pumpkin puree**
- ½ **tsp. salt**
- ½ **cup plus 3 Tbsp. sugar**
- 2 **tsp. cinnamon**

CARAMEL RUM RAISIN SAUCE

- ¾ **cup dark rum**
- 1 **cup raisins**
- 3 **cups sugar**
- 1 **cup heavy cream**

NOTE

The baked pudding can be refrigerated overnight. Cover with foil and rewarm in a 325° oven for 15 to 20 minutes. The sauce can be refrigerated for up to 1 week. Reheat gently.

This dessert from New York City pastry chef Melissa Murphy is an excellent alternative to pumpkin pie. Buttery brioche is soaked in a pumpkin crème brûlée base, then baked with a cinnamon sugar topping and served with a decadent caramel sauce.

1 MAKE THE PUMPKIN BREAD PUDDING In a medium saucepan, combine the milk and cream. Add the cinnamon sticks, ginger, vanilla bean and cloves and cook over moderate heat until just steaming; do not let the milk boil. Remove the saucepan from the heat, cover and let stand until the milk is fragrant, about 30 minutes.

2 Preheat the oven to 375°. Lightly butter a 9-by-13-inch glass or ceramic baking dish. On a rimmed baking sheet, toast the cubed brioche for about 8 minutes, until dry and golden, then spread in the prepared baking dish.

3 Rewarm the spiced milk over moderate heat until steaming, then strain it into a medium heatproof bowl.

4 Meanwhile, in another medium bowl, combine the eggs, egg yolks, pumpkin puree and salt and whisk until blended and smooth. Whisk in ½ cup of the sugar. Gradually whisk 1 cup of the hot milk into the pumpkin mixture, then whisk the mixture back into the remaining milk.

5 Pour the pumpkin custard evenly over the brioche and cover with plastic wrap. Let stand until the brioche has absorbed the custard, about 30 minutes. Discard the plastic wrap.

6 In a small bowl, combine the remaining 3 tablespoons of sugar with the cinnamon and sprinkle over the bread pudding. Set the baking dish in a large roasting pan and add enough hot water to the pan to reach halfway up the side of the baking dish. Bake the bread pudding, uncovered, for about 45 minutes, until puffed and set.

7 MEANWHILE, MAKE THE CARAMEL RUM RAISIN SAUCE In a small saucepan, warm the rum with the raisins. Remove from the heat and let soak for 20 minutes. In a medium heavy saucepan, combine the sugar and ½ cup of water and cook over moderate heat until a deep amber caramel forms. Remove from the heat. Carefully add a little of the heavy cream to stop the cooking. Add the remaining heavy cream and stir in the raisins and rum.

8 Let the bread pudding cool slightly, spoon into bowls and serve warm, with the caramel rum raisin sauce drizzled on top. —*Melissa Murphy*

th Baked
ls, p. 122

Recipe Index

Page numbers in **bold** indicate photographs.

Pappardelle with Summer
Squash and Arugula-Walnut
Pesto, p. 104

Photo Credits

ANTONIS ACHILLEOS 18

QUENTIN BACON 102

CHRIS COURT 199

TARA FISHER 166

NICOLE FRANZEN 160, 233

CHRISTINA HOLMES 11, 37, 60, 63,
78, 84, 116, 119, 120, 134, 151, 154, 176,
186, 193, 217, 226, 247, 251, 254, 257

CLARKSON POTTER 205

NICHOLAS HOPPER 194

JOHN KERNICK 17, 31, 32, 64, 70, 83,
91, 138, 163, 229

DAVE LAURIDSEN 189

JONATHAN LOVEKIN 258

JOHNNY MILLER 23

MARCUS NILSSON 4, 12, 44, 53, 88,
202, 206, 222, 237, back cover

MICHAEL PIAZZA 59

CON POULOS front cover, 26, 38, 41,
42, 47, 50, 54, 75, 105, 113, 129, 130, 133,
137, 141, 146, 169, 175, 179, 185, 190, 209,
212, 225, 230, 234, 267

ANDREW PURCELL 244

TINA RUPP 180, 218

LUCY SCHAEFFER 243

FREDRIKA STJÄRNE 8, 69, 94, 99,
108, 123, 126, 157, 172, 248, 262, 270

FOOD&WINE
BOOKS

More books from
FOOD&WINE

Annual Cookbook

More than 680 recipes from the world's best cooks, including
culinary legends Alice Waters and Jacques Pépin and
star chefs like Mario Batali, Carla Hall and Tyler Florence.

Cocktails

Over 150 new and classic recipes from America's most brilliant
bartenders. Plus, an indispensable guide to cocktail
basics and the top new bars and lounges around the country.

Wine Guide

An essential, pocket-size guide focusing on the most reliable
producers, with over 1,000 stellar wines.

TO ORDER, CALL 800-284-4145
OR VISIT **FOODANDWINE.COM/BOOKS**